D1431652

Freedom by Degrees

FREEDOM BY DEGREES

Emancipation in Pennsylvania and Its Aftermath

GARY B. NASH
JEAN R. SODERLUND

New York   Oxford
OXFORD UNIVERSITY PRESS
1991

Oxford University Press

Oxford   New York   Toronto
Delhi   Bombay   Calcutta   Madras   Karachi
Petaling Jaya   Singapore   Hong Kong   Tokyo
Nairobi   Dar es Salaam   Cape Town
Melbourne   Auckland

and associated companies in
Berlin   Ibadan

Published by Oxford University Press, Inc.,
200 Madison Avenue, New York, New York 10016

Oxford is a registered trademark of Oxford University Press

Library of Congress Cataloging-in-Publication Data
Nash, Gary B.
Freedom by degrees :
emancipation in Pennsylvania and its aftermath /
Gary B. Nash and Jean R. Soderlund.
p. cm. Includes bibliographical references and index.
ISBN 0-19-504583-1
1. Slaves—Pennsylvania—Emancipation.
2. Slavery—Pennsylvania—History—18th century.
3. Afro-Americans—Pennsylvania—History—18th century.
4. Pennsylvania—History—Colonial period, ca. 1600–1775.
5. Pennsylvania—History—1775–1865.
I. Soderlund, Jean R., 1947– .
II. Title. E445.P3N37   1991
974.8′00496073—dc20   90-38380

2 4 6 8 9 7 5 3 1

Printed in the United States of America
on acid-free paper

For the staff members of the
Manuscripts Department and Library
of the
Historical Society of Pennsylvania

Contents

Introduction

On April 19, 1730, the 24-year-old co-owner of the *Pennsylvania Gazette* advertised "A likely Negroe Woman to be Sold." Prospective buyers could see the slave "at the Widow Read's in Market-Street."[1] Thus began Benjamin Franklin's more than half-century direct involvement with slavery, for he, along with Samuel Meredith, was the recent purchaser of the *Pennsylvania Gazette,* and Franklin was living as a boarder in Widow Read's house and hence knew personally the slave woman he was advertising for sale.

Over the next sixty years, until his death in 1790, Franklin remained engaged with the issue of slavery—as a buyer, seller, and master of slaves; as reluctant abolitionist; and, finally, as outspoken critic of the institution. Oddly, his experience with slavery encapsulates the history of slavery in his adopted city, Philadelphia, and in the state to which he devoted so much of his life. To sketch Printer Ben's awkward and shifting relationship to the peculiar institution is to foreshadow several major themes of this book.

The massive collection of papers that have been gathered from around the world for a modern edition of the papers of Benjamin Franklin do not reveal when Franklin first purchased slaves. But it was probably in the late 1740s, after Franklin achieved financial security as a result of his astounding success with the *Pennsylvania Gazette, Poor Richard's Almanack,* and other publishing ventures. The black couple—Peter and Jemima—bought by Franklin and his wife Deborah (the daughter of the landlady whose slave woman he had advertised in 1730) were not working out, he wrote his mother in Boston in

1750. "We conclude to sell them both the first good Opportunity; for we do not like Negro Servants."[2] It is fair to infer from this remark that Deborah and Benjamin Franklin had been untouched by the antislavery voices heard in Pennsylvania in the late 1720s and 1730s—Benjamin Lay and Ralph Sandiford in particular—although Franklin had published the appeals against slaveholding of both of these early trumpets of abolitionism. Nor had he been affected by the teachings of John Woolman in the late 1740s, when the New Jersey Quaker began his crusade against the evils of slavery.

For Franklin, the problem with Peter and Jemima stemmed not from any moral qualms that ownership of them brought to the master but from their less than satisfactory work habits. Just a few months after the letter to his mother, Franklin penned his *Observations Concerning the Increase of Mankind,* which included a revealing passage about the desirability of excluding Africans from America "where we have so fair an Opportunity, by excluding all Blacks and Tawneys, of increasing the lovely White and Red." Franklin concluded this thought with the admission that "I am partial to the Complexion of my Country, for such Kind of Partiality is natural to Mankind."[3]

If Franklin was much like most other Pennsylvanians in his prejudice against the "Sons of Africa" and in his obliviousness to the moral indictments against slavery that were beginning to grow on the eve of the Seven Years' War, he was also discovering, as they were, that free labor could be more profitable and convenient than slave labor. In the *Increase of Mankind* Franklin argued that chattel property was uneconomic, most of all because of the "Neglect of Business" that came naturally to a person "who is not to be benefited by his own Care or Diligence."[4] Moreover, slaves ruined the white children in the families that owned them because "the white Children become proud, disgusted with Labour, and being educated in Idleness, are rendered unfit to get a Living by Industry."[5] To the father of 19-year-old William Franklin, such a remark may contain a special poignance.

Despite their growing distaste for slave owning, Benjamin and Deborah did not sell Peter and Jemima, as Franklin had told his mother in 1750 they intended to do. The onset of the Seven Years' War in 1754 dried up the supply of indentured servants because hundreds of Scots-Irish and German servants fled their masters and answered the call of British recruiting sergeants, making the purchase of white servants much too risky for the prudent investor in human labor. In this situation, slaves became the preferred form of bound labor. Resisting the quickening currents of antislavery ideology, Franklin joined scores of other Pennsylvanians in purchasing Africans during the war years. No evidence remains to say just when, but Franklin purchased King sometime before leaving for England with son William on April 4, 1757.

Deborah Franklin bought another slave, Othello, shortly thereafter. He would help Deborah around the house, replacing Peter, who Franklin had taken with him to England.[6]

While mirroring fellow Pennsylvanians in suppressing doubts about the efficiency of slaves in order to shift to black labor during the dislocations of the Seven Years' War, Franklin, like many around him, could not escape the nagging questions regarding the morality of slavery that were being raised on both sides of the Atlantic, principally by members of the Society of Friends. As the following pages will recount, the tireless Woolman had spread his message of antislavery in the early 1750s, and the leadership of the Society of Friends began to respond. Philadelphia Yearly Meeting, previously unwilling to sponsor antislavery advocates, took its first stand against slaveholding in 1754, and in 1755 warned Friends against any further importing or purchasing of slaves. Within three years, the Society took the first step to cleanse itself of slaveholding. Franklin was well apprised of all of this, and it is likely that his own decision to free Peter and Jemima at his death—a decision made as he rewrote his will while waiting in New York for ship's passage to London in 1757—may have been influenced by the newly forged resolve of Quaker leaders in Philadelphia Yearly Meeting to end the involvement of their members in the ownership of other human beings.[7]

So too, the Quaker hand can be seen, at least faintly, in the decision Franklin made in 1758, just after reaching England, to revise a phrase for the fourth edition of his *Observations Concerning the Increase of Mankind,* where Franklin changed the observation that "almost every Slave being by Nature a Thief . . ." to "almost every Slave being from the nature of slavery a Thief . . . ."[8] Franklin and his wife were not willing to give up their slaves, but the antislavery message was beginning to penetrate the armor of economic interest and personal convenience.

Despite the bold new ideological commitment of Quakers against slavery, the war years increased the involvement of Pennsylvanians in the system of coerced labor as the demand for labor rendered infertile the soil in which the antislavery Quakers were trying to plant seeds. Franklin's private experience with slavery during the war years adumbrated the larger movements under way in Pennsylvania. First, his slave King, whom he had given to his son William Franklin to serve as manservant, ran away in London, while Benjamin and William were visiting in the country. King was soon found in Suffolk, in the service of a lady who had taught him to read and write and to play the violin and French horn; but Franklin and his son consented that King should stay with her with a possibility that she might purchase him from William.[9] Thus, the Franklins learned first hand of the precariousness of slave property in the wartorn world of the mid-eighteenth century. Then, in 1760, Othello died in Philadelphia, a single statistic in what Franklin had noted a decade before—that in the northern colonies, slave deaths always outnumbered births, necessitating "a continual Supply . . . from Africa" to maintain their number.[10]

The tension between economic interest and antislavery ideology, a main theme in this book, continued for Franklin—and for Pennsylvanians—in the 1760s and 1770s as the American Revolution brewed. Franklin was reconsidering his notions of African inferiority, as became evident in 1763, when he visited the Anglican school for blacks in Philadelphia. He "conceiv'd a higher Opinion of the natural Capacities of the black Race, than I had ever before entertained," Franklin wrote. "Their Apprehension seems as quick, their Memory as strong, and their Docility in every Respect equal to that of white Children."[11] But such new attitudes did not keep Franklin from acquiring a fifth slave, George, valued at £100 in New York currency, in partial payment of a debt from Franklin's old friend James Parker in 1763. George would assume Othello's role, helping Deborah around the house.[12]

Franklin's ambivalence about slavery, like that of many fellow Pennsylvanians, increased during the years leading up to the Revolution. In 1770, Franklin was dubbing a conversation between an Englishman, a Scotchman, and an American in which the American was put immediately on the defensive for making "a great Clamour upon every little imaginary Infringement of what you take to be your Liberties," while at the same time being "Enemies to Liberty" in their holding of thousands of slaves.[13] Franklin's ideological pendulum swung even farther toward antislavery in 1772 through his association with Anthony Benezet, Philadelphia's stalwart abolitionist of the Revolutionary era. By June of that year Franklin was openly questioning the morality of slavery. In an unsigned letter to *The London Chronicle* on "The Somerset Case and the Slave Trade," he wrote: "Can sweetening our tea, &c. with sugar, be a circumstance of such absolute necessity? Can the petty pleasure thence arising to the taste, compensate for so much misery produced among our fellow creatures, and such a constant butchery of the human species by this pestilential detestable traffic in the bodies and souls of men?"[14] A year later, he wrote a friend that he "had the Satisfaction to learn that a Disposition to abolish Slavery prevails in North America," and to Benjamin Rush in the same year he opined "that the Friends to Liberty and Humanity will get the better of a Practice that has so long disgrac'd our Nation and Religion."[15]

Yet like so many Pennsylvanians, who by the outbreak of Anglo-American hostilities in early 1775 had become convinced that slavery was incompatible with the natural rights on which they were basing their protests against Great

Britain, Franklin held on to his slaves. Though admitting that slavery might disgrace "our Nation and Religion," Franklin could find no way to follow the path away from slavery that the Society of Friends was paving. When Deborah died in December 1774, Franklin was preparing to return to Philadelphia. Upon reaching the city in May 1775, he passed ownership of his slave George, who had been deeply distraught at his own wife's death only three years before, along to his daughter Sally and her husband Richard Bache.[16] Six years later, when Franklin was in Paris, his daughter reported that after much illness George had been sent to the Pennsylvania Hospital "as it was impossible to attend him . . . up four pairs of stairs from the Kitchen" (that is, in the attic). Several months later, Sarah Bache wrote her father, his former slave died.[17]

Peter, who had remained with Franklin throughout his two sojourns in England, fared no better. While serving Franklin, he had been separated from his wife Jemima for thirteen of the sixteen years between 1759 and 1775, just as his master had been separated from his wife Deborah. When Franklin came ashore in Philadelphia in May 1775, Peter was apparently at his side.[18] What became of him and his wife Jemima after 1775 is not known; but it is highly likely that if Franklin had released them from slavery, the manumissions would have been recorded in the court records or in the manumission books of the Pennsylvania Abolition Society or noted in the newspapers. Most likely, they died after Franklin's return to Philadelphia; possibly Jemima had not lived to see her husband come back from England, just as Deborah failed by five months to live long enough to see Benjamin step ashore on the Delaware wharves.

Slavery in Franklin's personal family was dying, just as it was beginning to die in Philadelphia. But Franklin, like many Pennsylvanians, was dissociating himself from the system of coerced labor not by giving freedom to his slaves but through the flight or death of his bondspeople or his transfer of them to other owners. Franklin promised his slaves freedom when he died, but while he lived, which was for a very long time, they remained unfree.

By his eighty-first birthday, in the year that the Constitutional Convention met in Philadelphia in 1787, Franklin was speaking openly against slavery. As president of the Pennsylvania Abolition Society, he signed a public exhortation that declared:

It having pleased the Creator of the world, to make of one flesh, all the children of men—it becomes them to consult and promote each other's happiness, as members of the same family, however diversified they may be, by colour, situation, religion or different states of society.[19]

Three years later, Bonhomme Richard, the consummate American, died. So far as we know, Franklin held no slaves at his death. Peter, Jemima, King, Othello, and George were all gone, but none had been released outright by Philadelphia's most famous citizen. Slavery came to an end in Franklin's life by degrees and amid feelings and interests that pulled incessantly against each other. He never did, so far as we know, release any of his five slaves unconditionally. Yet once separated by circumstance from the institution that he grew to abhor, he became a committed antislavery spokesman. In his final will and testament, Franklin made a grant to his son-in-law Richard Bache that was conditional on Bache's release of his slave Bob.[20] Finally, just before he died in 1790, he wrote a biting parody against a Georgia congressman, who had attacked the Society of Friends for introducing a petition before the first federal congress for ending the slave trade. Signed "Historicus," the piece was alleged to be a speech of an Algerian prince, Sidi Mehemet Ibrahim, to the Divan of Algiers defending the ancient practice of enslaving Christians who had fallen into the hands of Barbary pirates. In this mock defense of slavery, Franklin came perilously close to his own long connection with slavery. "If we forbear to make Slaves of [the Christians]," asked Sidi Mehemet Ibrahim, "who are to perform the common Labours of our City, and in our Families?"[21]

   This book is about the tug of war between ideological commitments and economic interests, between leaders and followers, between slaves and masters that occurred in Pennsylvania in the eighteenth century over the issue of slavery. It also explores how slaves, once freed, were fitted back into the labor force and how a recognition of the possibility of recapturing the labor of former bondspeople played a role in the emancipation process.

   In a larger sense, the book is concerned with reform movements in American history and how reform comes about. Of all reform movements, abolitionism has always seemed the premier case of moralism transcending materialism. Indeed, the word "fanatical" has been used by generations of historians to describe (and often to deplore) those who so uncompromisingly put moral principle ahead of political and economic realities. Yet abolitionism in recent years has also been seen less nobly—as the calculating adjustment of people who understood that bound labor was becoming less profitable than free labor, or as a diversionary attempt to draw attention away from the wage-slavery that became part of the Western industrializing process.

   Pennsylvania's experience with slavery in the Revolutionary era has attracted much notice, but almost entirely from historians who have seen abolitionism there as a triumph of two kinds of ideological commitment—both

Christian moralism and the philosophy of natural rights. The state was the home of American Quakerism and Philadelphia was its capital. Hence, the testimony of the Society of Friends against slavery during the upheaval of revolution and the passage of the first legislative act against slavery by the Pennsylvania legislature in 1780 have often been seen by historians as a stirring victory of ideology over economic interest.

The Pennsylvania case is indeed noteworthy. Of the states south of New England, slavery died first in Pennsylvania and it died there the fastest. But its death was a complicated matter in which slaves themselves were far more involved than has been understood and in which masters were more notable for shrewd calculations of how to extricate themselves at little cost from an involvement in owning fellow human beings than for a rise in their moral sensibilities caused by participation in commercial enterprise or anything else. Nor was the transition to a free labor system smooth, because while masters might give up their slaves, they did not easily relinquish ideas about the people whose labor they formerly commanded absolutely.

This book delves into ideas that began to effect a sea change in thinking about slavery in this country, but it examines these ideas as they emerge from the grit of economic, political, and social experience. It tests large-scale explanations against small-scale patterns of behavior and asks whether the particularities of the Pennsylvania experience with ending slavery and incorporating free black labor into the economy are consistent with the broad generalizations that historians have made.

The business of extracting, collating, and computerizing data from some two thousand individual cases of manumission—buried in wills, court records, and the manumission books of the Pennsylvania Abolition Society—along with combing a dozen newspapers for runaway slave advertisements for more than half a century could never have been accomplished by the co-authors of this book without student research assistance. Our first debt, then, is to the following undergraduate and graduate students studying at the University of California, Los Angeles, and the University of Maryland, Baltimore County, who endured with good cheer a kind of bound labor—or at least an apprenticeship: Holly Brewer, Christopher Brown, Margaret Clark, Mariquita Davison, David Finch, Rachelle Friedman, Tom Ingersoll, Daniel Johnson, Michael Johnson, David Lehman, Randy Parraz, and Paula Scott.

Many colleagues and friends read parts or all of the manuscript and offered invaluable criticism. They include Paul Clemens and Thomas Slaughter, Rutgers University; William Forbath, UCLA; Graham Hodges, Colgate University; James C. Mohr, University of Maryland, Baltimore County; Lucy

Simler, University of Minnesota; Billy G. Smith, Montana State University; Marianne S. Wokeck, Biographical Dictionary of Early Pennsylvania Legislators; and members of the Seminar of the Philadelphia Center for Early American Studies, University of Pennsylvania; and the Los Angeles Labor History Group.

We are also grateful to the staffs of the Library of the American Philosophical Society, the Chester County Historical Society, Friends Historical Library of Swarthmore College, the Lancaster County Historical Society, the Library Company of Philadelphia, the Division of Archives and Manuscripts of the Pennsylvania Historical and Museum Commission, the Philadelphia City Archives, the Presbyterian Historical Society, the Quaker Collection of Haverford College, and the Rare Book Room of the Van Pelt Library, University of Pennsylvania. Not included in this list are the staff members of the manuscripts department and library of the Historical Society of Pennsylvania, to whom we have dedicated this book, in recognition of their decades-long partnership in interpreting Pennsylvania's past.

Freedom by Degrees

1

Slavery in the
"Best Poor Man's Country"

In 1811, ironmaster Colonel Thomas Bull of East Nantmeal Township, Chester County, registered with the county clerk a six-month-old black girl Haney. In doing this, Bull ensured that he could keep Haney as his servant until she reached age 28, which, if she did serve that long, would make her one of the last blacks in Pennsylvania to serve under terms of the state's gradual abolition act of 1780. Bull, nearing age 70 at Haney's birth, had carefully safeguarded ownership of his slaves under the act, which held that owners could retain permanently all slaves born before the law went into effect and keep for 28 years all babies born to slave mothers thereafter, as long as the masters registered the blacks with the county government. Colonel Bull had claimed ownership of two young men, Jem and Judge, in 1780, and apparently acquired one or more slave women soon after that date because he listed two boys and a girl in 1789, and another child in 1802. As far as we know, he freed none of his slaves born before 1780 or their children born thereafter.[1]

In clinging to his slaves and his legal right to the service of their children, the aged Thomas Bull gave testimony to his continued interest in their labor while at the same time holding fast to the symbols of the elevated social status to which he had risen in the late eighteenth century. Born in 1744, Bull was first a stone mason and then became manager of the Warwick Furnace of

Rutter and Potts in East Nantmeal, a major employer of slave labor. He served in the Revolution under Anthony Wayne. After the war, while still managing the Warwick Furnace, he bought a 500-acre tract at the headwaters of French Creek, where he built a large house, gristmill, sawmill, and blacksmith shop. Bull also bought a substantial interest in Joanna Furnace in Berks County. He served in the Pennsylvania Assembly and was a prominent member of St. Peter's Episcopal Church in the Great Valley.[2] He established his plantation and purchased slaves to help meet his considerable need for labor just as the state legislature ordained the gradual demise of slavery. In 1780, his two black lads, aged 19 and 16 years, were in their prime and promised years of service on his estate. Like other well-to-do slaveowners of southeastern Pennsylvania who cultivated large tracts, had interests in milling, ironworks, or crafts, and assumed a comfortable lifestyle with retinues of servants, Bull resisted emancipation. It was for Thomas Bull and others like him that the Assembly passed an abolition law that actually freed no slaves and could have kept blacks in bondage as late as the 1840s and beyond.

Bull, however, was one of the last Pennsylvanians to perpetuate the institution and in fact was unrepresentative of the Revolutionary generation of slaveholders in Pennsylvania. In 1765, near the conclusion of a period of high slave importation, about 6000 slaves toiled on Pennsylvania farms, in artisan shops and kitchens, and on wharves and ships (Table 1–1). Twenty-five years later, the number of slaves in the state stood at 3,760; and by 1810 the number had dropped to 795. In the capital city of Philadelphia, where nearly 1500 blacks lived in perpetual bondage in 1767, only fifty-five remained enslaved in 1800 and two in 1810. In outlying Chester County, where tax lists indicate the presence of about 550 slaves in 1765, 493 remained in 1780 but this number plummeted to 53 in 1800 and to 7 in 1810. This decline was far more precipitous than was mandated by the provisions of the 1780 law. Not only did the act prevent further growth of slavery in the state, but it undercut the legitimacy of the institution and thus spurred slaves to free themselves, and owners to release their bondsmen and women. The decision to emancipate did not come easily, however, as slaveholders like Thomas Bull prized their slaves' labor over any intangible benefits they might receive for freeing them. Slaveowners in western Chester, Lancaster, York, Cumberland, Westmoreland, and Washington counties—all located along the border with Maryland and Virginia—held on to their slaves most persistently. They had invested in blacks recently, enjoyed greater success than Philadelphians with slavery because of lower slave mortality in rural areas, and shared a common border with slaveholders to the south. In 1790, residents of Lancaster (including Dauphin), York, Cumberland (including Franklin), Westmoreland, and Wash-

TABLE 1–1. Slave Population in Pennsylvania, 1765–1800

	c. 1765–70	1780–82	1790 (% of Total Pop.)[a]	1810[b]
Philadelphia (incl. No.Libs. & Swk.)	1,481[c]	539[c]	301 (0.7%)	2
Phila. Co. (remainder) & Montgomery	412[d]	est. 400	196 (0.6)	9
Bucks	n.a.	520[e]	261 (1.0)	11
Berks	n.a.	290[f]	65 (0.2)	4
Chester & Delaware	552[g]	493[g]	194 (0.5)	7
Lancaster & Dauphin	106[h]	838[i]	586 (1.1)	70
York & Adams	n.a.	793[f]	499 (1.3)	93
Cumberland, Franklin, & Perry	n.a.	1,149[f]	553 (1.6)	394
Westmoreland, Washington, Allegheny, & Fayette	n.a.	1,140[j]	834 (1.3)	159
Remainder	n.a.	est. 693	271 (0.4)	46
Total Slaves	5,561[k]	6,855[k]	3,760	795

Sources: (a) U.S. Bureau of the Census, *Heads of Families at the First Census of the United States Taken in the Year 1790: Pennsylvania* (Washington, D. C., 1908), 9–11; Chester Co. figure from U.S., manuscript census, 1790. (b) U.S. Bureau of the Census, *Third Census* (Washington, D. C., 1810), 51a. (c) See Table 1–4, below. (d) Gary B. Nash, "Slaves and Slaveowners in Colonial Philadelphia," *William and Mary Quarterly,* 3rd ser., 30 (1973): 246; adjusted to exclude the Northern Liberties. (e) This figure is from William W. H. Davis, *History of Bucks County Pennsylvania,* 2nd ed. (New York, 1905), 296–97. The microfilmed Bucks Co. Register of Slaves [1780], available from the Pennsylvania Historical and Museum Commission, Harrisburg, lists only 506 slaves, perhaps because a page has been lost since Davis consulted the manuscript. (f) Data for taxable slaves (ages 12 to 50 years), 1779, in Evarts B. Greene and Virginia D. Harrington, *American Population Before the Federal Census of 1790* (New York, 1932), 119; we used a multiplier calculated from the 1780 Chester Co. slave register (1.77) to estimate total slave population. (g) See Table 1–8, below. (h) Nash, "Slaves and Slaveowners," 244–45. (i) Copy, Lancaster Co. Register of Negro and Mulatto Slaves and Servants, Lancaster Co. Historical Society, Lancaster, Pa. (j) Washington Co. Negro Register (1782), available on microfilm from the Pennsylvania Historical and Museum Commission; George Dallas Albert, ed., *History of the County of Westmoreland, Pennsylvania, with Biographical Sketches* (Philadelphia, 1882), 60. (k) Estimate of Pennsylvania black population published in U.S. Bureau of the Census, *Historical Statistics of the United States, Colonial Times to 1970* (Washington, D. C., 1975), II, 1168, reduced by our estimate of 200 free blacks in 1770 and 1000 free blacks in 1780.

ington (including Allegheny) counties comprised just 44 percent of the state's population but held two-thirds of the slaves. In 1810, with about the same proportion of the total population, they owned 94 percent of men and women yet in bondage.

Of the original thirteen states, only Rhode Island and Connecticut approximated Pennsylvania's decline in slavery in the post-Revolutionary era. Both of

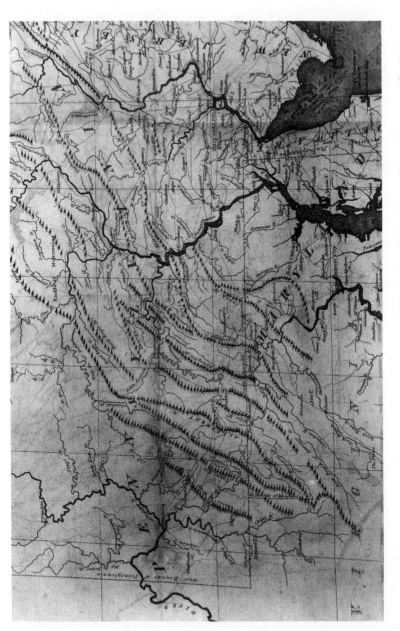

Detail of "A Map of Pennsylvania, Delaware, New Jersey & Maryland, with the Parts adjacent," engraved for Robert Proud, *The History of Pennsylvania, in North America* (Philadelphia, 1798), vol. 2. Courtesy of The Historical Society of Pennsylvania.

these states contained slave populations that were somewhat larger in proportion to the white population than was the case in Pennsylvania, but the rate of decrease in slaveholding from 1780 to 1810 was very similar in all three states. Few slaves lived elsewhere in New England. But in neighboring New York, New Jersey, and Delaware, where the demise of slavery might be expected to have followed a course similar to Pennsylvania, the institution remained vibrant into the early nineteenth century (Table 1–2). The proportion of slaves among all inhabitants generally declined throughout the mid-Atlantic region after 1750, but the absolute numbers of slaves continued to climb until 1790 in New York and Delaware and through the end of the century in New Jersey. Contrary to the case of Philadelphia, the number of slaves grew in New York City until 1800. In the South, with continued importation and natural increase of slaves, the black and white populations grew at about the same rate. The number of slaves grew rapidly, confounding the Revolutionary generation's belief that slavery would wither, especially if the slave trade ended. Slaves made up about one-third of the southern population in 1790: they maintained that proportion in the old South in 1820, while in the new states, Alabama, Mississippi, and Louisiana, slaves composed 40 percent of the total population.[3]

TABLE 1–2. Slavery in the Mid-Atlantic Region, 1750–1800

	New York		New Jersey		Delaware		Pennsylvania	
	No.	%*	No.	%*	No.	%*	No.	%*
1750	11,014	14.4	5,354	7.5	5,740	20.0	2,822**	2.4
1760	16,340	13.9	6,567	7.0	6,650	20.0	4,309**	2.3
1770	19,062**	11.7	8,220**	7.0	7,050**	20.0	5,561**	2.3
1780	20,954**	10.0	10,060**	7.2	8,477**	19.0	6,855**	2.1
1790	21,193	6.2	11,423	6.2	8,887	15.0	3,760	0.9
1800	20,903	3.5	12,422	5.9	6,153	9.6	1,706	0.3

*Percentage of total population.

**Data on black population reduced by our rough estimate of number of free blacks.

Sources: For 1750 to 1780, the New York and New Jersey data are from U.S. Bureau of the Census, *Historical Statistics*, II, 1168, verified with census data available in Greene and Harrington, *American Population*, 100–102, and reduced by rough estimates of the number of free blacks based on Arthur Zilversmit, *The First Emancipation: The Abolition of Slavery in the North* (Chicago, 1967), 242; Thomas E. Drake, *Quakers and Slavery in America* (New Haven, 1950), 75, 80; and Jean R. Soderlund, *Quakers and Slavery: A Divided Spirit* (Princeton, 1985), 106. The Delaware data for 1750–80 are from Patience Essah, "Slavery and Freedom in the First State: The History of Blacks in Delaware from the Colonial Period to 1865" (Ph.D. diss., University of California, Los Angeles, 1985), 21, 100–101; and the Pennsylvania data are from Table 1–1 above and U.S. Bureau of the Census, *Historical Statistics*, II, 1168. All figures for 1790 and 1800 are from U.S. Bureau of the Census, *A Century of Population Growth from the First Census of the United States to the Twelfth 1790–1900* (Washington, D. C., 1909), 57, 133.

Thomas Bull, then, was synchonized more with plantation owners in the South and in other parts of the Middle Atlantic region than with his neighbors of southeastern Pennsylvania. Long after most Pennsylvanians, whether for ideological or economic reasons, judged slavery obsolete, Bull held fast to a labor system that had thrived in his locality in his youth. Few blacks living in the state in the early nineteenth century suffered under thralldom. But the institution had flourished only a generation before and had been an important source of labor through the pre-Revolutionary period.

For most of the eighteenth century, slavery had significance as a labor system beyond the bounds of plantation society. Regions outside the tobacco, rice, and sugar producing areas of the Chesapeake, Carolinas, and West Indies depended on African slaves to fill their labor needs. At times during the pre-Revolutionary period slaves accounted for one-third to one-half of the work-force employed by merchants on ships sailing from northern ports and in city shops, tanneries, ropewalks, and houses. Outside the cities, slave men and women worked fields and ran mills, shops, and forges. Slaves did a wide range of jobs in the North and could perform a variety of tasks over the course of a day, week, year, or lifetime. The requirements of urban production and trade, mixed agriculture, and rural manufacture imparted distinct characteristics to slave life on the periphery of plantation areas.

Pennsylvania was a good case in point. The rise and fall of slavery in eighteenth-century Pennsylvania, in both the city of Philadelphia and its hinterland, provide a counterpoint to the growth of slavery in the southern colonies. Without a staple crop to monopolize the energies of large numbers of bound laborers for most of the year, Penn's colony experienced no dramatic transition from white to black bondsmen and women like that of Barbados, South Carolina, and the Chesapeake tidewater. Farmers, rural and urban artisans, merchants, and professionals turned to white indentured servants, black slaves, free laborers, and family members as the supply and price of different kinds of labor varied and their labor needs changed. While some wealthy Philadelphians and rural entrepreneurs marked their social status with a retinue of slaves, most producers viewed black and white labor as interchangeable and probably preferred whites. No occupation became associated solely with slaves. The flexibility of Pennsylvania's labor system facilitated abolition of slavery in the state in the last two decades of the eighteenth century. Advocated first by Quakers and Revolutionary Whigs for religious and humanitarian reasons, emancipation gained momentum in the late 1780s and 1790s as slaveowners learned that they could recoup their investment and retain access to the services of blacks while manumitting their slaves. At the turn of the century black indentured servants and wage laborers joined white workers to provide a ready supply of cheap labor.

The experiences of Africans who landed in Pennsylvania and their progeny were therefore different in many respects from slaves who toiled in fields of rice, tobacco, and sugar cane. But different too were aspects of the lives of African-Americans who worked in Pennsylvania's capital city and in the countryside. Throughout the colonial period slaves composed a higher proportion of the population of Philadelphia than of its hinterland, and thus urban slaves enjoyed greater opportunity to create a richer social life. High mortality and cramped living quarters in the city, however, worked against the formation of families. While adverse conditions prevented slaves in Philadelphia from sustaining their numbers by natural population growth at any time before the Revolution, after 1750 the population of slaves in the country began to grow naturally, primarily because mortality was lower outside the city. The work slaves performed in Philadelphia and the countryside also had distinct characteristics, of course, but in both places women provided mostly domestic service, and men could be expected to do a variety of jobs, including domestic chores. Indeed, slaves were sold so frequently and transferred back and forth from city to country that it is impossible to separate completely the experience of a rural Pennsylvania slave from that of her or his counterpart in Philadelphia.

Black bondage played an important role in the social and economic life of early Pennsylvania, especially its capital city, Philadelphia. Slaves lived in Pennsylvania before the Quakers came with William Penn in 1682. Johan Printz, who governed New Sweden, the first significant European settlement in the region, had a black man Anthony in his service, and the Dutch West India Company in the 1660s employed black slaves along the Delaware. A few of the Swedish and English farmers who preceded Penn's arrival owned slaves, including Lasse Cock, a prominent Swede who served as Penn's interpreter to the Lenni Lenape.[4]

Like the Swedes and Dutch before them, the English, Irish, and Welsh who came to Pennsylvania to launch Penn's "holy experiment," the majority of them Quakers, made use of slave labor. They desired workers to help build houses, shops, sheds, wharves, roads, breweries, brick kilns, taverns, and all other "improvements" that in less than a decade literally created out of the wilderness a city and its appendaged farmlands. They cared little about the status or color of their workers, only that they toiled. The wealthy Quaker merchant James Claypoole, soon after he decided to move his family and business from London to Philadelphia, urgently wrote to his brother Edward in Barbados to request four black slaves: "2 good stout Negro men, such as are like to be pliable and good-natured and ingenious . . . [and] a boy and a girl to serve in my house; I would not have either of them under 10 years or above 20. But principally observe their nature and capacity." Claypoole had already sent to Penn's colony a white servant skilled in brickmaking and husbandry and was looking in England for several carpenters and laborers, a bricklayer, and a farmer. He envisioned a large estate in Pennsylvania, knew he needed many hands to fulfill his dream, and therefore turned to Africans as well as to his countrymen to meet his needs. In his frantic quest for labor, he did not shrink from bringing into his provincial household a completely alien and alienated people, which he never would have done in England.[5]

The settlers who in November 1684 purchased in a matter of days the 150 Africans delivered to Philadelphia on the ship *Isabella* still lived in temporary housing: crude structures like the dirt-floored and unchimneyed post-and-hole houses suggested by Penn to prospective settlers, or cellars dug in the ground and covered with planks.[6] These new colonists had brought large numbers of indentured servants with them and used their own hands and energies and those of their children who were old enough, but still they grasped any available and affordable laborers. Slavery quickly became part of the cultural and economic landscape of the Quaker colony, in the same way it was taking hold in other parts of North America. Penn and his associates founded Pennsylvania just as the English slave trade expanded to meet the needs of colonists in Virginia, Maryland, and the West Indies, and so Pennsylvanians too adopted the institution with enthusiasm. Immigrants to Pennsylvania from the West Indies (like those who went to South Carolina at the same time) brought slaves with them, and others imported blacks from the islands. Pennsylvania settlers, like employers throughout the British colonies, took advantage of the burgeoning slave trade of the late seventeenth and early eighteenth century.[7]

Among the first Quaker slaveholders in Pennsylvania was William Frampton, a wealthy merchant who moved to Philadelphia from New York. He was the agent of Charles Jones and Company of Bristol, England, who had imported the 150 Africans in 1684. Frampton's estate, probated in 1686, included four slave men, one called "a great Sambo," two women, and one slave whose sex was not recorded. Apparently Frampton took advantage of his position as agent and had the cash or credit needed to acquire what was for seventeenth-century Philadelphia a large number of slaves. He owned a brewery and a bakery, enterprises that required dependable and steady labor.[8]

Another early slaveholder was George Guest, a much more ordinary man than Frampton, who also died in 1686. Guest's personal estate, at £58 sterling, was less than one-tenth of the Quaker merchant's property. His inventory listed shared ownership of a "Negro boy" and a white boy servant with five years remaining on his indenture. Guest and his partner Joseph Browne had set up a brickmaking business by 1685, when they received a black man Jack (the "Negro boy" of the inventory?) from Patrick Robinson in payment for a load of bricks.[9] City craftsmen of all wealth brackets—brewers, bakers, brickmakers, carpenters—needed labor to build and carry on their businesses.

Despite early warnings by several Quakers that slaveholding violated their beliefs, Philadelphians in the highest ranks of the colony's power structure bought slaves to perform domestic service, build their wharves, houses, and stores, and labor on outlying plantations. Even before the city's establishment in 1682, George Fox, the founder of Quakerism, and the Irish missionary William Edmundson had already questioned the morality of owning slaves. And in 1688, four Germantown Quakers voiced their dismay about the burgeoning trade in human chattel. For them, "the traffick of men-body" undermined the spirit of Penn's experiment in brotherly love and made "an ill report in all those countries of Europe."[10] These sentiments fell on deaf ears: the Quakers who settled Philadelphia showed little compunction about drafting Africans to do their work. Of the twenty-seven Philadelphians who died before 1701 and are known to have owned slaves, at least twenty were Quakers; 70 percent of the men who led Philadelphia Yearly Meeting before 1706 owned black bondsmen and women.[11] Slaveholders included some of the most important people in the province. James Claypoole, the wealthy Quaker merchant and member of William Penn's inner circle, died in 1687 owning two slaves. John Eckley, appointed judge of the Provincial Court in 1684, was probably a slaveowner because his widow Sarah died in 1692 owning a black man Thom, his wife Betty, and their daughter Maria aged about two years old. Thomas Lloyd (d. 1694), who became president of the Provincial Council when Penn returned to England in 1684, directed in his will that his five slaves—Mingo, Wissen, Julius, Maria, and Sarah—be hired out and the wages paid to Lloyd's wife, Patience, and their children. The Irish Quaker Robert Turner, who served as provincial treasurer and judge of the Provincial Court in the 1680s, became a close associate of the schismatic George Keith in the 1690s and died in 1700 owning a black man Tony, as well as the slave's collar and chain. Thomas Fitzwater, another Friend and an assemblyman and coroner of Philadelphia County, ordered his executors to pay his debts by selling his slave man to the highest bidder.[12]

Thus, the newly established Quaker colony was no haven for blacks. Penn's "holy experiment" included an attempt to treat the Lenni Lenape fairly so as to avoid the bloodshed experienced in other regions of North America, but the

Quaker proprietor and his associates made no effort to prohibit black slavery in the City of Brotherly Love and its environs. Indeed, Penn owned at least twelve slaves himself and stated at one point that he preferred them to white indentured servants because slaves could be held for life. Though in one early will the proprietor provided for manumission, slaves worked on his Pennsbury estate in Bucks County throughout his tenure. One of these slaves was Black Alice who died in 1802 at age 116. She recalled often lighting the proprietor's pipe.[13]

The earliest laws of Pennsylvania, including *The Frame of Government*, the *Laws Agreed Upon in England*, and subsequent acts of the Assembly, neither legalized specifically nor prohibited slavery. Slaveholding colonists simply relied on custom to protect their property rights. Blacks accused of crimes were tried in the same courts and under the same laws as whites, and on at least some occasions, received the same punishments. In 1700, however, the Assembly recognized in law differences between the terms of servants, who served for a specified number of years, and slaves, who served for life. At about the same time, the lawmakers established separate courts for blacks and until 1780, when the courts were eliminated by the gradual abolition act, all blacks—free and slave—were tried by two justices of the peace and "six of the most substantial freeholders of the neighborhood," not by a jury. Murder, rape of a white woman, buggery, and burglary were declared capital offenses for blacks. Whites found guilty of these crimes (except murder) would not be subject to execution until 1718. The law further stated that a black man convicted of attempting to rape a white woman should be castrated. An act passed in 1706 altered the penalty for attempted rape to be the same as that for theft. The 1706 law held that "for an attempt of rape or ravishment on any white woman or maid, and for robbing, stealing, or fraudulently taking and carrying away any goods living or dead, above the value of five pounds, every negro, upon conviction of any of the said crimes, shall be whipped with thirty-nine lashes, and branded on the forehead with the letter R or T, and exported out of this province."[14]

In 1726, the Pennsylvania legislature established a full-fledged black code that, while less rigorous than legislation regulating the activities of slaves in most other colonies, formalized a caste system on the basis of skin shade and is most notable for the restrictions it placed on free blacks. The code required slaves to carry a pass from their masters when traveling and prohibited them from "tippling or drinking in or near any house or shop where strong liquors are sold." But in comparison with laws in effect in South Carolina and Georgia during the colonial period, the Pennsylvania code was positively enlightened. In the former colonies slaves were classified as property rather than as people, could not be taught to write (or read in the case of Georgia), were prohibited from certain occupations, and were subject to a bounty system in which slave hunters would be paid for the return of runaway slaves, alive or dead, the proof of the latter being a "scalp with Two ears." Under the Quaker colony's law, whites—including owners—were subject to the same punishment for killing or maiming a slave that they would receive if the victim were white. In South Carolina and Georgia, in many situations a person who murdered or assaulted a slave was required only to compensate the owner.[15]

For free blacks, however, the 1726 Pennsylvania law was severe, especially considering the moderate restrictions on slaves. The law required a master who wished to manumit a slave to put up a £30 bond in case the freed person should become a burden on his or her locality at some future time. This bond was considerably less than the £200 New York and New Jersey required, but still its effect was to discourage those with the inclination to emancipate their slaves. Further, blacks who managed to obtain freedom were liable to reenslavement. The 1726 law specified "if any free negro fit and able to work shall neglect so to do and loiter and misspend his or her time or wander from place [to place], any two magistrates next adjoining are hereby empowered and required to bind out to service such negro from year to year as to them shall seem meet." A freed black could also be reenslaved for marrying a white. And the children of ex-slaves could be taken from their parents until age 21 years for females and age 24 years for males, whether or not the family was poor or negligent, and with or without the consent of the parents. Freed men and women also could not trade with slaves or entertain them in their homes without the master's permission.

Despite creating this uncongenial environment for free blacks, Pennsylvania, in other ways, conferred advantages upon freed persons that other colonies lacked. New Jersey law prohibited free blacks from owning property; Pennsylvania law did not. Unlike South Carolina and Virginia, blacks liberated in Pennsylvania did not have to leave the colony and, indeed, the province placed no restrictions on in-migration from other places.[16]

Thus, the Quakers who controlled the Pennsylvania Assembly early in the eighteenth century followed the lead of other colonies by establishing a black code. They codified a social hierarchy based on color, placing special restrictions on free blacks and making them liable to reenslavement at the whim of a court. Still, slaves retained their status as persons. They could learn to read and write if the opportunity availed itself, were banned by law from no occupation, and liberty remained possible. But freedom for blacks did not mean equality—they remained, by law and custom, a separate, subordinate class.

Urban Slavery

From its founding, Philadelphia was an urban district, distinct economically, socially, and culturally from the rest of southeastern Pennsylvania. The city did not evolve gradually as a market town because it had a superior harbor or was in a central location. Rather, the city was planned. Penn took great pains in nurturing his capital: he approved the site, devised the plat, named its streets, sold the lots, and encouraged craftsmen and merchants to settle there. Philadelphia of course was inextricably tied to its environs. First Purchasers who bought tracts in the country were to receive both town lots and "liberty" lands, which were somewhat larger parcels in the immediate suburbs. This scheme, in theory, linked the urban and rural areas through the interests of the province's wealthiest investors. Over time, trade connections that facilitated production and marketing of the colony's chief exports—wheat, flour, and bread, livestock, beef, and pork, flaxseed, and wood products—kept Philadelphia closely tied to its hinterland. In addition, churches held lines of communication between members in town and country, while government maintained the legal framework under which all residents lived and worked.[17]

Notwithstanding its mercantile, religious, and political bonds with the countryside, Philadelphia evolved differently from the farmlands of early Pennsylvania. The city's population was densely settled, regularly received disease-ridden ships, and always contained a large component of new immigrants. Disease sustained by inadequate waste removal and the constant introduction of new germs created an extraordinarily high death rate.[18] Housing was generally compact and combined with the workspace of the craftsperson or shopkeeper, and was often rented. Residents purchased most of their food, but their access to the markets also introduced them to such luxuries as fine clocks and mirrors, a variety of books, tea and the equipage needed to brew it, coffee, chocolate, and exquisite cloth. Consequently, the urbanites encountered social pressure to buy such items. Most obviously, and almost by definition, the occupational structure of Philadelphia was unique in the province. The merchants, shoemakers, sea captains, carters, tavernkeepers, brewers, bakers, clerks, ship chandlers, shipbuilders, and wheelwrights often had different needs from the farmers who dominated the rural economy. Of course, artisans, merchandisers, and innkeepers inhabited the countryside, but they usually combined their trade or business with farming for both home use and the market.

Slavery developed in different patterns in the Quaker city and in rural Pennsylvania. Philadelphia's population included a higher percentage of slaves than could be found in the countryside for much of the pre-Revolutionary period, a circumstance that held important consequences for the lives of the slaves, as well as for their masters. Slavery grew far more rapidly and became more prevalent in the city than in the rural districts as urban dwellers invested substantial amounts of capital in labor and could use slaves productively on ships at sea, docks, boatyards, and construction sites, in taverns, artisan shops, and the homes of prospering merchants, professionals, and officeholders.

Slaves were most critical to the urban economy during the first forty years of the city's existence (see Table 1–3).[19] The percentage of slaves in the Philadelphia population peaked early in the century. In the first two decades of the eighteenth century, 12 to 17 percent of city residents were slaves, close to the proportion found in the Chesapeake during these years.[20] During the 1720s, economic depression severely weakened the demand for labor, and the slave population dropped below 8 percent. By the end of the decade, however, the city's economy had recovered and was embarked on a course of long-term expansion that would last for thirty years. To fill their need for workers, Philadelphia employers bought slaves, who in the late 1720s were available at cheaper prices than before. The period from the end of Queen Anne's War in 1713 through the 1740s witnessed an enormous expansion of slavery in the American colonies. Philadelphia slave prices, which declined after 1705 and reached their nadir in the mid-1730s, reflected this increased supply. The

TABLE 1–3. Slave Population of Philadelphia (City Only)
Calculated from Probate Inventories, 1691–1770

	No. Slaves* per Inventoried Decedent[a]	Houses[b]	Calculated Slave Pop.	Est. Percentage of Total Pop.[b]
1691–1700	.44	485	213	10.4%
1701–10	.84	750	630	17.4
1711–20	.65	940	611	12.4
1721–30	.42	1145	481	7.5
1731–40	.53	1335	708	9.1
1741–50	.51	1565	798	8.5
1751–60	.47	2080	978	7.6
1761–70	.52	2645	1375	8.2

*In inventories.

Sources: (a) Phila. Co. Probate inventories (testates and intestates), 1691–1770 (for city wards only), Phila. City Hall, Register of Wills. (b) P. M. G. Harris, "The Demographic Development of Colonial Philadelphia in Some Comparative Perspective," *Proceedings of the American Philosophical Society* 133 (1989): 274; adjusted to exclude Northern Liberties and Southwark. See n. 19 in this chapter for further discussion of sources.

lowering in 1729 of the duty paid on each slave transported into Pennsylvania from £5 to £2 also spurred substantial importation of blacks. Quaker Ralph Sandiford attacked the increased trade in his pamphlet, *A Brief Examination of the Practice of the Times* (1729). He warned in his revised edition published the next year, "We have *negroes* flocking in upon us since the duty on them is reduced to 40s *per* head for their importation, which makes a revenue of the evil instead of removing it; for we have frequently slaves sold twice a week in sight of my habitation which is in the center of this city, by vendue or auction, with the beasts, in sight of our christian magistrates called *Philadelphians.*" The view of the auction block from his shop window led Sandiford to risk disownment by the Friends, who would not approve his tract.[21]

During the three decades following the 1730s, slavery remained an important source of labor in Philadelphia, as about 8 percent of city dwellers were slaves, but from the late 1730s to 1754 heavy immigration of Scots-Irish and Germans provided an alternative labor supply. The immigrants frequently offered themselves and their families as indentured servants in order to pay the cost of their passage. About 58,000 Germans and 16,500 Irish came up the Delaware between 1727 and 1754. When the flow of German immigrants stopped during the Seven Years' War, however, and white servants fled to the British army to avoid serving the remainder of their terms, many Philadelphians, especially artisans, purchased slaves to fill their labor needs. From 1757 to 1766, approximately 1,290 African and West Indian slaves disembarked in Philadelphia or directly across the river in West Jersey.[22] Thus, 15 percent of Philadelphia's households possessed slaves in 1767, with the highest concentrations of slaveownership in Chestnut, High, Walnut, and Lower and Upper Delaware wards, all a part of the commercial core of the city and home to many of Philadelphia's most prosperous citizens. Slaveholding was least frequent in Mulberry Ward and in the adjacent Northern Liberties, where laboring class people made up the bulk of the population. After 1767, slaveholding decreased quickly in the city. About 1500 slaves lived in Philadelphia, Southwark, and the Northern Liberties in 1767, but by 1775 this number had been halved—to about 728 slaves—while the total population of the city and its immediate suburbs grew by one-fourth (Table 1–4). The percentage of slaves in Philadelphia's population dropped from 5.6 percent to 2.2 percent in eight years. The city's slave population continued to decline, to about 539 in 1780, 301 in 1790, and 55 in 1800. By the turn of the century, black bondage was virtually extinct in Pennsylvania's capital.

The rise and fall of slaveowning did not occur in a uniform manner throughout the ranks of free Philadelphians. Among wealthy city dwellers, those who died with personal estates worth £200 sterling or more, slaveholding reached its zenith during the first decade of the eighteenth century when over two-

During the 1750s and 1760s, when shiploads of slaves from Africa and the West Indies arrived in the Delaware, the London Coffee House, at Front and Market streets in Philadelphia, was the scene of slave auctions. Detail of watercolor by Edward Mumford. Courtesy of The Library Company of Philadelphia.

TABLE 1–4. Black Population in Philadelphia,
Including Southwark and the Northern Liberties, 1767–1810

	Total Population	Slaves	Free Blacks	Total Blacks (% of Total Pop.)	
1767	26,460[a]	1481[b]	57[c]	1538	(5.8%)
1775	33,290[a]	728[d]	114[c]	842	(2.5)
1780	36,946[a]	539[d]	241[c]	780	(2.1)
1790[e]	44,096	301	1849	2150	(4.9)
1800[e]	67,811	55	6028	6083	(9.0)
1810[e]	88,987	2	8942	8944	(10.0)

Sources: (a) Harris, "Demographic Development," 274. (b) Philadelphia tax assessment list, 1767, Rare Book Room, Van Pelt Library, University of Pennsylvania;
adjusted to include nontaxable slaves (estimated to be 35% of the total). (c) Manumissions from wills, records of Philadelphia Monthly Meeting (Quaker Collection of
Haverford College), Phila. Co. deeds (City Archives), and records of the Phila. Court
of Quarter Sessions (City Hall). (d) Constables' returns, 1775 and 1779–80 (City Hall
Archives), adjusted to include Southwark and the Northern Liberties (estimated from
the 1767 tax list to be 16.5% of the total). (e) U.S. Bureau of the Census, *Heads of
Families,* 10; U.S. Bureau of the Census, *Return of the Whole Number of Persons
within the Several Districts of the United States: Second Census* (Washington, D. C.,
1800), 2a; U.S. Bureau of the Census, *Third Census,* 33–33a.

thirds of affluent decedents owned slaves. In the period before 1711,
slaveholding was most pervasive among wealthy merchants, professionals,
and "gentlemen": over three-fourths of these inventoried decedents held
blacks. After that, every decade except the 1740s marked a steady decrease in
slaveownership among the city's wealthy. In the 1730s, fewer than one-half of
wealthy decedents owned slaves, and by the 1770s, the proportion dropped
below one-fourth.[23]

Among the wealthy Philadelphians who owned slaves early in the eighteenth century were several merchants who had a house and businesses in the
city and an outlying plantation or two. They kept slaves in both places. For
example, John Jones was a carpenter, merchant, and planter who died in 1708
owning a total of twenty-three blacks. One lived with his son, eight lived at
his residence in Philadelphia, and fourteen labored at his plantation north of
the city in Southampton, Bucks County.[24] Samuel Carpenter, one of Penn's
commissioners of property, provincial treasurer, and a long-time provincial
councilor, also owned a Bucks County plantation in addition to his real estate
in town. When he died in 1714, he owned seven slaves: two men, Mingo and
Stepney; an old man, "Malagascar Jack," and his wife, Sarah; a little girl,
Pegg; an old woman, Hagar, "past her labour;" and a boy, Ishmael. Jonathan

Dickinson, who owned two plantations in Jamaica and two in Pennsylvania—in addition to his city property—had a total of twenty-one slaves in Pennsylvania when he died in 1722.[25]

A large proportion of the wealthy merchants and gentlemen who owned five or more slaves during this early period had migrated from the West Indies or had close contacts there; these connections suggest the source of many of Philadelphia's slaves. Émigrés from other colonies, especially the West Indies, brought slaves with them to the new province. In addition to Jones, Carpenter, and Dickinson, examples include Magness Popell, a merchant and shipowner from Barbados who owned seven slaves when he died, and merchant Andrew Duany, formerly of Jamaica, who possessed twelve slaves. The city's merchants imported parcels of slaves as part of their ongoing trade with the islands. Dickinson and fellow Quaker Isaac Norris received numerous consignments of slaves from West Indian traders during the first three decades of the eighteenth century. Both men expressed discontent about being involved in the trade, but their complaints seem to have resulted more from the unhealthiness of the bondspeople they received than from any moral abhorrence of the slave trade. In a letter written on May 2, 1715, to his brother in the West Indies, Dickinson acknowledged the existence of antipathy towards the trade among some Pennsylvania Quakers but nevertheless requested that more slaves be sent, as long as they were young and healthy.[26]

The trend of slaveownership among less affluent Philadelphia craftsmen, merchants, and professionals followed a different course than among the wealthy. Among inventoried decedents whose personal wealth was £50 to £200, slaveownership peaked in the 1730s and 1740s, when 30 to 40 percent died owning slaves. Employers with limited resources could take advantage of decreased slave prices to increase their productive capacity during an era of economic expansion. Bricklayers Samuel Hall and Samuel Nicholas and tailors Thomas Roberts and Joseph Webb, who died in the 1730s leaving personal estates worth £55 to £86, all had acquired slaves. The bricklayers each owned a male slave who were individually valued at £12, considerably below the average price of about £20 for slave men in Philadelphia in the early 1730s. Apparently these craftsmen had purchased slaves, who, for whatever reason—youth, poor health, surliness—commanded low prices, to assist them in their trade. The two tailors, Roberts and Webb, both owned women, a sensible choice for the sewing trade since slave women on average cost less than men. Roberts's young woman and Webb's girl Bess were valued at £15 and £17, respectively, about average for women at that time.[27]

After the 1730s, as prices of slaves began to rise, less affluent employers turned from slaves to white immigrant labor. However, when German immigration stopped during the Seven Years' War, middling craftsmen and merchants bought up imported slaves. To take a famous example, Benjamin Franklin acquired at least four slaves, Peter, King, Jemima, and Othello, in the 1750s. When Franklin and his son William left Philadelphia for London in 1757, they took Peter and King with them, leaving Peter's wife, Jemima, in Philadelphia to serve Deborah Franklin, his wife.[28]

In 1767, in Philadelphia and its suburbs, Southwark and the Northern Liberties, craftsmen were the largest occupational group among slaveholders, composing over one-third of slave masters. Another 30 percent were merchants, 12 percent were proprietors of taverns, shops, chandleries, and inns, and 10 percent were sea captains and mariners. Throughout the pre-Revolutionary period, over 40 percent of Philadelphia's slaves worked for artisans, mariners, and owners of ropewalks, shipyards, breweries, tanneries, and brickyards (Table 1–5).[29]

Philadelphia slaves worked at a wide range of occupations and could be expected to fill a number of roles during the course of a day, year, and lifetime. The work slaves did varied from Philadelphia to the countryside, but because many slaves in both city and hinterland performed domestic service (women more often than men) and practiced trades (men much more often than women), and because owners frequently sold or transferred bondspeople from one place to another, no sharp distinctions can be made. Differences in the composition of slave contingents working at John Jones's Philadelphia residence and Bucks County plantation, with more women in the city and more men and boys on the farm, suggest some variations in how owners

TABLE 1–5. Sex and Age of Slaves Owned by Occupational Groups in Philadelphia, 1682–1780

	No. of Slaves	Percentage of Slaves					
		Women	Men	Girls	Boys	Unk.	Total
Widows/Single Women	96	40%	22%	18%	10%	10%	100%
Innkeepers	37	35	24	14	19	8	100
Mariners	78	31	27	10	18	14	100
Artisans	287	27	37	11	19	6	100
Merchants/Shopkprs.	282	24	30	12	22	12	100
Gents./Professnls.	89	24	36	14	24	2	100
Total	869						

Sources: Phila. Co. Probate inventories, 1682–1780 (for city wards only); Jean R. Soderlund, "Black Women in Colonial Pennsylvania," *PMHB* 107 (1983): 60.

employed black labor in the town and country. Jones's Philadelphia crew included one man, Cudgo, who was a sawyer, five women, and two girls. While Cudgo's skills were obviously suited to carpentry (Jones's trade), the women and girls labored in Jones's townhouse and shop. Perhaps Jones hired out several of the women. The slaves who worked at Jones's plantation included five men, a woman with her three-month-old baby, another woman, five boys, and a girl. According to his 1708 will, Jones wanted these slaves to stay on his plantation and cultivate, improve, and manage it until its sale. Those who could not be used on the plantation were to be hired out for the highest wages, and if any "prove[d] untoward or refractory neglecting their duty" Jones's trustees and widow were to sell "them that so evilly demean themselves." Jonathan Dickinson also tended to assign more women to Philadelphia and more men to his farms, but he did not segregate them absolutely by sex. Two males, three females, and four slaves of unknown sex lived in the city; six males, one female, and three other blacks toiled on his plantations at Frankford and on the road to Wissahickon, and two other females had unspecified dwelling places.[30]

In Philadelphia, craftsmen, merchants, shopkeepers, and professionals preferred to own slave men who performed a wide variety of jobs, working side by side with their masters, white servants, and free laborers (Table 1–5). In its advertisements the *Pennsylvania Gazette* gave wide notice of the skills of slaves. They were blockmakers, barbers, masons, coopers, butchers, biscuit and sugar bakers, mariners, tanners, distillers, carpenters, shipbuilders, and blacksmiths.[31] However, a slave craftsman or assistant could carry out household chores in addition to his artisanal duties; a slave in town could be transferred to the country to help with the harvest. As slaves passed from owner to owner by sale or inheritance, they were expected to adapt quickly and learn new trades. Tom, the slave of Ann Reardon of Society Hill, was a biscuit baker who, before starting work at the bakery, "followed whitewashing." Daniel Badger's slave Ben had been a farmer and butcher before joining Badger's crew on the *Lovely Lass*. He jumped ship near Marcus Hook in June 1770, perhaps because the sea was not his calling, perhaps to return to friends and family in the city. William Chesney's slave Will, also known as William Keith, was both "very handy about a Farmer's House" and a cooper, having learned his trade with a former owner in Philadelphia before moving to York County.[32]

Throughout the colonial period, widows and innkeepers in Philadelphia favored slave women over slave men, presumably because their primary need was for domestic help; and despite the preference of craftsmen, merchants, and professionals for men, they too owned women who assisted in their homes, shops, and sometimes in trades. Most slave women did housework, which required diverse skills. One twenty-year-old woman, advertised for sale in 1767 "for no fault" could "do all kinds of house-work extraordinary well, such as cooking, washing, ironing, &c." An earlier sale notice, perhaps for the same slave, mentioned that she could sew "coarse plain Work" in addition to her other duties. Another woman could "cook well, and do all Sorts of House Work in Town or Country."[33] With this flexibility and multiplicity of talents and skills, slaves remained an important source of labor in Philadelphia through the colonial period. Though never dominant in numbers they provided a necessary alternative for labor-hungry colonists.

Beyond their work, what was life like for slaves in Philadelphia? How did the conditions for bondsmen and bondswomen change over the century prior to the Revolution and how was the situation of urban slaves different from what it would have been had they lived in the surrounding countryside of southeastern Pennsylvania? The overarching reality for enslaved blacks, of course, was their legal subjection to their masters, who not only extracted their labor but dictated their physical well-being, held sway over marriages and families, and determined their residence and occupation.

The initial indignity for enslaved Africans was their capture, sundering them from kin and community. Booty in war or kidnapped merchandise, the new slaves endured a march to the sea where they boarded crowded disease-ridden slave ships that would take them across the Atlantic. Prior to 1758, most Africans who ended up in Pennsylvania went first to the West Indies. They worked on island plantations until migrating north with their owners or until sold in small groups on consignment to a Philadelphia merchant like Isaac Norris or Jonathan Dickinson, who had lived in the West Indies and maintained close ties with island merchants and planters. From 1758 to 1765, many of the slaves brought up the Delaware River came directly from Africa. When the Seven Years' War interrupted the European servant trade, Philadelphia merchants responded to the critical need for labor by sending ships directly to the west coast of Africa to pick up whole cargoes of slaves for Philadelphia's market.[34]

It is difficult to know what proportion of the city's black population at any given time was born in Africa and how many were "country-born"—native to Pennsylvania and surrounding colonies. We know from Darold Wax's work, and from population data and probate records, that slave importation into Pennsylvania was high relative to the number of slaves already living in the province in the 1680s, from 1705 to 1720, in the 1730s, and from 1758 to 1766. Frequent importations meant that a high proportion of Philadelphia slaves were African-born—whether brought from the West Indies or directly from their homelands.[35] It is impossible, however, to make a firm estimate of the proportion of city slaves who were "new Negroes" because there is no way of determining how many of the slaves brought into the province stayed in Philadelphia and how many were sold to masters in rural Pennsylvania, West Jersey, Delaware, and Maryland.

Advertisements that owners placed in the *Pennsylvania Gazette* in an effort to track down runaway slaves provide some evidence about the backgrounds of slaves who dared to escape their owners. Jo, who ran away from his master George Smith of Philadelphia in 1740, had been born in Bermuda and spoke "good English." Richard Swan's man Cuffy was born in Montserrat and knew both English and French, while John Winckles's James was "Carolina born." The importation of a large number of slaves directly from Africa in the late 1750s and early 1760s is reflected in descriptions of Pennsylvania slaves. Phebe (or Sarah, as she called herself) had "three or four large Negroe Scars up and down her Forehead," evidence of her African origins. Robert Shewell's "Negroe lad, named Limerick . . . [was] remarkably black, 3 scars each side of his face, well made."[36]

Data from the Philadelphia probate inventories and other sources provide insight into the possibilities for family life among slaves in the city. The sex ratio of slave men to women was highest in the first decade after settlement, when almost all of the slaves in the province had only recently arrived, either directly from Africa on the *Isabella,* in 1684, or from the West Indies. From 1690 on—with the exception of 1711–20, which was also a time of high importation—the ratio of slave women and men stayed even (Table 1–6). White Philadelphians brought both men and women to the city: the greatly skewed sex ratios denoting high importation of men into the plantation areas of the West Indies, Carolinas, and Chesapeake did not exist in the Quaker city. City employers wanted slaves for domestic work as well as for jobs in construction, crafts, maritime work, and hauling. And because Philadelphia purchasers were offered the least desired of any slaves shipped from Africa by way of the West Indies, they received a higher proportion of women than the sugar colonies.

While the number of slave women matched the number of men for most of the pre-Revolutionary period, Philadelphia slaves were not able to make the transition to a self-sustaining population that blacks in the Chesapeake colonies achieved by the 1720s and 1730s.[37] If Philadelphia slaves had been able to maintain their numbers by reproduction, at least one girl per woman would be found among them.[38] Instead, the number of slave girls never surpassed 0.8 per woman during the colonial period and actually declined to about 0.4 per woman after 1750 (Table 1–6). Thus, the city's pre-Revolutionary slave

TABLE 1–6. Sex Ratios and Girl/Woman Ratios
of Philadelphia Slaves, 1682–1780

	No. of Slaves*	Ratio of Men to Women	No. of Girls** per Woman
1682–90	20	1.40	0.2
1691–1700	34	.89	0.6
1701–10	87	1.13	0.7
1711–20	108	1.38	0.7
1721–30	76	.67	0.7
1731–40	110	1.00	0.8
1741–50	179	1.22	0.7
1751–60	178	1.21	0.4
1761–70	265	1.10	0.5
1771–80	143	.92	0.4

*In inventories. Native American slaves are not included.

**Girls are counted rather than children to minimize the count of imported children, among whom boys predominated.

Source: Phila. Co. Probate inventories, 1682–1780 (for city wards only).

population, though women and men might find mates, could not replenish itself and required continued importation for growth. When the Pennsylvania Assembly placed a £10 per head duty on imported slaves in 1761 and twelve years later raised it to £20, thereby in effect legislating the slave trade out of existence, the number of slaves in the city plummeted. In the years between 1767 and 1775, when the slave population of Philadelphia (including Southwark and the Northern Liberties) declined from about 1500 to 728, fewer than 100 children were born and survived. During the same period 679 slaves and free blacks were buried in the city.[39]

Available evidence does not permit precise determination of the factors that impeded natural population growth among black Philadelphians, but enough is known about mortality and morbidity in the city and about the conditions under which slaves lived to provide some general observations. Mortality among whites was much higher in Philadelphia than in the Middle Atlantic countryside, and for the city's blacks it was higher still. While residents of rural areas died at an estimated average rate of 15 per thousand each year, the crude death rate for all Philadelphians, slave and free, generally ranged from 34 to 52 per thousand, primarily because a high proportion of city residents were recent immigrants, who had lived under harsh conditions on board ship, were susceptible to diseases endemic to the new land, and brought other illnesses with them which in turn infected city residents. Poor sanitary conditions and crowded housing added to Philadelphia's insalubrity.[40]

Blacks were more vulnerable to disease than were whites. In the forty-three years during the colonial period for which evidence exists, Susan Klepp finds that the annual death rates averaged 67 per thousand for city blacks, as opposed to 46 per thousand for whites. Klepp suggests this differential resulted from the fact that slaves had poorer nutrition and housing, and were more susceptible than whites to measles, smallpox, and respiratory infections, especially pleurisy and influenza.[41]

Contributing to this soaring death rate, and perhaps most significant for whites and blacks, was high infant and child mortality. Klepp's study of white Philadelphia families revealed that one-fourth of children died in their first year and one-half died by age 15. For Philadelphia blacks, child mortality was at least as high, and probably higher.[42] Quaker abolitionist and teacher Anthony Benezet observed in 1773 that black Philadelphians, especially infants, died in such numbers that their population would dwindle without new arrivals.[43] The conditions of urban slavery—inability to care adequately for a child because of duties required by the master, poor diet, mistreatment, rarity of husband and wife living in the same household—all contributed to high infant mortality and reduced fertility. Some slave women may have induced abortions and committed infanticide to relieve their own situations and to avoid raising a child who would grow up only to live out his or her life as a slave.[44] In addition, the likelihood of having children sold or apprenticed outside the city was no incentive to produce them.[45]

Runaway advertisements from the *Pennsylvania Gazette* testify to the liability to injury, disease, and rough usage of Philadelphia slaves. Richard Swan's slave Cuffy had a "large scar on his forehead and both feet sore." James, the slave of John Winckles, a Philadelphia painter, was "much scarr'd on the small of his back and shoulders." A slave man owned by Philadelphian Silas Parvin was "hip-shot" and in consequence could go "very lame." Greenwich, owned by David Franks, was "blind of an Eye." Joe, a young black man committed to Chester jail in November 1763, who said his master was blacksmith Edward Brown of Philadelphia, had a rupture; and Ann Willing's 17-year-old slave was "knock kneed, and marked with the small-pox, and [had] a large wen on his neck, under the right ear." Blathwaite Jones described his 21-year-old mulatto man Ned, who called himself Ned Levy, in this way: "5 feet 6 inches high, he squints much, or rather has a cast in his eyes, bow legged, with a scar on the left side of his nose, and is very apt to shut his right eye." And Ishmael, the slave of William Thomas of Southwark, was "25 years of age, about 6 feet high, strong made, his colour between a mulattoe and a black, rocks in his walk, or rather somewhat lame, occasioned by his having his thigh bone broke when a boy."[46] Slaves were not the only persons who suffered injury and disability in the eighteenth century, but the indifference of owners toward the health of their slaves, and the brutality of some, increased susceptibility to accidents, infectious diseases, and chronic illness. Benjamin Lay, the ardent Quaker abolitionist, decried the poor conditions in which slaves lived. Bondsmen and women had insufficient clothing, he thought, for harsh Pennsylvania winters. Lay dramatized this point by standing in deep snow without a shoe.[47] As late as 1806, in January, Robert Sutcliff observed a 12-year-old boy near Philadelphia dressed in only "a light linsey jacket and trowsers, without hat, shoes, or stockings." He had a locked iron collar around his neck "and from each side of it an iron bow passed over his head."[48]

Thus, while slavery in Pennsylvania by many standards was less brutal than in plantation areas, still, like the institution everywhere, it relied on physical force. Though most slaves were not in chains, some runaways had them on when they escaped because, according to their owners, they had tried to run off before. Philip Syng's man Cato "had irons on his legs, and about his neck, but probably has cut them off, as he has done several times before on the like occasion." Brickmaker John Coats kept his slave workers in iron collars with hackles to prevent them from fleeing his Philadelphia brickyard.[49] Quakers, who dominated the provincial legislature for most of the colonial period and were about one-third of slave masters in the 1730s and one-sixth by the 1760s, were forbidden by their religious beliefs from using violence.[50] But given the severe penalties accorded blacks convicted of crimes—significantly harsher than punishments prescribed for white criminals—Quakers did not shrink from using state violence to control their slaves.

Slaves countered the will of their masters most often by running away and by resistance, both overt and covert, such as theft, vandalism, insolence, and work slowdowns. In his *Observations Concerning the Increase of Mankind* (1751), Benjamin Franklin noted in reckoning the costs of slave labor that in addition to the initial purchase price, cost of food and clothing, and risk of death, masters also suffered "Loss by [the slave's] Neglect of Business (Neglect is natural to the Man who is not to be benefited by his own Care or Diligence), Expence of a Driver to keep him at Work, and his Pilfering from Time to Time." Isaac Norris I, the Quaker slave trader, found that slaves frequently feigned illness or acted in an unruly manner to prevent being sold. One man from Jamaica in 1702 "pretended he could not work. Sd. his hand was broke and he was good for Nothing." The next year a woman whom

Norris sold to a Maryland buyer was "very averse to going & Just as the Boat was to put off gave us the Slip. I shall dispose of her as Soon as I can (for she has plaid [played] some Ill pranks in the family)." Others pretended to be lame or warned potential buyers that if they were sold they would refuse to work. In 1772, George Nagel of Reading attempted to sell George, the slave of Bernard Gratz of Philadelphia. George was so disruptive that Nagel sent him to the jail and later put him up for auction at a local tavern, "where there was a Number of Persons who inclined to Purchase him. But he protested publickly that he would not be sold, and if Any one should purchase him he wou'd be the Death of him and Words to the like purpose which deter'd the people from biding." Nagel finished by reporting that George was "now almost Naked and if not furnish'd soon with some Cloathes I fear he'll perish. . . He's now Chain'd & Hand Cuff'd on Account of his threats." Slaves also committed suicide, as documented in Philadelphia in 1743, 1748, 1759, 1761, and 1764. Quaker John Smith witnessed an episode in 1748 in which he "perceived a Bricklayer who works at Building Capt. Dowers's house & his negro differing—saw the master strike him upon which the negro ran down to the End of the wharf—& several after him—when he got there he swore if his master struck him again he would jump off & drown himself—which the master unhappily doing—the fellow was as good as his word—jumped off & perished before anybody could save him."[51]

Slave families were vulnerable to the needs and whims of their owners. Billy G. Smith, in his analysis of advertisements published in the *Pennsylvania Gazette,* 1728 to 1790, finds that masters supposed that 6 percent of their runaways left in order to rejoin family members or friends from whom they had been separated by sale, a smaller percentage than indicated by newspaper notices in the Chesapeake and Lower South. Smith also discovered that Delaware Valley owners expected 17 percent of the fugitives to flee to Philadelphia and 10 percent to travel to other specific locations. Presumably the slaves had unstated reasons for heading in those directions, including the intent to reunite with kin or otherwise pick up the pieces of a disrupted life. Thus owners in Virginia, Maryland, New Jersey, and outlying counties in Pennsylvania purchased space in Philadelphia newspapers in the hope that their slaves might be found in the city or elsewhere in the region. Will had learned coopering in Philadelphia before being sold to William Chesney of York County. Joseph Hugg, who lived near Gloucester, West Jersey, thought his slave man Grig probably returned to Philadelphia, as he had been owned by a Mr. Wilcox and then Mr. Mullen, innkeeper, of that city. In November 1771, Thomas Cullen of Pottsgrove gave his " Mullatoe wench" Hagar Jones a pass for eight days to visit her child in Philadelphia. When she had not returned by January, Cullen had her picked up and taken to the Philadelphia workhouse but she was released because he neglected to obtain a commitment from the mayor. By February, Jones still had not returned to service. Cullen described her as "a very lusty Indian looking hussy, remarkably fond of spiritous liquor, very turbulent in her temper, drunk or sober, is supposed to have gone to New-Jersey or New-York, and being an artful jade, may probably obtain a pass under pretence of being a free woman; she has a large scar on her forehead, is about 34 years of age."[52]

Thus family ties for Philadelphia slaves remained tenuous. If a slave couple established a relationship and had children, they could expect to see the children hired out, apprenticed, or sold to masters elsewhere in the city, the colony, or beyond. City houses had limited space and feeding slave children meant added expense. In January 1767 an anonymous owner wanted to sell his 20-year-old slave woman because she had given birth to a baby girl, "it being inconvenient in the family she now lives, to have a breeding wench."[53] The tax lists, constables' returns, censuses, and probate records all show that only a minority of Philadelphia slaves could have lived in the same household as family groups, even when the low average size of families is taken into consideration. Most lived in households with three or fewer slaves: only about 5 to 7 percent of slaveowners listed on the 1767 tax list, the constables' returns of 1775 and 1780, and the 1790 and 1800 censuses had four or more blacks. In the period up to 1780, 42 percent of slave women listed in the probate inventories lived in the same household with a potential spouse. Of the men, 39 percent lived with slave women. More women than men had slave children under the same roof: 47 percent of women but only 35 percent of men lived with one or more children who were possibly their own. Moreover, the fact that women and men, and adults and children, had the same master did not necessarily mean that the slaves were kin. While an owner's slaves were sometimes related—for example Quaker Samuel Preston's eleven slaves were a three-generation family—just as likely was the possibility that the slaves had no relationship to each other. The records of two Philadelphia Anglican churches further show that slave husbands and wives rarely lived in the same household. Of sixty-four black couples married in Christ Church and St. Peter's Church between 1727 and 1780, both partners were free in seventeen marriages and one person was free and the other slave in nine marriages. Of twenty-nine marriages between slaves, only seven couples were owned by the same master and twenty-two had different masters. The status of the remaining nine couples is unknown.[54]

Thus, while Philadelphia slaves had little chance to establish households and raise families under their own roofs, some were able to form relationships with blacks living nearby. And urban slaves, unlike those living in the Pennsylvania countryside, could benefit from proximity to a large number of slaves. If they were willing to live apart from spouses, they could marry and have children, though this separation likely reduced fertility among black women.

In addition, the city with its substantial black population offered social and cultural resources that rural slaves lacked. White churches and individuals established schools specifically for blacks and provided opportunities for worship whether in separate meetings or in regular services. Both Anglicans and Friends started schools for black children in the 1740s and 1750s. Robert Bolton, who had been Philadelphia's dancing master, renounced his former role and established a school for black children in 1740. Bolton, like many of the city's slaves, was moved by great awakener George Whitefield's message of spiritual equality. In 1747 the Society for the Propagation of the Gospel (SPG) sent William Sturgeon, a Yale graduate, to catechize Philadelphia blacks and hold special services for them. And in 1758, with the assistance of Benjamin Franklin, a slaveholder himself, the Associates of Dr. Bray, an Anglican philanthropic society, set up a school for free black and slave children.[55] Quaker abolitionist Anthony Benezet had begun in 1750 to hold evening classes for blacks in his home, and in 1770 he convinced Philadelphia Monthly Meeting to open an "Africans' School." He was one of very few eighteenth-century whites who considered black and white children to have the same intellectual potential. As in other schools of the time, all of the scholars in the Quaker school studied reading, writing, and arithmetic, and while the girls learned sewing and knitting the boys did more advanced academic work.[56]

Friends and Anglicans also concerned themselves with the spiritual welfare of blacks, but their contrasting definitions of church community led them to fulfill their missions in different ways. The patterns are familiar to anyone cognizant of the history of American race relations: by the 1770s the Quakers wanted slaves free but would not welcome them as regular members of the meeting; the Anglicans would incorporate them within the church, but in a subordinate role. Friends had encouraged, indeed required, members to bring their slaves to meeting since 1696 and permitted black attendance at regular meetings for worship throughout the colonial period. Philadelphia Quarterly Meeting set up a separate meeting for blacks in the 1750s, perhaps to interest them in coming. But Friends did not permit blacks, free or slave, to join the church until the 1790s, after a long internal conflict over the issue. Pennsylvania Quakers, especially after the 1750s when tribalistic tendencies were exacerbated, defined the boundaries of their group narrowly and did little to encourage outsiders of any sort to join.[57]

Pennsylvania Anglicans, on the other hand, while distinctly less interested than Friends in assuring the freedom of slaves, were more willing to include them within the church. As the established church in England and several American colonies, though not in Pennsylvania, the church accepted as its mission to minister to everyone regardless of their station in society. Christ Church had recorded just one marriage and no baptisms of blacks before 1741, but after that date, free blacks and slaves married and were baptized at the city's Anglican churches with increasing frequency. The SPG missionary Aeneas Ross arrived in town in 1741 and, though he stayed only until the next year, baptized eighteen adults, of whom twelve were blacks. Robert Jenney, the next rector of Christ Church, continued Ross's efforts, reporting in 1744 that "our Negroes are numerous & many of them inclined to be religious." The connection between Philadelphia's African-Americans and the Anglican churches—Christ Church, St. Paul's, and St. Peter's—lasted through the Revolution. The Christ Church records show that more than 250 blacks were baptized and 45 couples wed in the church between 1745 and 1776.[58]

Beyond these white-dominated activities, there is evidence that self-ordained slave ministers preached and performed rituals within the black community. Preaching Dick, who fled first from Robert Grace and then from

Philadelphia, Sept. 4. 1746.

RUN away on the 16th of July, from Thomas Rutter, of this City, a Negro Man, named Dick, commonly call'd Preaching Dick, aged about 27 Years: Had on when he went away, a Bearskin Jacket, and a light Duroy Jacket, without Sleeves, Oznabrigs Shirt and Trowsers, and one Pair of brown Linnen Trowsers, blue Stockings, new Shoes, a new Castor Hat, and blue Worsted Cap. Whoever takes up and secures the said Negro, so that his Master may have him again, shall have Thirty Shillings Reward, and reasonable Charges, paid by   THOMAS RUTTER.

From 1730 through the 1780s, newspaper advertisements for escaped slaves appeared with increasing frequency, as bondsmen and women claimed freedom from reluctant owners. Such notices tell the stories of defiant slaves like Preaching Dick, who fled his owners at least twice. *Pennsylvania Gazette,* September 4, 1746. Courtesy of The Historical Society of Pennsylvania.

butcher Thomas Rutter, was well known in the city in the 1740s, and Moses Grimes, the slave of John Hales of Lombard Street, was "very religious," preaching "to his colour, walk[ing] before burials," and performing the marriage ceremony in the 1770s. Mary Deklyn of Callowhill Street lamented the loss of her slave Rachel, who was about 30 years old, had "a remarkable austere countenance," and had taken her owner's hymn book with her. Penn, the slave of Thomas Savin of Cecil County, Maryland, could be expected to "make a great shew of religion." Penn adopted the name of James Pemberton (after the eminent Friend?) and ran away from his master at least twice, in 1769 and in 1774. The first time he passed as a freeman and indented himself to a currier named Meredith in Philadelphia.[59] The section of the "Strangers burial ground" that was set apart for blacks was the gathering place for the city's slaves and free blacks throughout the colonial period. According to one woman's memoirs, slaves could be seen "going to the graves of their friends early in the morning, and there leaving them victuals and rum." On holidays and fair days, blacks "divided into numerous little squads, dancing, and singing, 'each in their own tongue,' after the customs of their several nations in Africa."[60]

The slave Penn, like other runaways, hoped to pass in anonymity among the large and constantly changing population of blacks in Philadelphia. Many owners believed that their escaped slaves were "lurking" about the city, supported no doubt by friends and kin. Philip Syng wrote that 20-year-old Cato "generally skulks about this City." Thomas Barnard of Marcus Hook, Chester County, expected that 30-year-old Phebe was "harboured by some of the free Negroes in or near Philadelphia or Germantown." Masters also thought that their slaves might try to board ship at Philadelphia and thereby make good their escape. Joseph Johnson of Southwark wrote that his black man Quaco, who called himself William Murrey, had run off about six weeks earlier. "He has a certificate of his being baptized," Johnson continued, "which he shews as a pass, and says he is a free man; and, as he is a sly arch fellow, may have a forged pass from me of his freedom; he has been seen in several parts of the town, and on Friday last he was seen at the barracks." Johnson warned, "Whoever harbours or conceals said Negroe, may depend on being prosecuted to the utmost rigour of the law; and all captains of vessels are forbid to carry him off at their peril." William Dunscomb believed that his slave Dick, who had jumped ship in Baltimore, was headed for Philadelphia, "intending it is thought to get into some vessel, as he followed the sea."[61]

Thus, while a Philadelphia woman remembered later that her grandfather had claimed that "he not only knew every gentleman in town, but every gentleman's black servant and dog,"[62] runaways counted on the anonymity of the city to protect their self-acquired freedom. As would happen later to a much greater extent, the Quaker city was a magnet for refugees from the southern colonies and elsewhere. Philadelphia's substantial slave population, growing number of free blacks, and role as an entrepôt, which both offered the sea as an additional avenue of escape and constantly infused new elements into the city, gave some hope to slaves searching for freedom that they might find it in Penn's capital city.

Slavery in the Countryside

Slavery followed a trend in rural Pennsylvania different from that in Philadelphia. Until 1750, black bondage was a far more important source of labor for urban residents than for farmers, craftsmen, and entrepreneurs in the countryside. While 80 percent of the colony's total population lived in the hinterland in 1720 and 89 percent in 1750, only 60 to 65 percent of Pennsylvania slaves lived outside Philadelphia during the first half of the century.[63] After 1750 slavery started to grow more quickly in parts of rural Pennsylvania than in the city. Though the total populations of Philadelphia and the rest of Pennsylvania expanded at about the same rate from 1750 to 1790, the proportion of the colony's slaves living in the countryside rose from about two-thirds in 1750 to three-fourths in the 1760s, to over 90 percent in 1780 and 1790 (Table 1–1). In the late 1750s and 1760s, with increased importation, the number of slaves rose in both Philadelphia and outlying areas, but after 1767 the two patterns diverged: while the number of slaves fell sharply in Philadelphia between 1767 and 1780, no such dramatic decrease occurred in the country. The number of slaves dropped only slightly in Chester County and probably remained level in Philadelphia County (not including the suburbs of Southwark and the Northern Liberties which are counted with the city). In Lancaster County the slave population grew eightfold between 1759 and 1780; Lancaster Borough's taxable slaves increased from thirteen in 1756 to at least fifty-seven in 1782. Slaveholding rose similarly in Yorktown, York County, after the mid-1760s.[64] After 1780, when the gradual abolition act prevented by law further growth of the institution, slavery began to decline in rural Pennsylvania as well as in the city. The number of enslaved men and women in the countryside dropped from 6,316 in 1780 to 3,459 in 1790, and to 793 by 1810.

Chester County, southernmost of the three original Pennsylvania counties and located to the west and southwest of Philadelphia on the Delaware and Maryland borders, provides a rural contrast to the city. Swedes, Finns, and

Dutch first settled the eastern part of the county along the Delaware, then Penn's settlers filled the rolling hill lands west of the river's edge, and subsequent natural increase and immigration, especially during the years from 1730 to 1760, pushed settlement westward. Except for the town of Chester, a landing place for ships going upriver and the local seat of government, Chester County (including Delaware County, which was formed from the eastern part of Chester County in 1789) remained primarily agricultural throughout the eighteenth century. Medium-sized family farms, sometimes combined with trades such as weaving, smithing, and tanning, characterized the economic landscape of the county as a whole. By 1760, farm families owned tracts averaging about 135 acres, on which they grew wheat, rye, flax, and Indian corn, and raised horses, cattle, hogs, and sheep; they sold wheat, flour, flaxseed, meat, cheese, and butter at market.[65]

As in Philadelphia, slaves provided one source of labor in Chester County throughout the eighteenth century, albeit on a smaller scale than in the city. Again there was no dramatic and permanent shift from servant to slave labor as on the plantations of the West Indies, South Carolina, and the Chesapeake. For most of their labor needs Chester County farmers, like those throughout southeastern Pennsylvania, employed free labor: themselves, their families, apprentices, and hired laborers. The volume of farm work varied by season in wheat-growing areas so that most farmers required additional field labor for only part of the year.

However, Chester County residents who farmed fairly large tracts, had mills, tanyards, forges, inns, or similar holdings that required workers year-round, and were wealthy enough to afford domestic servants, frequently invested in bound labor, more often indentured white servants than slaves during most of the pre-Revolutionary period. In Thornbury Township in 1726, for example, fourteen of twenty-three landholding households employed additional labor, including a total of seventeen bound white servants, five slaves, and two hired servants.[66] Three-eighths of inventoried decedents in eastern Chester County before 1700 owned white servants (Table 1–7). Then, during the first decade of the eighteenth century, the proportion dropped to about one-fifth and continued on a downward trend to the 1770s when only one-tenth of inventoried decedents owned indentured servants. While the indentureships declined, slaveownership increased. After an initial high point before 1710, the proportion who owned slaves at death plummeted to less than 4 percent during the years 1711–20, and then generally rose through the rest of the pre-Revolutionary period. If the probate records are an accurate guide, nearly one-third of the area's households contained bound laborers throughout the coloni-

TABLE 1–7. Slave and Servant Ownership
in Eastern Chester County, 1682–1780

	% Owning Slaves	% Owning Servants
1683–1700	18.8%	37.5%
1701–10	16.7	22.2
1711–20	3.3	16.7
1721–30	9.5	19.0
1731–40	14.5	14.5
1741–50	9.8	16.0
1751–60	13.1	15.5
1761–70	10.6	11.5
1771–80	19.0	10.1

Source: Probate inventories of Chester, Ridley, Springfield, Nether
Providence, Upper Providence, Middletown, Aston, Edgmont, and Marple townships. Chester County Archives, West Chester, Pa.

al era.[67] The demand for bound labor remained fairly steady, but in contrast to
Philadelphia, the use of slave labor increased at the end of the colonial period.

Among slaveholders in Chester County was Robert Wade, who immigrated
first to Salem, West Jersey, with John Fenwick in 1675, went briefly to
Burlington, and then settled in Upland on a large estate. Wade was a Friend
and the earliest Quaker meetings in Chester met in his house. He served in the
Assembly and as a justice of the peace. When he died in 1698, he owned a
white man-servant Alexander, an Indian "servant," and three black slaves,
probably the man and woman John and Jane and their daughter Jane, whom
Wade's widow Lydia freed when she died in 1701.[68] Ralph Fishbourne was
another wealthy Quaker who lived in Chester and died owning slaves. A
merchant and farmer, he owned at least three plantations, a bolting house, a
bakehouse, and a shop. When Elizabeth Fishbourne died in 1709, one year
after her husband, she owned a slave man Jack, who had been hired out to a
neighbor, another man Cull, his wife Betty, and their infant Cull. Ralph
Fishbourne had also given two slaves to his son William. Widow Fishbourne
split up her slave family in her will, giving the young Cull to her brother as
soon as the child was weaned.[69]

Other early Chester slaveowners included James Sandelands, who lived in
Pennsylvania prior to Penn's coming. He owned an old black woman, a young
woman, and a child. Alice Trumain, an Aston Township widow with little
inventoried wealth, owned a "Nagor" and two Scots servants. Quaker farmer
John Bristow of Chester owned at least two plantations, a malt-house, and a

slave man, woman, and children. Retired farmer Samuel Levis, Sr., gave his slave Jeffrey to his daughter Elizabeth Shipley, an eminent Quaker minister. John Camm, a farmer and frame-work knitter; Joseph Baker, Andrew Morton, and Joseph Cobourn, farmers; cooper Richard Finiken; and tanner Frederick Engle, all owned slaves when they died.[70]

A more famous slaveholding Quaker couple were David and Grace Lloyd, who moved to Chester from Philadelphia around 1714. David Lloyd, a lawyer, held a number of provincial offices, including speaker of the Assembly and chief justice. Leader of the "country" party of early Pennsylvania politics, he engaged in battle with the proprietor over the rights and powers of the Assembly. When he died in 1731, a gentleman and a farmer, Lloyd owned four slave men, three women, and three children. Grace Lloyd, who served as presiding clerk of the women's Philadelphia Yearly Meeting and Chester Monthly Meeting, owned five slaves when she died nearly thirty years later. She freed two men and two women in her will, but gave another man, Will, to Francis Richardson, a Philadelphia merchant.[71]

Slaveholding reached its height in rural Pennsylvania during the period from about 1765 to 1783 (Table 1–8). Slaveownership became most frequent by the mid-1760s, soon after large numbers of blacks were imported to replace white servants whose immigration was cut off by the Seven Years' War. Between 1760 and 1765, the number of slaves nearly doubled, from 293 to 552, and over the next decade and a half—contrary to the urban trend and despite numerous manumissions by Quakers—the number dropped only slightly.[72] After 1783, slavery in Chester County declined quickly: by 56 percent between 1783 and 1790 and by 88 percent by the end of the century. Slaveholding was not evenly distributed across the county from 1765 to 1783 but rather clustered in several locations: along the Delaware River, in Westtown and Edgmont townships, in the Great Valley, in the Nottinghams along the Maryland border, and, to a lesser extent, along the Octorara and Brandywine creeks.

While the level and centers of slaveholding in Chester County changed little between 1765 and 1783, white indentured servitude first increased and then declined drastically during these years, a drop even more rapid than in Philadelphia. The number of taxable servants (aged 15 to 50 years) rose from 149 in 1760 to 436 in 1775, as immigration resumed after the Seven Years' War, then dropped precipitously to 43 in 1779. The Revolution of course had eliminated immigration to Pennsylvania as had the Seven Years' War twenty years before, but this time white servitude did not rebound. The labor structure in Chester County—and in southeastern Pennsylvania as a whole—changed fundamentally in the years after 1780.[73]

TABLE 1–8. Black Population in Chester County,* 1760–1820

	Total Population	Slaves	Free Blacks	Total Blacks (% of Total Pop.)
1760	24,281[a]	293[a]	28[b]	321 (1.3%)
1765	28,779[a]	552[a]	36[b]	588 (2.0)
1780	32,000[c]	493[d]	137[b]	630 (2.0)
1783	34,537[a]	442[a]	158[b]	600 (1.7)
1790[e]	37,298	194	826	1,020 (2.7)
1800[e]	44,902	53	1,790	1,843 (4.1)
1810[e]	54,330	7	2,617	2,624 (4.8)
1820[e]	59,261	8	3,842	3,850 (6.5)

*Includes Delware County after 1789.

Sources: (a) 1760 tax assessment list, Shippen Papers, Historical Society of Pennsylvania [HSP]; and 1765 and 1783 tax assessment lists, Chester County Archives, West Chester. Total population was estimated by using a multiplier (5.1) calculated from the 1783 tax list and census. Because the 1765 and 1783 tax lists included only slaves aged 12 to 50 years, the total number of slaves in 1765 and 1783 was estimated by using a multiplier calculated from the 1780 slave register (1.77). Lucy Simler shared her data from the 1760 and 1783 tax lists. See also Paul G. E. Clemens and Lucy Simler, "Rural Labor and the Farm Household in Chester County, Pennsylvania, 1750–1820," in Stephen Innes, ed., *Work and Labor in Early America* (Chapel Hill, 1988), 115. (b) Manumissions from Chester County wills, deeds, and records of the Court of Quarter Sessions (Chester County Archives); and records of Bradford, Chester, Concord, Darby, Goshen, Kennett, New Garden, Nottingham, Radnor, Sadsbury, and Uwchlan Monthly Meetings (Friends Historical Library of Swarthmore College). (c) Estimate based on number of 1779 taxables reported in Greene and Harrington, *American Population,* 117, 119. (d) Chester County Slave Register, 1780, Pennsylvania Abolition Society Papers, Reel 24, HSP. (e) U.S. Bureau of the Census, *Heads of Families,* 9; U.S. Bureau of the Census, *Second Census,* 2a–2b; U.S. Bureau of the Census, *Third Census,* 36a–37; U.S. Bureau of the Census, *Fourth Census, 1820* (Washington, D.C., 1821), 20.

No hard and fast lines separated owners of slaves and indentured servants in Chester County. In 1765, both groups were wealthier on average than tax-payers who controlled no bound labor. They owned more land and were more likely to be involved in milling, tavernkeeping, tanning, distilling, and other activities where labor needs were beyond the capacity of family members. While all Chester County landholders averaged 134 acres each, landholding slaveowners had 222 acres and landholding servant-owners had 196 acres. And though innkeepers and the owners of iron furnaces and forges were more likely to own slaves, a greater number of distillers, millowners, and tanners held white servants. As a whole, investors in such enterprises were more likely to own bound laborers than was the average taxpayer. Part of this difference can be explained by wealth, but the opportunity to keep workers busy year-round was important too.

Like their counterparts in Philadelphia, rural slave women spent most of their time engaged in domestic chores, though in the country these tasks extended to the farmyard and meadow. In 1762 an owner wanted to sell his 18-year-old "wench" who could "do all manner of house-work, and is used to milking and being among cows; she can spin flax and wool well, and is a good washer." Another woman was "able to do town or country work, but most suitable for the country, as she was brought up there, and is very handy and active in tending cattle and horses, and can do many sorts of out-door work."[74]

While most slave men in the hinterland did field work and a variety of chores required on an eighteenth-century mid-Atlantic farm, some had skills such as masonry, sugar making, coopering, and tanning.[75] A number worked at the iron forges that dotted the Pennsylvania countryside. In 1765, forge owners John Potts and Samuel Flower of East Nantmeal were taxed for eight men and seven men respectively, and Jonathan Vaughan of Aston held six men, more than the norm of at most one or two slave men per owner. At ironworks, most slaves toiled at unskilled jobs, including mining and wood-cutting, or were semiskilled colliers, who made charcoal. In 1768, for example, Persifor Frazer of Thornbury Township sought the return of Isaac, a 26-year-old man who "understands the Coaling Business, having been employed therein for 3 or 4 years at Sarem Forge" on Chester Creek. Many slaves also worked as apprentices to skilled forgemen, however, and became skilled themselves.[76] At New Pine Forge in Berks County, in 1760, a labor agreement specified that a skilled forgeman take "charge of a Negro man called Tom and [promise] to use his utmost Endeavors to Learn him the Said Negro." Two skilled men, Pompey, a "tiner," and Cyrus, a "hammerman," who were owned by Philadelphian David Caldwell, were each valued at £115, much higher than the average slave man.[77]

Runaway and sale notices in the *Pennsylvania Gazette* depict a slave population on the move, sold from owner to owner and escaping owners to rejoin families and friends—or simply to find freedom. Blacks from a wide area landed in Chester jail: they came southwest from the city of Philadelphia and south and east from Lancaster, York, Berks, and Cumberland counties in Pennsylvania, as well as from Delaware, Maryland, Virginia, and New York. Dublin, who worked at Berkshire Furnace in Berks County, was captured in Chester in 1769. Samuel Martin of Paxton Township, Lancaster County, advertised for his escaped 18-year-old woman, who was wearing an iron collar when she left and had formerly been the property of Samuel Kennedy (probably of Chester County). Slaves also escaped from Chester County masters. A mulatto, Jacob, born in the town of Chester and brought up in the house of James Mather, a tavernkeeper, left his current owner James Sharp of Sadsbury Township in 1760. Black Joe, formerly the slave of Nathan Hayes, in 1761 left owner John Bell of West Fallowfield. One of Joshua McDowell's men was jailed in New Castle in 1764, and another, Coco, ran away in 1768. Coco was a sugar maker who had formerly lived with John Edwards in Philadelphia. A boy who ran away from a Chester County tavernkeeper was caught in Lancaster. Persifor Frazer's man Isaac had lived near both Pequea and Wilmington, Delaware, before Frazer bought him. And Esther, before being purchased by William Kennedy of West Nantmeal, had been owned by John Jackson of Kent County, Delaware. A country-born slave with "a cunning Turn of Wit," she was captured in Philadelphia. On June 19, 1776, John Telles of West Caln Township advertised the loss of his mulatto slave Frank who had been born in Portugal, noting "he is well known on the roads, and in Philadelphia."[78]

The demographic composition of the slave population in rural Pennsylvania in 1780, when slavery was at its peak, suggests that conditions were more conducive to natural population growth in the countryside than in Philadelphia. Of the 487 slaves registered by Chester County masters in response to the gradual abolition act and identified by sex and age, 238 were aged 16 years and above. These adults were evenly divided between men and women. The 249 children were also closely divided, with 123 boys and 126 girls. Lancaster County slaveowners reported 838 slaves in their possession. Of those whose age and sex are known, 399 were aged 16 years and over and 437 were under age 16. There were 202 men and 197 women. In Bucks County the numbers of adults and children were almost even (254 to 252), with 132 men and 122 women (1.08 adult sex ratio). The numbers of adults and children in Washington Country were exactly even, but the adult sex ratio was somewhat skewed, with 97 men and 119 women.[79] Thus, by 1780, slave men and women in all four of these counties had more children survive infancy than city slaves, and in Chester, Lancaster, and Bucks adults had favorable sex ratios.

As the case of Chester County shows, however, equal numbers of men and women did not ensure ease in finding a mate. Slaves of both sexes were not evenly distributed throughout the county, so the opportunity for them to marry and establish families was not as favorable as these data for the entire county suggest. The small numbers of slaves added to the problem of unequal distribution, creating serious obstacles for women and men looking for companionship. For instance, in the fifteen townships closest to the Delaware River, men outnumbered women thirty-three to twenty-two. In contrast, in the townships along the western county line, except for East Nantmeal where slave men worked at the Warwick Furnace, women exceeded men, thirty to twenty-one.[80]

Thus, while rural Pennsylvania slaves achieved natural population growth by 1780, they did so in spite of serious hindrances. Owners generally considered their own convenience and needs, not their slaves' emotional ties, when organizing their labor force. Only one-third of Chester County slave women and men lived in households with potential husbands or wives. The situation of Bet and Plato of East Nottingham was exceptional for they and their five children, aged one to eleven years, shared the same owner, farmer Patrick Power. More typical was the case of Jim, also Power's slave, who had no wife or children in the household. He either had no spouse and children or was separated from them by some distance. Jim's wife may have been one of the thirty-seven Chester County slave women (almost one-third) who lived in households with children but no potential spouse, or she and their children may have been free. Or Jim's children might have been sold. At least 36 percent of Chester County slave children lived in households without their parents.[81]

Philadelphia and rural Pennsylvania slaves, then, lived under significantly different demographic regimes, but in both places they experienced obstacles to establishing and maintaining families. In the city, dense settlement and a balanced sex ratio facilitated marriage but children died at discouraging rates because of urban conditions. In rural districts like Chester County, finding a mate was made more difficult by distance and disadvantageous local sex ratios, but slaves who did marry had greater expectation that their children would survive because of greater salubrity of the environment, though they might lose them well before maturity by sale to another owner.

Black Pennsylvanians contributed to the society and culture of their colony in ways that can only be inferred from available evidence. During the pre-Revolutionary period, no slave who lived in Philadelphia or the surrounding countryside kept a diary or journal, wrote descriptive letters to friends, or crafted essays or poems that have survived. Our knowledge of blacks and slavery comes through the eyes and pens of whites who, whether hostile, sympathetic, or apathetic toward African-Americans, lacked understanding of their thoughts and lives. Thus we too cannot know about such questions as how new arrivals adjusted to Middle Atlantic society, whether urban or rural; how pervasive was their resistance to slavery; in what ways they established communities and to what lengths they went to sustain such communities and the families that composed them; and what specific cultural influences blacks had on the larger society. White colonial Pennsylvanians, like most whites since, were insensitive to the ways in which Africans had an impact on the forging of North American culture.

For most of the colonial period—indeed until the eve of the Revolution—slavery was more important in Penn's capital than in the rural areas surrounding it. Slaves composed about one-twelfth of the urban population and were a significant part of the labor force. New arrivals brought skills, knowledge, and beliefs from their African homelands, the Caribbean, and nearby northern American colonies, with which they undertook the tasks that Philadelphia owners assigned. Urban blacks worked to create a community against incredible odds. High mortality, separation of husbands and wives, myriad ethnic backgrounds and experience, and frequent sales made community-building difficult, though in the long-run they were successful, after manumissions and escapes freed most slaves in the city and the favorable climate toward blacks of late eighteenth-century Philadelphia drew refugees from the southern colonies.

Slaves in the hinterland lacked the advantages that accompanied the relatively high density of slaves in the city. While urban slaves enjoyed the fellowship of neighbors at school, church, festivals, and on the streets, rural slaves often lived long distances from one another and lacked such contacts. After the late 1750s, however, with increased slave importation and a generally healthful environment, the rural slave population grew. Pennsylvania farmers, rural artisans, and innkeepers purchased slaves from Africa and nearby colonies to fill their labor needs when the Seven Years' War cut off their supply of European servants. And for the next quarter-century many held on to these slaves tenaciously, even in the face of growing abolitionist sentiment among Quakers and Revolutionary patriots.

2

The First Emancipators

William Southeby, a substantial, well-respected Philadelphia Friend, approached the Quaker-dominated Pennsylvania Assembly in 1712 with a bold request. He petitioned for the "Enlargement," or general emancipation, of all slaves in the province. A septuagenarian, Southeby took up abolition toward the end of a lifetime in which he had prospered, served as a public official, and achieved recognition as a "weighty Friend." With his antislavery crusade he risked losing status within both the Society of Friends and the larger society. Raised a Roman Catholic, he had settled in Maryland first in 1659 and then again in 1663, and became a Friend sometime before 1668. He was a farmer and boatwright on the Eastern Shore until 1684, when white Marylanders began to substitute black for white labor. Moving on, Southeby bought land first at Jones's Creek in Kent County, Delaware, and then in Philadelphia. In 1684 he was named acting register general for Pennsylvania and sat on the Provincial Council. When he moved to Philadelphia he served as justice of the peace and in 1688 was elected a member of the Assembly. He purchased land, including frontage on the Delaware between Sassafras and Vine, and became a tallow chandler.[1]

Southeby's 1712 petition was well timed because the Assembly was concerned about the expansion of slavery in Pennsylvania, especially in light of the bloody slave uprising that had only recently shocked New Yorkers. Pacifist Quakers must have recoiled at the violence produced by slavery. In April 1712 a group of about twenty slaves had laid a trap by setting fire to a building in New York City and attacking the white men who came to put it out with knives, axes, and guns. They killed nine whites and injured others, but the retribution wreaked upon the black community far surpassed this toll. White New Yorkers hanged thirteen slaves, burned three at the stake, and broke one on the wheel. Another starved to death in chains, and six committed suicide to deny the authorities the opportunity to inflict their barbaric tortures. Terror spread up and down the seaboard. But in the minds of Pennsylvania's legislators, Southeby's proposal to free the blacks was not the answer. Indeed many of the assemblymen owned slaves and looked forward to many years of service from them. The House decided "it is neither just nor convenient to set them at Liberty." However, they saw in a petition to curtail the slave trade, which was "sign'd by many Hands" and presented to them at the same time, a way to slow the growth of slavery without hurting present owners. In fact, such regulation would increase the local market value of slaves. And so in response to this second petition, the Assembly laid a prohibitive duty of £20 Pennsylvania currency on each slave imported into the colony. This measure might have forestalled further importation had it been approved by Queen Anne. When she denied it, the Assembly enacted a lower duty on slaves and, because their intention was to raise revenue rather than prevent importation, the Crown let these laws stand.[2]

The divergent petitions of 1712 represent well the divisions in early Pennsylvania over the question of slavery. The colony was the scene of a lively debate over the issue—a debate carried on almost entirely among Friends, who dominated Pennsylvania's population and power structure during the first decades after settlement. They kept control of the legislature for most of the pre-Revolutionary period (the exception being the duration of the Seven Years' War), despite the fact that they declined as a proportion of the population as large numbers of immigrants of other religions, particularly Germans and Scots-Irish, arrived in the colony. The Quakers were the first religious body in Pennsylvania, and indeed in the Atlantic world, to grapple with the morality of slavekeeping, but their decision to ban the practice came only after a century of strife. Even so, before the Revolution, no such discussion at all took place within the other major denominations, including the Anglican, Presbyterian, and Lutheran churches.

A few Quakers like Southeby opposed the institution absolutely and would use legislative fiat to bring about its demise. Before moving to Pennsylvania Southeby had witnessed the beginning of an influx of slaves into Maryland to work that colony's tobacco fields, and he feared that the same process would take place in Penn's colony. Southeby and other abolitionists saw slavery contaminating the "holy experiment."

On the other hand, the majority of Friends doubted that slavekeeping was wrong. Everywhere that Europeans colonized the New World they filled the shortage of labor typical of developing frontier societies with African slaves. Quakers bought slaves because they needed the labor and believed they could avoid offending God as long as they treated their slaves well. Most Friends, including the legislators of 1712, were more easily convinced that the slave trade violated Quaker doctrine—because it involved systematic violence— than that they themselves sinned by employing black labor in their homes, shops, and farms. Early Pennsylvania Friends, like American colonists in general, believed that their own labor needs and property rights took precedence over any right of Africans to be free.

Though Southeby's appeal was the first such petition to reach the Assembly, Quakers had been debating whether slavery was consistent with their beliefs for a quarter-century before 1712. Influential Friends like Southeby, who could easily have afforded to buy slaves but rejected the institution on moral grounds, submitted a series of papers to Philadelphia Yearly Meeting. Four Germantown Friends, including Francis Daniel Pastorius, Derick op den Graeff, and his brother Abraham op den Graeff, founders and political leaders of the German settlement, were the first to petition their meeting about slavery. The Germantown Friends, writing in 1688, were appalled that the Quaker colony, established for liberty of conscience, should deny men and women "liberty of the body." Friends should consider the golden rule, to do unto others as you wish others to do to you, when separating wives from husbands and children from parents. They warned that Europeans had been shocked at reports "that the Quakers doe here handel men as they handel there the cattle. And for that reason some have no mind or inclination to come hither." Pennsylvanians must stop robbing and stealing the bodies of men, women, and children, or surely the blacks would rise up "and handel their masters and mastresses as they did handel them before; will these masters and mastresses take the sword at hand and warr against these poor slaves, licke, we are able to believe, some will not refuse to doe; or have these negers not as much right to fight for their freedom, as you have to keep them slaves?" Both the Philadelphia Quarterly and Yearly Meeting refused to take action against slavery in response to this appeal.[3]

Then in 1693 followers of George Keith, a Scottish Quaker who arrived in Philadelphia in 1689 to teach school and then quickly challenged Philadelphia Yearly Meeting over doctrinal matters including the bodily resurrection of Christ, issued the tract, *An Exhortation and Caution to Friends Concerning Buying or Keeping of Negroes.* The Keithians, among them one of the Germantown petitioners, Abraham op den Graeff, may have been attempting to embarrass the dominant Quaker faction by urging Friends "not to buy any Negroes, unless it were on purpose to set them free, and that such who have bought any, and have them at present, after some reasonable time of moderate Service . . . they may set them at Liberty, and during the time they have them, to teach them to read, and give them a Christian Education."[4] But while the schismatics may have been trying to preempt the issue for their own purposes, no clear line separated the two sides on slavery. Several prominent Keithians, including the Irish merchant Robert Turner, owned slaves, while abolitionist William Southeby stayed with orthodox Friends. Several of Keith's followers did take seriously the admonition to free slaves, however, for they were among the colony's first manumitters.

In 1696 the Friends meeting responded more favorably to papers written by Southeby and Cadwalader Morgan, a leading member and minister of Merion meeting, who urged prohibition of slave importation and ownership. The Yearly Meeting, recognizing that the slave trade required force and therefore was in clear violation of the Quaker creed of nonviolence, in 1696 advised members to "be Careful not to Encourage the bringing in of any more Negroes, & that such that have Negroes be Careful of them, bring them to Meetings, or have Meetings with them in their Families, & Restrain them from Loose, & Lewd Living as much as in them lies, & from Rambling abroad on First Days or other Times."[5] Like the Assembly fourteen years later, the meeting hoped by condemning the slave trade to stunt the growth of slavery and appease their consciences on this issue, without damaging the economic interest of the many prominent members who already owned slaves. The advice, however, had little effect in stopping slave imports. When in 1698 importation continued and Pentecost Teague of Philadelphia Monthly Meeting wrote a paper opposing "the selling of Negroe's at the publick Markett place & Outcry," the meeting appointed Southeby and other weighty Friends to write to Quakers in Barbados asking them to stop sending slaves to Pennsylvania. Teague's case illustrates the distinction Friends made between importing and owning slaves. A well-to-do merchant who served in the Assembly and was for two decades a leader of Philadelphia Monthly Meeting, he owned a black man when he died in 1719.[6]

Also in 1698, Robert Pyle, a prominent member of Concord Monthly Meeting in Chester County, justice of the peace, and long-time assemblyman, submitted a paper describing the process by which he decided not to buy a slave. With the exception of racist overtones that are present in his work but not in the writing of other Quaker abolitionists, Pyle's epistle provides a good idea of the arguments these early polemicists used. Pyle explained that he considered purchasing a slave when the terms of his English servants expired because he had many young children and hoped that a slave, who could be kept for life, would give him and his children "more liberty." He called to mind, however, the Christian dictum, "Do unto all men as ye would have all men doe unto you," recognized that the slave trade encouraged Africans to "make warr one with another, and [sell] one another for slaves," and feared that blacks "might rise in rebellion and doe us much mischief; except we keep a malisha [militia]; which is against our principles." He also asked himself if he was not doing well enough financially and should not "theyrwith be content." Even after considering these arguments, Pyle might have purchased a slave, had he not had a dream in which he found that he could not climb a ladder to heaven, which stood "exact upright," while trying to carry a black pot, which he interpreted to be a slave. This convinced him "to lett black negroes or pots alone." He wrote further that Friends should free their slaves after a term of years, with the guidance of the Quaker quarterly meetings.[7]

Except in contributing to the growing body of opinion against slavery, Pyle's paper about the morally encumbering nature of slavery had little practical effect. Quakers continued to import and buy slaves despite the Yearly Meeting's 1696 advice. The West Indian immigrant, Isaac Norris I, who became presiding clerk of Philadelphia Yearly Meeting in 1711, was a frequent importer before 1730, as was Jonathan Dickinson, another worthy Friend who had come from the Caribbean.[8] As shown in the last chapter, in relation to the total population, slavery expanded in Philadelphia to a greater extent during the first two decades of the eighteenth century than at any later time. In response, segments of the Quaker meeting continued to call for stronger measures. They wanted to ban slave trading altogether, not simply advise members that the practice was undesirable.

Organized resistance to the slave trade emerged first in Chester Monthly Meeting, composed primarily of farmers with a liberal sprinkling of artisans and country traders. Through Chester Quarterly Meeting they petitioned the Yearly Meeting in 1711, 1715, and 1716 to place a ban on buying imported blacks. The Yearly Meeting leadership of this period, of whom about 60 percent owned slaves (including clerk and slave trader Isaac Norris) agreed only to "caution" Friends to avoid purchasing such slaves, a somewhat stronger and more far-reaching minute than the 1696 advice but not a rule of discipline. Writing about the 1715 meeting, Norris observed that it "was large and comfortable, and our business would have been very well were it not for the warm pushing by some Friends, of Chester chiefly, in the business of negroes. The aim was to obtain a minute that none should buy them for the future. This was opposed as of dangerous consequence to the peace of the church, for since they could not tell how to dispose of those we have, and that many members must still possess them, and then it might fall to their lot in duty to deal with future offenders, which as it could not in itself be equitable, such must do it with an ill grace, and at best it would be a foundation for prejudice and evil speaking one of another, *so that it was got over.*"⁹ Norris's concern for the sensibilities and reputations of Quaker slaveholders who might find it necessary to discipline purchasers of slaves, and for justice toward such potential offenders, must have frustrated the abolitionists whose chief concern was justice towards blacks.

In 1729 Chester again requested a more stringent ban. This time an urgency resonated in their request because country Friends witnessed an upswing in slave importation that was fueled by the emergence of eastern Pennsylvania from a severe economic contraction in the 1720s and a reduction in the tariff on slaves from £5 to £2. In response, the Yearly Meeting decided in 1730 that purchasing newly imported slaves was "Disagreeable to the Sense of this Meeting" and instructed monthly meetings to admonish members who did so, but again failed to prescribe any penalty such as disownment from the Society. After this, the Friends made no substantial progress on the issue of slavery until 1754.¹⁰

While Chester meeting focused on curbing purchases of imported slaves and failed to get the wholehearted support of Philadelphia Yearly Meeting even for this limited proposal, individual Quakers continued to speak out for total emancipation. When they published their abolitionist tracts, these Friends risked being disowned—in fact some were—because Quaker discipline forbade publishing without approval of the Society's overseers of the press. Since most of Philadelphia Yearly Meeting's overseers of the press owned slaves, and at least one—Isaac Norris—imported blacks, they approved no antislavery writings. The meeting viewed these works primarily as attacks on Friends rather than as arguments against the institution of slavery. Thus, Quakers expelled the offending members for "disunity," a disciplinary violation of much greater concern at that time than buying imported blacks.

William Southeby, for example, did not remain quiet after he failed in 1712 to convince the Assembly to enact a law for general emancipation. In 1714, despairing of action by the Society or the Assembly to stop the slave trade, Southeby in an unpublished paper reproved Philadelphia Friends for avoiding the issue with the excuse that London Friends would not ban the trade. He argued that the Pennsylvanians, who included so many "ministers and other ancient Friends," should "be exemplary to other places, and not take liberty to do things because others do them."¹¹ A few years later, when Philadelphia Yearly Meeting resisted Chester Quarter's petition against buying imported slaves, Southeby published several abolitionist papers (which have not survived) without Friends' permission. Philadelphia Monthly Meeting threatened him with disownment but apparently did not follow through. At about the same time, an English Quaker, John Farmer, was disowned by Rhode Island Friends for demanding in print that all Quakers free their slaves. He appealed his disownment to Philadelphia Yearly Meeting, which upheld the New England meeting. In 1729, Philadelphia merchant Ralph Sandiford, an English immigrant who, had he wished, was wealthy enough to engage in the slave trade himself, rushed a pamphlet to press that reprimanded slaveholding Friends, the leaders of his meeting. Greatly upset by the upswing in slave importation, he published the tract even though the overseers of the press denied him permission. The Philadelphia meeting condemned him for his actions.[12]

Up through Sandiford those who spoke out against slavery were well-situated men. Though not at the pinnacle of power, their stations in society were similar to those of the slaveholders they challenged. Pastorius and Abraham op den Graeff, two signers of the 1688 petition, were assemblymen, as were Pyle and Southeby. Derick op den Graeff was a prominent officeholder in Germantown. Though not political leaders, Morgan and Sandiford were men of substance and influence. These men took up an unpopular cause, one that served for them no class interest. Their motives in opposing slavery were deeply moral and religious, though also practical because they saw the spread of slavery as threatening the stability and welfare of Pennsylvania society. Their morally based position ran directly counter to the interests of merchants dealing in slaves and an upper stratum with money to invest in cheap labor, and therefore found little favor. They spoke out against the influx of slaves in the years before 1720 and following 1729, responding to the very real possibility that Pennsylvania might become a slave society like Virginia or Carolina. They questioned the wisdom of their equals who imported slaves, warning them that slavery was wrong and would lead to violence and social upheaval.

These early Quaker abolitionists fit no category put forth by David Brion Davis, Thomas L. Haskell, and John Ashworth in their extended debate about the origins and triumph of abolitionism.[13] These were not the "deviant personalities" Davis presents in *The Problem of Slavery in Western Culture*,[14] except to the extent that their abolitionism brought opprobrium. They found contempt because they opposed slavery, but they did not pursue abolitionism because they were outcasts. Nor were Southeby and the others nascent capitalists who hoped, consciously or unconsciously, to promote the growth of wage labor in Pennsylvania. Obviously these men were not factory owners and consequently had no need for disciplined free workers of the sort Davis describes for the post-1780 period. By denouncing involuntary bondage, these early abolitionists did not justify a new economic order or allay pangs of guilt springing from new forms of oppression.[15] On the contrary, they attacked slavery when importation, relative to the total population, was at its height because they feared that the colony, like those to the south, was becoming a slave society. They could have imported and used slave labor like many of their peers, but for moral and religious reasons they rejected that option. The early reformers interpreted Quaker teaching to mean that slavery was wrong—because of violence inherent in the slave trade and slavery, because slaveholding represented conspicuous consumption, and, most important, because ownership by another human being impeded the slave's ability to reach God. Though these antislavery Quakers also did not fit Thomas Haskell's mold of altruists inspired by the rise of capitalism to believe that they should, and could, alleviate the suffering of slaves, they did have the formalist turn of mind, described by Haskell, that saw "the difference between a free worker and a slave [as] not a matter of degree but of quality."[16] Freedom and slavery were not at opposite ends of a continuum on which the lots of master craftsmen, wage workers, indentured servants, and slaves could be placed; they were morally antithetical. For the abolitionists, slavery was an unmitigated evil because slaves lacked control of their souls.

Quaker opponents of slavery had limited influence in the years before 1750. In Davis's words, the conditions "that favored the acceptance of antislavery ideology" did not yet exist.[17] Abolitionism served no ruling class interest— indeed it challenged the ways of life of most affluent Pennsylvanians, both Friends and non-Friends. Like settlers throughout the American colonies, residents of Penn's province turned to black slaves when they had the capital and incentive to purchase them. In a society where free labor was chronically short because land was plentiful, slaves bound in perpetuity and indentured white servants bound for four to seven years provided labor for craftsmen, merchants, farmers, millers, and mariners who needed more assistance than their families could supply.

After Sandiford a different sort of reformer took up the abolitionist mantle. While Southeby, Farmer, and Sandiford had placed their church membership in jeopardy by publishing antislavery tracts without the meeting's permission, they—and Morgan, Pyle, and the Germantown Friends—otherwise conformed generally with their neighbors. The next reformers, who renounced worldly pleasures and material wealth, dedicated their lives to eliminating slavery. Benjamin Lay, John Woolman, and Anthony Benezet wrote tracts, to be sure, but they also adopted ascetic lifestyles, hoping in this way to foster spiritual growth and avoid dependency on slave labor and slave-produced goods.

Lay, the most uncompromising of Quaker abolitionists, had been born to poor Quakers in Colchester, England, and apprenticed to a glovemaker. He then spent seven years at sea before returning to his trade in London. Considered a troublemaker by Friends, Lay was disowned for accusing ministers in meeting of preaching their own minds instead of restricting themselves to the words of God. He and his wife Sarah then left England, migrating first to Barbados and subsequently to Philadelphia in 1731. He witnessed barbaric conditions of slavery in Barbados, and when he discovered the institution entrenched in Pennsylvania as well, he started his crusade, using personal example and dramatic acts to portray the evil of the institution. Lay made his own clothes to avoid materials grown with slave labor and publicly smashed his wife's teacups to discourage use of slave-produced sugar. On one occasion during the 1730s, he stood with one bare foot in snow outside a Quaker meeting to make those who owned slaves realize how badly they clothed their blacks in winter. He also kidnapped a Quaker child to bring home to Friends the grief suffered by African families when their children were snatched by slave traders or when their owners separated parents and children. Lay interrupted religious services of other denominations as well.

The events that made leading Philadelphia Quakers lose patience altogether and openly repudiate Lay were his publication of *All Slave-keepers, That Keep the Innocent in Bondage, Apostates* (1737), which denounced Friends, and his "bladder of blood" demonstration at the 1738 Yearly Meeting. At the meeting, Lay plunged a sword into a hollowed-out book that resembled a Bible and contained a bladder of red pokeberry juice, splattering those sitting nearby with "blood." His intention was to show Friends that they committed spiritual and physical violence by holding slaves, whether or not they treated them well and taught them Christian principles.[18] The conservative Friends confronted by Lay in 1738 were not moved by his unconventional behavior. In the midst of a period of economic growth that continued through the 1750s, Philadelphia Yearly Meeting made no significant change in its policy concerning slaves for a generation.

Not until mid-century did abolitionism begin to acquire for Friends what Davis calls "ideological hegemony."[19] In the 1750s, Philadelphia Yearly Meeting underwent momentous changes, as reformers attempted to rid the Society of laxity and corruption. A new generation of leaders took control, including Israel, James, and John Pemberton, sons of wealthy Philadelphia merchant Israel Pemberton, Sr.; Daniel Stanton, a Philadelphia joiner; and prosperous farmers John and George Churchman and William Brown of

Benjamin Lay, a committed abolitionist, denounced slaveholding in public demonstrations and in his book, *All Slave-Keepers, Apostates* (1737). As suggested in this portrait, he was a vegetarian and lived in a cave on his small farm near Abington, Pennsylvania. Engraving by Henry Dawkins (restruck after 1790), after an oil painting by William Williams (ca. 1760). Courtesy of The Historical Society of Pennsylvania.

Chester County. Joining them in their labors to enforce more rigorously the Society's rules against marrying outside the faith and such worldly pursuits as gambling, shooting matches, and extravagant display were British Friends Mary Peisley, Catherine Payton, and Samuel Fothergill. The reformers interpreted the outbreak of war on the Pennsylvania frontier in 1755 as God's punishment for their waywardness and resolved to cleanse the Society of sin. To do so, they believed they must build a wall around the church, excluding those who married non-Friends or in other ways refused to adhere to the strict Quaker code.[20]

Abolitionists John Woolman and Anthony Benezet were able to hitch their campaign to ban slaveownership among Friends to the more general reform movement. Woolman, a shopkeeper and tailor of Burlington County, New Jersey, who purposely limited his business in order to devote himself to traveling in the ministry, had awakened to the evils of slavery during the 1740s. Around 1742, when he was 22 years old and working in a Mount Holly shop, he wrote a bill of sale for a black woman, whom his employer had sold to an elderly Friend. Woolman regretted the act as soon as he had done it and told both men that he "believed slavekeeping to be a practice inconsistent with the Christian religion." When subsequently asked to write another "instrument of slavery," Woolman refused.[21] In 1746, he made his first journey to Maryland, Virginia, and Carolina, returning home full of remorse because he had eaten and "lodged free-cost with people who lived in ease on the hard labour of their slaves." He saw in the "southern provinces so many vices and corruptions increased by [the slave] trade and this way of life that it appeared to me as a dark gloominess hanging over the land."[22]

Soon after he returned from the South, Woolman wrote his essay, *Some Considerations on the Keeping of Negroes,* which was directed not only to the Friends he had visited on his journey but to his neighbors in New Jersey and Pennsylvania as well. He did not submit the manuscript immediately to the Quaker overseers of the press, however, because in 1746 fully two-thirds of that body owned slaves. Woolman waited until 1753, after the deaths of several slaveholding censors and their replacement by antislavery-minded Friends, to request permission to publish his tract.[23] In the essay, published in 1754, he gently reminded readers that blacks had not forfeited "the natural right of freedom" and were equal to whites in God's eyes. He warned that slaveholders tested divine benevolence: "If we do not consider these things aright, but through a stupid indolence conceive views of interest separate from the general good of the great brotherhood, and in pursuance thereof treat our inferiors with rigour, to increase our wealth and gain riches for our children, what then shall we do when God riseth up; and when he visiteth, what shall we answer him?"[24]

One of the new overseers of the press appointed in 1752 was Anthony Benezet, who in 1736 had married Joyce Marriott, a member of Woolman's monthly meeting in Burlington, and had begun serving on Yearly Meeting committees in 1747, just one year after Woolman. Benezet was born in France in 1713 of Huguenot parents whose estate was confiscated, and with them escaped to England in 1715 and sixteen years later immigrated to Pennsylvania. He rejected a mercantile career, believing that a life seeking wealth was not his calling. Instead he began teaching school in Germantown in 1739 and in 1742 became an instructor of poor children at the Friends' English School in Philadelphia. Like Lay and Woolman, Benezet was an ascetic. He chose schoolteaching knowing that his income would be small. His intention was to adhere strictly to the Quaker doctrine of plainness, and in fact he was considerably less affluent than most of his fellow reformers.[25]

In 1750, Benezet began holding free classes for black students at his home in the evening while continuing to teach white children by day. He found that his black pupils were as capable as whites in both academic work and in "moral and religious advancement." He continued to teach free blacks and slaves on this informal basis for twenty years, until he convinced Philadelphia Monthly Meeting to open an "Africans' School" in 1770.[26] The foundation on which he built all of his labors—for abolition of slavery, justice for native Americans and the poor, education, pacifism, and temperance—was his abhorrence of wealth. "The great rock against which our society has dashed" is "the love of the world & the deceitfulness of riches, the desire of amassing wealth."[27]

Soon after Woolman submitted his essay to the overseers of the press, Benezet laid a proposal to denounce slave trading before Philadelphia Monthly Meeting. This meeting referred the paper to the quarterly meeting, which in turn sent it to Philadelphia Yearly Meeting. Both Woolman and Benezet were now members of the inner circle that held sway over Yearly Meeting policy, and both attended the Yearly Meeting in 1754, which after revision issued Benezet's paper under the title *An Epistle of Caution and Advice, Concerning the Buying and Keeping of Slaves*. The tract was a stirring renunciation of slaveholding itself, not just importation, and marked acceptance of the abolitionist position by the Yearly Meeting leadership. The Friends noted that the number of slaves "is of late increased amongst us" and thought, therefore, the time was ripe to make their concerns public. "To live in Ease and Plenty by the Toil of those whom Violence and Cruelty have put in our power, is neither consistent with Christianity, nor common Justice; and we have good reason to believe, draws down the displeasure of Heaven, it being a melancholy but true Reflection, That where Slave keeping prevails, pure

Religion and Sobriety decline, as it evidently tends to harden the Heart, and render the Soul less susceptible of that holy Spirit of Love Meekness and Charity, which is the peculiar Character of a true Christian." The epistle further urged slavekeepers to consider that separation of husbands and wives tempted blacks to commit adultery and suggested that they educate their slaves in Christianity and prepare them for eventual freedom.[28]

Approval of Woolman's essay and Philadelphia Yearly Meeting's *Epistle* were the first steps toward abolition of slavery within the Society of Friends. With the publication of these two tracts in 1754, the Quaker antislavery field shifted from "voices crying in the wilderness"[29] to the centers of meeting power. Before British reformers arrived in Philadelphia to spread their message of rebuke and rejuvenation, before the outbreak of war on the Pennsylvania frontier confronted Friends with the possibility that God would punish them for past and current sins, and before any economic downturn made slave labor less profitable, Woolman, Benezet, and allies from local meetings managed to convince the Yearly Meeting that slaveholding was wrong. By the 1750s, many fewer leaders of the Yearly Meeting owned slaves (10 percent, compared with about 60 percent before 1730). Over the years since the 1720s, though conservative, well-to-do Friends stayed in charge of the Yearly Meeting, abolitionism had taken root within certain local meetings—Shrewsbury and Woodbridge in East Jersey, Wilmington in Delaware, Gwynedd in Philadelphia County, and Philadelphia. The antislavery bloc gradually grew within Philadelphia Yearly Meeting during the twenty- to thirty-year period before 1754. Some slaveowning Friends manumitted their slaves and other Quakers, reasoning in much the same way as had Robert Pyle, chose not to buy any at all. During the twenty years before 1755, the continuing availability of white immigrant and native-born labor, both free and indentured, made this choice easier for Pennsylvanians.[30]

Though Philadelphia Yearly Meeting announced its abhorrence of slaveholding in 1754, much work needed to be accomplished before abolitionism permeated the ranks. Benezet, Woolman, and other conscience reformers, whose primary concern was the welfare of slaves, by 1754 won the approval of enough Yearly Meeting leaders to issue the tracts. With the outbreak of the Seven Years' War the next year, the prophecies of Woolman, Benezet, and even those of Lay, seemed fulfilled. In 1756, John Churchman, an ardent reformer who, as far as we know, had not previously spoken against slavery, wrote in response to watching the bodies of slain frontier inhabitants carried through the streets, "How can this [calamity] be? Since this has been a land of peace, and as yet not much concerned in war; but as it were in a moment, my eyes turned to the case of the poor enslaved Negroes. And however light a matter they who have been concerned in it, may look upon the purchasing, selling, or keeping those oppressed people in slavery, it then appeared plain to me, that such were the partakers of iniquity."[31] Abolitionism became part of the drive for purification. Friends who had little humanitarian concern for blacks took up antislavery ideology in the hope that purging the Society of sin would pacify an angry God. The Quaker leadership embraced abolitionism as part of the crusade for moral revitalization; the challenge now was to convince rank-and-file Friends, as well as slaveholders outside the Society, that this stance was right.[32]

Philadelphia Yearly Meeting struck first at importing and buying slaves. In 1755, it instructed monthly meetings to discipline any Friend who engaged in this activity. Because the leadership failed to specify how offenders should be punished, local meetings requested clarification, and in 1758 Friends decided to place under discipline (exclude from participation in meeting business but not actually disown) any member who imported, bought, or sold a slave. They also appointed John Woolman and four other abolitionists to visit slaveholders in every local meeting to explain the Society's new attitude toward black bondage. Once the Yearly Meeting leaders had adopted the new position, they sought cooperation of local Friends to enforce it. In 1755 the Yearly Meeting had made a similar move by appointing a large committee to circulate among local meetings to evaluate their enforcement of the rules concerning marriage and proper behavior. The 1755 committee reported on its progress and targeted problem meetings and by 1761 forced the last recalcitrant meeting into line. The antislavery committee of 1758 had a similar mission but was less immediately successful. Woolman, John Churchman, Daniel Stanton, John Sykes of Chesterfield Monthly Meeting in West Jersey, and John Scarborough of Bucks County visited local meetings and individual slaveholding families, advising them of the Society's stand. They performed their visits over a five-year period, reporting at each Yearly Meeting that they continued the service and felt opposition to slavery was growing. They believed they had fulfilled the mission of this committee when they had visited slaveholders in all parts of the Yearly Meeting. When they began their visits in 1758 they may have hoped to convince all Quaker slaveowners to release their slaves, but by 1762 they knew this was impossible. Now aware that the task would take many years and individuals would require repeated visits, the committee requested local meetings to carry on the work.[33]

Coinciding with the years of the committee's service was a drastic labor shortage that severely tested the Friends' commitment to abolition and quickly demonstrated that the moral reform movement succeeded in establishing the claim of morality over economic interest in the minds of Society leaders but not in the minds of more ordinary Friends. In the mid-1750s, during the excitement of revitalization, Woolman, Benezet, and their allies had won over fellow Yearly Meeting leaders to their cause. Weighty Friends who had earlier given little thought to the plight of slaves were swept up in the fervor of moral rearmament and needed little prompting to view slavery as the embodiment of worldliness and sin. As far as we know, relatively few of these leaders owned blacks. During the 1740s and early 1750s, the huge wave of German and Scots-Irish immigration provided sufficient labor for their needs. By 1755, however, the tide had turned: German immigrants arrived only in very small numbers and Irish immigration declined by one-third. From 1749 to 1754, 115 ships carrying almost 35,000 German immigrants reached Philadelphia, but in 1755–56 only three ships came and only one more arrived before 1763.[34] And while the war interrupted ocean traffic from Europe, most indentured servants who came before 1755 had, by the late 1750s, either served out their terms or run away to join the British army. To fill the gap in the labor supply, which was especially ill-timed with the war-stimulated economy, Philadelphia merchants turned to West Africa. In just four years, from 1759 to 1762, they brought at least 857 blacks up the Delaware River, selling them in Philadelphia and—after the Pennsylvania Assembly placed a £10 tariff on each slave in March 1761—in Delaware and West Jersey, where they could easily be transferred to Pennsylvania.[35] Labor-starved Quakers and non-Quakers alike bought these slaves.

Thus the Yearly Meeting leadership, imbued with the belief that slaveholding was wrong, had a doubly difficult task in convincing more worldly Friends. In the midst of a labor crisis, not only did they have to persuade members who already owned blacks to give them up, but they now also faced Friends who, desperately needing workers for their shops and farms, made new purchases of imported slaves. In defiance, or perhaps ignorance as some alleged, of the 1758 Yearly Meeting decision, Quakers eagerly bought black workers. And then when the economy crashed after 1760 and members sold slaves they no longer needed, meeting leaders confronted even more tragic situations in which offending Friends might acknowledge their wrongdoing but the victims could no longer be helped. In the years from 1760 to 1764, local Pennsylvania meetings dealt with sixty-four disciplinary cases concerning the buying and selling of slaves, over half of all such cases heard in these meetings between 1757 and 1776. In Philadelphia the offenders were often Quakers of ordinary means, considerably less affluent on average than the local leaders who judged them. Many pleaded economic necessity. Blacksmith Nathaniel Brown, for example, explained in 1760 that he purchased a slave because his apprentices had joined the army and he could hire no journeymen. Benjamin Mifflin and Samuel Massey acknowledged in 1762 that they had bought a slave because their bakery required "a constant & steady sett of hands" and then sold him when they abandoned the business.[36] In rural Pennsylvania, where slaveholding was confined to a fairly small group of affluent farmers, farmer-artisans, millowners, and innkeepers, Quaker slavemasters were on average wealthier than the local meeting leaders who attempted to convince them of their wrongdoing. But these rural offenders also justified their actions by citing economic need.[37]

During the years immediately following publication of Woolman's essay and Philadelphia Yearly Meeting's *Epistle* in 1754, therefore, economic cross-currents first encouraged and then hindered the growth of abolitionist ideology. For leaders, abolitionism fitted the purification movement exactly: slavery was one more corruption to be purged from the Society. When the labor shortage beginning about 1756 spurred renewed slave importation, these Friends resisted any temptation to buy slaves. Their commitment to moral rearmament transcended contrary economic trends. For less conscientious Quakers, however, the imperative to free slaves or refrain from buying and selling them registered only weakly, if at all. Responding to market factors, many purchased slaves to increase production during the boom years and sold them during the post-1760 depression. The hopes of Woolman, Benezet, Stanton, and others that slavery would be purged quickly from their church—and indeed from the face of the earth—were dashed. It would take until the mid-1770s, when slaveholding had declined precipitously in Philadelphia and few slaveowners still held positions of influence in Philadelphia Yearly Meeting, before the meeting would take decisive action against the practice.

The 1758 Philadelphia Yearly Meeting debate over slavery had been stormy. John Pemberton wrote, "I am Sure I even dreaded the meeting, least some Debates might arise, that might prove painful." Woolman recalled "though none did openly justify the practice of slavekeeping in general, yet some appeared concerned lest the meeting should go into such measures as might give uneasiness to many brethren."[38] Friends took a significant step by threatening to place under discipline members who imported, bought, or sold slaves, but they did not prohibit slaveownership entirely. The leadership had adopted an abolitionist stance: if they hoped to eradicate slaveholding from the Society of Friends—and indeed from the wider society—they must marshal support from the membership.

The best records available to help us measure the early growth of abolitionism are the manumissions that Pennsylvanians of various walks of life and different religions wrote, primarily in their wills. Persons who penned no essays or journals produced in their final testaments expressions of antislavery sentiment.[39] Slaveowners touched by doubts about the justice of holding human beings in perpetual servitude began demonstrating their concern even before 1700 by releasing their blacks in their wills. Such emancipations were compromised, of course, by the fact that the owners retained their slaves for their own lifetimes and often those of their wives or other heirs, but nevertheless the manumitters did admit uncertainty about the practice. Thus manumissions provide evidence about the pervasiveness of opposition to slavery over the late seventeenth and eighteenth century.

Throughout the pre-Revolutionary period manumissions were rare. They were least frequent before 1741 but even after that date remained unusual in both Philadelphia and Chester County (Table 2–1). According to our evidence, fifty-two Philadelphians manumitted ninety slaves in the sixty-five years before 1763. Certainly there were more, but the records for them apparently no longer exist. During this early period, men were more likely to be freed than women, despite a fairly even adult sex ratio throughout the colonial period (Table 1–6). Of manumitted blacks, thirty-seven were men, twenty-three were women, and twenty-eight were children (Table 2–2). Why men received freedom more frequently than women is unclear, but gender-related differences in the way manumitters freed women and men suggest that their masters had distinct expectations about their abilities to earn a living. Throughout the period to 1762, slaveowners who freed women often released them outright, eschewing the additional service or yearly payments that masters frequently required of men (Table 2–3). Many women, but few men, received bequests such as bed and bedding, other furniture, clothes, or a sum of money. Apparently slaveowners believed that freed women would have more difficulty than men supporting themselves and any children they might have, and therefore emancipated women more rarely, not wanting to become responsible for their support as specified by the 1726 law. When owners did manumit women, they often provided some assistance rather than saddling them with additional terms or sums to pay. Children almost never received immediate freedom, but instead were required either to complete terms of apprenticeship or bondage, or remain in the household of the owner's heirs for a specified number of years. Delayed freedom meant that they spent the most productive years of their lives in bondage.

In Philadelphia, in the years through 1740, owners seldom manumitted their slaves. On average only one slave was promised freedom every two years, with a rate of fewer than one in 1000 blacks liberated each year. Artisans, merchants, and proprietors of inns and shops purchased blacks with the intent of exploiting their labor and remained unimpressed by the exhortations of Southeby, Sandiford, and Lay.

TABLE 2–1. Manumissions, 1698–1800

PHILADELPHIA

	Slave Population	Manumissions		% of Slave Population Manumitted Annually
		Total	No./Year	
1698–1740	600–700	23	0.5	0.08%
1741–1762	800–1,500	67	3.0	0.2–0.4%
1763–1774	1,481 (1767)	87	7.2	0.5%
1775–1779	728 (1775)	199	39.8	5.5%
1780–1790	539 (1780)	239	21.7	4.0%
1791–1800	301 (1790)	190*	19.0	6.3%
1800	55			

CHESTER COUNTY**

	Slave Population	Manumissions		% of Slave Population Manumitted Annually
		Total	No./Year	
1698–1740	200–300?	11	0.25	0.1%
1741–1762	293 (1760)	35	1.6	0.5%
1763–1774	552 (1765)	36	3.0	0.5%
1775–1779	432 (1774)	98	19.6	4.5%
1780–1790	493 (1780)	73	6.6	1.3%
1791–1800	194 (1790)	22	2.2	1.1%
1800	53			

*Does not include Africans from the *Ganges* who were freed and indentured through the Pennsylvania Abolition Society.

**Includes Delaware Co., which separated from Chester in 1789.

Sources: Probate records, Phildelphia and Chester County; Philadelphia tax assessment list, 1767, Rare Book Room, Van Pelt Library, University of Pennsylvania, adjusted to include nontaxable slaves; Phila. constables' returns, 1775 and 1779–80 (City Hall Archives), adjusted to include the Northern Liberties and Southwark; U.S. Bureau of the Census, *Heads of Families*, 59–75, 98–104, 199–245; U.S. Bureau of the Census, *Second Census*, 2a; Chester Co. tax assessment list, 1760, Shippen Papers, Historical Society of Pennsylvania; Chester Co. tax assessment lists, 1765 and 1774, adjusted to include nontaxable slaves; Chester Co. slave register, 1780, PAS Papers, Reel 24, HSP. Manumissions are from Philadelphia and Chester Co. wills, deeds, court of quarter sessions records, minutes and manumission books of monthly and quarterly meetings of Philadelphia Yearly Meeting, and records of the Pennsylvania Abolition Society.

The earliest emancipators in the city were followers of George Keith who in the early 1690s were involved in a bitter dispute among Friends that started over a confession of faith, quickly mushroomed into a full-scale political battle, and left the Society deeply divided. The Keithians had issued an antislavery pamphlet, and at least three of their number considered its contents when they wrote their wills. The first recorded manumission in the city was that of George Hutcheson, a merchant who died in 1698. He had been a

TABLE 2–2. Sex and Age of Manumitted Slaves, 1698–1762

PHILADELPHIA

	No.	Males			Females			Unknown Sex
		16+	16−	Unk.	16+	16−	Unk.	
1698–1740	23	9	3	1	7	2	0	1 (child)
1741–1750	29	13	7	0	6	3	0	0
1751–1762	38	15	7	1	10	5	0	0
TOTAL	90	37	17	2	23	10	0	1
			62%			37%		1%

CHESTER COUNTY

	No.	Males			Females			Unknown Sex
		16+	16−	Unk.	16+	16−	Unk.	
1701–1740	11	5	0	0	3	3	0	0
1741–1750	12	4	0	5	2	0	1	0
1751–1762	23	10	2	3	5	0	3	0
TOTAL	46	19	2	8	10	3	4	0
			63%			37%		

Sources: Manumissions (see notes 39, 59 of this chapter).

distiller in England and migrated first to Burlington, West Jersey, and then to Philadelphia. Originally a Friend, Hutcheson supported Keith and did not return to the Quaker fold. Unlike fellow Keithian Robert Turner, who failed to free his slave when he died in 1700, Hutcheson apparently had some reservations about black bondage. He ordered in his will that his slave Tony, aged

TABLE 2–3. Conditions on Manumissions, 1698–1762

PHILADELPHIA

	Men	Women	Children	Unknown Age	Total
			(Percentage Freed with Conditions)		
1698–1740	67%	57%	67%	—	65%
1741–1750	69	33	90	—	69
1751–1762	67	10	92	0%	58

CHESTER COUNTY

	Men	Women	Children	Unknown Age	Total
1701–1740	40%	0%	100%	—	45%
1741–1750	100	0	—	100%	83
1751–1762	50	20	50	83	52

Sources: Manumissions.

about 15 years, be free if he arrived to the age of 40. Hutcheson could not know if Tony would live that long, but nevertheless he exhibited scruples about the institution. And while it is unknown whether he had helped to write the Keithian tract against buying and keeping slaves, regardless, his will reflected its concern.[40] About a year after Hutcheson's death, his son-in-law and fellow merchant and Keithian, James Stanfield, also died. In his 1699 will, Stanfield emancipated one of his slaves, Jack, after he had served Stanfield's friend Mary King, a widow, for five years. Stanfield had apparently joined the Anglicans in the wake of the schism because he bequeathed one of his slaves to the Rev. Thomas Clayton, rector of Christ Church.[41]

During the first decade of the eighteenth century, when slaveholding was at its height among wealthy Philadelphians, only one freed a slave—the former deputy-governor William Markham, an Anglican, who died in 1704. A cousin of William Penn, Markham had considerable practical influence on the development of early Pennsylvania: as Penn's first deputy he made initial contacts with the Lenni Lenape, Swedes, and leaders of neighboring colonies, established the first government under Penn's proprietorship, and supervised selection of the site of Philadelphia and survey of lands. Markham gave his wife Joanna the right to sell or free any of his servants and slaves, but singled out a 4-year-old Indian boy named Titus Frankson whom he wanted freed at age 24. The widow, however, could make the final decision on Frankson's freedom.[42]

Following Markham, Philadelphians of various faiths freed blacks—or expressed their intention to free them—in scattered years. William Lee (d. 1711), a Keithian who subsequently joined the Baptists, took some pains to keep his heirs from circumventing his plans for manumission, but still he encumbered his slaves with long terms. His 28-year-old black woman Betty and her children Cuff, aged 2, and Judith, aged 5, would be free and receive freedom dues at age 45. Lee specified that his heirs should not sell the slaves outside the province and if sold within Pennsylvania, indentures for their freedom at age 45 should be drawn up. Captain John Baily, a mariner, bestowed freedom on two of his nine slaves. In 1714, he was the first Philadelphia manumitter to release blacks immediately upon his death. He also requested William Trent, an Anglican merchant of the city, to assist them "if there shall be Occasion."[43]

During the years 1720–24 the pace of manumission quickened a bit, as six owners freed eight slaves. Economic depression had beset the city around 1720, slave importation declined and, as would occur later in the 1760s and 1770s, high mortality (and perhaps sales to other colonies and rural areas of Pennsylvania) drastically reduced a slave population not supplemented with fresh imports (see Table 1–3). As demand for labor fell, concern about the immorality of slavery gained sway in the minds of a handful of Philadelphians. At a time when "the ship Builder & Carpenter starve for want of Employment," these testators worried less about the labor needs of their heirs. Samuel Monckton, a physician and apothecary who died in 1720, for example, directed his executors to set his slave Virgil free three months after his death but stipulated that the ex-slave must assist brother Philip Monckton in the shop one day a week. Philip would provide Virgil with clothes "for decent Wearing" from Samuel's wardrobe.[44] Had Philadelphia's economy been booming, Samuel might have perpetuated Virgil's bondage, requiring him to serve Philip full-time.

Lionel Brittin, who left the Society of Friends and was described as a "Philadelphia Mugletonian," wrote in 1721 that his slaves Quan and Dinah should "have their freedom within Three months after my wifes decease if she shall so think fit by deed or will to declare and that they have their respective bedding & Cloathing." It is not known whether Quan and Dinah became free, or indeed how they established themselves with only their beds and clothes, but when Brittin's widow Elizabeth died about twenty years later, she mentioned no slaves in her will.[45] Richard Aldeburgh, a "gentleman," in 1724 liberated one of his three Philadelphia slaves, a woman Sarah, and sent her to Jamaica, where he owned an estate.[46]

Not before the mid-1720s is there evidence that any city Friend freed his or her slaves. The arguments of Southeby, Morgan, Pyle, and Farmer had as little impact on the moral consciousness of individual Quakers as on Philadelphia Yearly Meeting as a whole. Two Quaker women, widows of substantial officeholders, and Thomas Redman, a bricklayer, were apparently the first members of Philadelphia Monthly Meeting to heed in a practical manner the admonitions of the abolitionists. Patience Lloyd, widow of Thomas (d. 1694), who served as president of the Provincial Council, freed the slave woman Ambo and her youngest daughter Molly, but kept children Hannah and Sam in bondage. These young slaves she gave as presents to her granddaughters, Deborah Moore and Patience Story. Esther Shippen, whose husband Edward (d. 1712) had held numerous posts including assemblyman and mayor of Philadelphia, wanted her slave Moll to serve her sister-in-law for three years and then be freed. Thomas Redman freed Negro James after he worked for the widow for four years, eight months, and fifteen days from the signing of the will.[47]

During the late 1720s and 1730s, as the economy improved and went into a period of long-term expansion that lasted through the Seven Years' War, fewer Philadelphians chose to free their slaves in their wills. In addition to the renewed demand for labor that accompanied the economic upturn, the 1726 law requiring a £30 security bond undoubtedly discouraged some would-be emancipators. If legislators hoped by passing the law to nip a budding movement of voluntary emancipation, they achieved immediate success. In any event, Philadelphians who freed their slaves soon after 1726 showed greater concern for the financial well-being of the freed blacks than had earlier manumitters. William Goodwin, an Anglican carpenter and merchant who died in 1729, sent his slave man Sam to Jamaica (where Goodwin had recently lived) to be freed after four years of servitude. Thus Goodwin could avoid putting up the £30 bond. Mary Paschall (d. *ca.* 1734), a widowed shopkeeper, carried out her husband Benjamin's intentions by freeing their woman Sarah and giving her £20 freedom dues. She also freed Sarah's child but failed to manumit one other girl. Presbyterian Humphrey Morray (d. 1735), a distiller and planter, showed the greatest concern of these early manumitters for the economic security of the slaves he freed. Morray gave Cipio and Moll, husband and wife, their freedom and forty acres of land where they already lived at the south end of Morray's plantation. They could also keep, as long as they lived, the house, cart and gear, and livestock they had in their possession. If Cipio and Moll did not like their present farm, Morray's executors should buy another forty acres for them not more than eleven miles from Philadelphia and build a small log house. Their child Cipio was not freed and received no property. Morray allowed him to live with his parents until they died but he would then become the slave of Morray's cousin.[48] Morray was typical of Pennsylvanians who bequeathed property to their slaves by will. The testators tried to provide security for the freed blacks but would not go so far as to give them estates that the blacks themselves could hand down to their heirs.

Beginning in 1735, Quakers prominent in Philadelphia meeting began freeing a few slaves in their wills. Isaac Norris I, who had imported West Indian blacks as late as 1730 and was presiding clerk of Philadelphia Yearly Meeting from 1711 to 1729 and an overseer of the press, died in 1735. He had also been a long-time assemblyman allied with the Penn-Logan faction, and mayor of Philadelphia. Norris owned a house, lot, and wharf in Philadelphia and mills in Norriton Township, Philadelphia County, in addition to his Fairhill estate in the Northern Liberties. Norris freed his Indian slave Will within five years, providing that Will serve the widow Mary Norris faithfully during that time. Norris mentioned no other slaves in his will, but his widow owned a black girl Dinah, whom she did not free when she died in 1748. As no inventory of Isaac Norris's estate exists, it is impossible to know if he owned additional slaves when he died. Possibly he did not, because he hoped that Will would be able to assist son Joseph Norris at the mills in addition to serving Mary Norris at Fairhill. The widow likely acquired Dinah to replace Will after he had served his term.[49]

When Samuel Preston died in 1743 he manumitted eleven slaves, an extraordinary event for the time. Like Isaac Norris, he had helped to guide the Philadelphia Yearly Meeting policy that had resisted antislavery reformers for many years: he was treasurer since 1714, overseer of the press since 1717, and also served as clerk and correspondent with London Yearly Meeting. Of less importance politically than Norris, Preston served briefly as provincial councilor, assemblyman, and Philadelphia mayor. "Some time" before 1743, Preston had freed four of his slaves, husband and wife Ishmael and Judith, and Caesar and Cudgo, possibly their sons. Ishmael and Judith also had a child who was free-born. Their daughter Hagar, age 25, had two young sons of her own. Preston indentured Hagar and one of her sons to Ishmael and Judith till age 30. The other son Preston gave to his own grandson Preston Carpenter, also until the slave reached age 30. His remaining slaves, a man Occo, a boy Ishmael, and two girls, all probably children of Judith and Ishmael, would be free at age 30.[50]

The manumissions granted by first-rank Quaker leaders Norris and Preston signified the turmoil occurring in the Friends' minds during the 1730s and 1740s. These men had agreed in meeting to censure Ralph Sandiford and Benjamin Lay for their abolitionist activities and had refused to prohibit absolutely the purchase of imported slaves, but still they felt discomfort with the practice. Apparently Preston and Norris recognized the inconsistency of slaveholding with their religion but needed the labor and did not want to lose their investment. So they held on to their slaves, salved their consciences with a moderate meeting policy against importation, tried to silence antislavery critics who trumpeted their hypocrisy to the world, and then freed their slaves in their wills. A splotchy record on slavery, perhaps, but not a surprising one for such a complex and highly divisive issue. Abolitionists in Philadelphia Yearly Meeting forced all Pennsylvania Quaker slaveholders to weigh the justice of their actions well before masters of other religions had to make a similar choice.

During the 1740s and 1750s, an increasing number of Philadelphia Quakers followed in the footsteps of Norris and Preston (Table 2–4). Eight of eleven decedents who freed slaves during the years 1741–50 were Friends, and in the next decade eleven of sixteen were Quakers. Eighteen percent of slaveholding Quaker decedents in the 1740s and 30 percent in the 1750s manumitted slaves in their wills. In small but growing numbers, beginning in the decade before Philadelphia Yearly Meeting issued the *Epistle* of 1754, Friends fueled by individual manumission the first emancipation movement in Philadelphia. Indeed the *Epistle* and visits of the 1758 committee of five had a limited effect on the numbers of slaveholders deciding to free their slaves, as twelve Philadelphia Quakers freed slaves in 1741–54 and just twelve followed suit from

TABLE 2–4. Religious Affiliation of Manumitters, 1698–1762

	PHILADELPHIA					
	1698–1740	*1741–1750*	*1751–1760*	*1761–1762*	*Total*	
Quaker	4	8	11	5	28	(54%)
Presbyterian	1	0	0	0	1	(2)
Anglican	6	2	3	4	15	(29)
Baptist	1	0	0	0	1	(2)
Ex-Quaker	2	0	0	0	2	(4)
Unknown	2	1	2	0	5	(9)
TOTAL	16	11	16	9	52 (100)	
	CHESTER COUNTY					
Quaker	6	4	8	1	19	(70%)
Presbyterian	0	1	0	0	1	(4)
Anglican	1	1	1	0	3	(11)
Unknown	1	0	3	0	4	(15)
TOTAL	8	6	12	1	27 (100)	

Sources: Manumissions; church records.

1755 to 1762. From the 1740s, manumissions marked the existence of anti-slavery sentiment outside the bounds of Quaker meeting policy but the policy itself inspired no great surge of emancipation.

Over these two decades, however, manumitting Friends did become more generous toward their slaves. In the 1740s many of the Quaker manumitters continued to delay freedom for their slaves and some emancipated only certain individuals. Men had a better chance for freedom than women, but they were also more likely to have additional terms to fulfill. Mirroring the Society as a whole, which could not agree on a firm antislavery policy until the mid-1750s, individual Friends remained ambivalent. Nicholas Waln, a Northern Liberties planter who died in 1744, freed his man Oliver at age 30 and chairmaker Caleb Emlen manumitted a boy Peter when he reached age 32. Thomas Shute freed only four of six slaves. Three men, Peter, Samuel, and Ned, would be liberated six years after his death if they each paid £6 per year, presumably to cover the £30 surety bond; otherwise they would be sold. Shute also emancipated an old man Samuel, whom Shute's grandchildren would supply with necessities. Thomas Lloyd, a merchant and ship chandler, did not actually free his slaves, but was concerned that two of them, London and Tom, should not have to change masters in their old age. Thus, instead of bequeathing them to his heirs, he asked his executors to let the two men work for themselves and assist them as long as they behaved well.[51]

In the 1750s, more Friends began to free their slaves outright, although seven of ten Quaker slaveholders still refused to free their bondspeople at all. The chances of slave women to obtain liberty improved and they retained their advantage over men in avoiding conditional release. Mary Shubert freed her woman Dido immediately upon her decease, but failed to free a man Cato. Shopkeeper William Monington required his slave Sam to fulfill a 15-year bond to William Neat before he could achieve freedom, but Monington placed no restrictions on freed slaves Parthenia and her daughter Sall, to whom he gave bequests of £10 and £5 respectively. In addition to freedom, widow Elizabeth Holton gave her slave Nanny £3 yearly, her bed, and some of the decedent's clothes. Nanny's son Ishmael, a mulatto boy, would be apprenticed to cordwainer John Guest and then freed. John Jones, a cordwainer, freed slaves he had not released earlier and gave each £12 annually from his estate. He specified that if his personal estate and rents would not cover these legacies, his executors should mortgage some real estate.[52]

Prominent Friend Israel Pemberton, Sr., did not actually release his slave Betty, but would have set her free years earlier if she had agreed. In his will he expressed a certain concern for her welfare, even paternalism, that other manumitters hinted at but did not express in so many words. Pemberton wrote,

> As my Negro Betty hath lived with me many years her Mistress did some years since make her an offer of her freedom which she then refused to accept of, rather chusing to continue with us and as she is now further advanced in years it is not likely that she would be able to maintain herself long if she should now have the like offer made to her again therefore it is my mind & Desire that she should continue with her mistress or some of my children but if my wife declines letting her live with her and not any of my children are inclined she should live with them it is my mind & will that she have a Room or some convenient place provided for her & put upon some Business that she may be earning something toward a livelihood and in Case it appears she is not able to support herself that then she should be supplyed with such things as may be convenient & necessary for the making her Life as comfortable to her as the infirmitys of old age will admit of out of my Estate [not?] letting her want the Necessarys or Conveniences of Life Suitable for a Person in her Circumstances she having in her younger years approvd herself a good Servant.[53]

Pemberton's sons, Israel Jr., James, and John Pemberton, figured prominently in the Quaker reform movement of the 1750s and, especially James and John, were active abolitionists. Who took care of Betty after Israel Sr.'s death is not known.

Among non-Friends there was little momentum for emancipation. Five Anglicans and three persons of unidentified religion set their slaves free during the 1740s and 1750s and others promised to do so. Widow Ann McCall in 1744 freed one of at least five slaves she owned, and Michael Brown, a silk dyer, released his man Caesar after his widow's death. Both of these manumitters had some affiliation with the Anglican Church, as did John Hyatt, gentleman, who directed his executors to release Margaret and her child Lincon within a year of his death and give Margaret her bed, £10, and £3 worth of kitchen furniture. Hyatt also freed two slave children when they reached age 37, unless their father or someone else paid his heirs £20 for each, in which case they could be free earlier. He kept one other boy, named Quacimaney, enslaved. In 1754, Anglican Elizabeth Moore, a widowed shop-keeper, freed her "honest and faithful servant" Grace, bequeathed her £5, a bed, and clothes, and gave her an additional £5 a year for three years to take care of her own son who was sickly and whom Moore did not free. Flatman John Anderson freed his man Cutcho immediately upon his death.[54] In 1757, writing his first will, Benjamin Franklin promised freedom to Peter and Jemima, man and wife, after his death, a pledge that he would not have to keep since he outlived them both.[55]

Thus in the 1740s and 1750s, when a modest upswing in Quaker manumissions accompanied greater pressure within Philadelphia Yearly Meeting to take an antislavery stance, emancipations by non-Friends, most of them Anglicans, remained sparse and highly individualistic. Manumission among non-Quaker Philadelphians was the exception, a reward a few blacks received for faithful service or a promise to young slaves of liberty at some time far in the future. Within the context of an expanding economy, a morally based ideological movement could gain little ground when it required material sacrifices or inconvenience, especially if the church itself remained neutral on the issue. In the early 1760s, the numbers of Anglican manumitters began to challenge those of Friends (Table 2–4), but in proportion to the numbers of slaveholders belonging to their churches, Anglicans remained far behind. In 1761–70 one-half of Quakers, but only one-eighth of Anglicans, who died owning slaves freed them in their wills. Thirty percent of Philadelphia Anglicans dying in the 1760s owned slaves whereas only 18 percent of Quakers and 20 percent of all inventoried decedents were slave masters.[56]

During the period to 1762, abolitionism followed a somewhat different path in rural Chester County than in Philadelphia. Led by Chester Monthly Meeting in the eastern part of the county, Quaker farmers and artisans throughout the area encompassing Chester and Lancaster counties and northern Delaware in the 1710s and again in 1729–30 called for an end to the slave trade. Specifically, they wanted Philadelphia Yearly Meeting to prohibit members from buying imported blacks. Their targets in this crusade were Philadelphia merchants like Isaac Norris and Jonathan Dickinson, who were importing slaves from the West Indies. The 1710s was a time of particularly high importation, and 1729 witnessed an upturn in the trade after the duty was reduced to £2 per slave. Since Norris and Dickinson were members of the Philadelphia Yearly Meeting elite, and fellow leaders owned slaves and presumably bought and sold them as well, the Chester County petitions accomplished little.[57]

Not only did Chester County Friends demonstrate opposition to slavery before the 1730s through efforts to stop slave trading, but they also avoided buying slaves. After the first few decades of settlement when well-placed Friends like John Bristow and Robert Wade employed slave labor, the practice lost favor. Quaker Robert Pyle spoke for most of his neighbors when in 1698 he explained his decision not to purchase a slave. Following 1730, however, increasing numbers of Chester County residents turned to slaves when they needed additional full-time labor. In the 1730s, in the part of eastern Chester County served by Chester Monthly Meeting, eight of fifty-five (15 percent) decedents owned slaves when they died. All eight slaveholders were Friends, a result primarily of the fact that Quakers constituted the wealthiest segment of eastern Chester County society. By the 1760s the elite, as well as the population in general, of the Chester Monthly Meeting area had become more diversified, and of eleven slaveowning decedents (one-tenth of all inventoried decedents), seven were Anglicans and Swedish Lutherans and only four were Friends.[58]

These data on slaveownership, though they represent only the part of the county settled first, elucidate the record of manumission for the entire county found in Table 2–4. Chester County Friends represented three-fourths of manumitters before 1741 because Quakers were the primary slaveowners at that time. Over the period before 1763, twenty-seven Chester Countians freed forty-six slaves, about the same ratio as in Philadelphia, and the percentage of men and boys among the liberated slaves was also virtually the same—63 percent in Chester County versus 62 percent in Philadelphia (Table 2–2).[59] Like urban slave women, country women were less likely than men to obtain freedom but had a better chance of receiving outright freedom when they were emancipated (Table 2–3).[60]

Before 1763, Chester County masters were somewhat more likely than city dwellers to emancipate their slaves but in both places the rate of manumission was low (Table 2–1). Although data are lacking on slaveholding throughout Chester County for the period before 1760, a reasonable estimate is that Philadelphia slaveowners outnumbered the county's owners by at least two to one and probably by as much as three or four to one. The ratio of manumitters was two to one. The comparison changed over time, however, as we see in Table 2–4. Before 1721, six Philadelphians and only one Chester County resident, Quaker Lydia Wade, freed slaves. Since none of the city manumitters was a Friend and, with the exception of Wade, no Chester County Quaker slaveowner emancipated a slave, it is clear that most members of the Society of Friends in Pennsylvania who chose to purchase and keep blacks did not yet question seriously the morality of their actions. Only in the 1720s, when importation was reduced and the economy depressed, did both rural and urban Friends begin to free slaves. Chester Countians manumitted blacks at a higher rate than Philadelphians from the 1720s through the 1750s, largely because Quakers, who owned most of the county's slaves, were touched by abolitionist thought, but in the early 1760s the rural owners fell behind.

Philadelphia women were 17 percent and Chester County women were 22 percent of manumitters, and thus during this early period were considerably more likely to free their slaves when they died than were men: women were only 11 percent of slaveowners in Philadelphia and 4 percent in Chester County.[61] Among women only widows and other single women could normally own property (a woman's personalty, including slaves, became her husband's property upon marriage) and relatively few women left wills or appeared as household heads on tax lists. Women were also more likely to free their adult slaves without conditions. Eight of nine Philadelphia female slaveowners freed women, and only one of the eight, Esther Shippen, required additional service. Of five other slaves freed by Philadelphia women, two boys had to serve additional time. In Chester County, six women freed three men, three women, three children, and two slaves whose ages are unknown. Unlike male manumitters, they freed all of the adults outright. However, they required additional service or payments before permitting the children to go free. Of urban manumitting women, four were Quaker, three were Anglican, and the religious affiliation of two could not be identified. In Chester County all of the manumitting women were Friends.

Lydia Wade, widow of Robert, was the first person to free slaves in Chester County. In her 1701 will she freed husband and wife John and Jane one month after her death and their daughter Jane, who would first live with her parents for twelve years and then with Wade's brother-in-law John Wade for five. Elizabeth Clayton of Chichester, who died in 1738, liberated Dinah and specified that her daughter Molly should also be freed if Dinah or her husband paid the executor, Clayton's son Thomas, £10 within a year, and if not she should serve Thomas to age 28. Clayton's husband William had also provided for Dinah's freedom when he wrote his will in 1725, but he had mandated longer service, directing that Dinah and any children she might have remain enslaved till age 35. Deborah Nayle, a Thornbury Township widow who died around 1751, was much more generous to her slave than most manumitters. Nayle bequeathed £30 for the security bond, and in addition gave Bella £25, her bed and other household items and furniture, all of her provisions, clothes, a mare, and two books, a volume by Quaker author Elizabeth Stirredge and Ellis Pugh's *A Salutation to the Britains*.[62]

Grace Lloyd, the widow of antiproprietary leader David Lloyd, owned five slaves when she died in 1760, about thirty years after her husband had left her ten bondspeople. Grace Lloyd wanted Andrew to be hired out to age 30 and then freed, and Pegg should serve out her term of hire and be freed. But either slave could be sold if he or she proved "wicked" or "troublesome." Negroes Sam and Betty were to receive their freedom immediately upon Lloyd's death. Three of the freed blacks were given bequests—Andrew received a new scythe and falling ax and Pegg and Betty each received bedding. Lloyd did not free her fifth slave, a man named Will, but rather gave him to Francis Richardson, who liberated four slaves but not Will (if still a slave) in 1778. Lloyd also designated a forty- by seventy-foot lot in Chester as a burying ground "for Negroes who have belonged to my late husband or me & their descendants & those who belong to Friends of Chester meeting & such as in their lifetime desire to be Buried there but not for any that are Executed or lay violent hands on themselves."[63]

While it is possible that women were more sensitive to the plight of their slaves, and perhaps more susceptible to the arguments of abolitionists, it is also true that these widows, and those in Philadelphia, were in a better position to free slaves than their husbands had been. Slaveowning men expected their slaves to work for their widows and children, and many of those who promised freedom to their slaves required them to serve until after the wife's death. In contrast, the widows who left wills could dispose of their property more freely, because their children—if they had any—were mostly grown and had received their shares of the husband's estate. The widows' slaves were usually personal servants who could be manumitted, and the £30 bond covered by the decedent's estate, with little financial hardship for the heirs.

In the period to 1763, then, abolitionism in Pennsylvania remained a Quaker initiative. Except for the early Keithian movement, just a few Anglicans and other non-Quakers freed slaves in scattered years. Like manumitters in other colonies,[64] they often emancipated only one or two of their slaves, leaving the rest in bondage, and required terms of additional service or monetary payments before freedom. In light of the deep involvement in slavery of Anglicans, especially residents of Philadelphia, the number who freed slaves before 1763 was very small.

But even among Friends the growth of abolitionism was slow and fitful. Only one Quaker in Chester County and none in Philadelphia freed slaves before the 1720s, and almost no slaveowners responded to the pleas for emancipation before the 1740s. Antislavery activists found the Friends inhospitable until mid-century, when Philadelphia Yearly Meeting reformers incorporated slaveholding in the catalogue of sins to be purged from the Society. Increasing numbers of Quakers freed slaves in their wills during the 1740s and 1750s, but they did not always release all of the bondsmen and women they owned and often delayed freedom for years. Indeed, some rank-and-file Friends chose to purchase slaves during the Seven Years' War when labor was in short supply, and many refused to release slaves they owned. Philadelphia Yearly Meeting would not rid itself of slaveholding until the late 1770s.

Though colonial Pennsylvania had a stronger record on abolition than any other polity enmeshed in black slavery—the Germantown petition, Chester meeting's opposition to the slave trade, John Woolman's ministry, and Philadelphia Yearly Meeting's *Epistle* and ban on slave trading were all pathbreaking efforts—no mass movement for emancipation yet emerged. Between 1751 and 1762 fewer than one hundred of some six thousand blacks in the colony had gained their freedom. While slaveholding had been declining slowly in Philadelphia since the 1720s and had never been substantial in rural areas, the labor crisis of the late 1750s reversed the urban trend and put new life into the institution in the countryside. Before 1756 most Pennsylvanians considered slavery a viable labor alternative, and the Seven Years' War reinforced that view.

The period of that war and its aftermath was a cauldron spewing forth both the forces that would eventually destroy slavery in Pennsylvania and those that delayed its eventual demise. In the years from 1754 to 1758 Philadelphia Yearly Meeting leaders hopefully promulgated their new antislavery policy, then watched it founder as rank-and-file Friends in both city and country invested in imported slaves and adamently held on to those they already owned because they could turn nowhere else for the labor they needed. And almost as soon as the overheated wartime economy drove them to purchase Africans—in violation of the 1758 discipline—the postwar slump forced them to sell the slaves they had bought, thus breaking the rules once again. Others held on to bondspeople they had recently acquired, expecting to recoup the purchase price.

The peak in importation around 1760 inspired both renewed commitment to slavery and tentative movement against it outside the Society of Friends as well. Many residents throughout Pennsylvania, especially in areas of relatively recent settlement along the southern border in western Chester, Lancaster, York, and Cumberland counties, invested in African-American laborers for the first time and had no intention of manumitting them. But at the same time other citizens shuddered at the prospect that William Penn's colony might become another Barbados or South Carolina. They feared the threat of violence and alien customs that they believed the newcomers brought with them.

Thus in early 1761 the Pennsylvania Assembly placed a £10 per head duty on each slave imported into the province. Their intent was to stop the influx of bondsmen and women from Africa and other colonies, but the legislation would prove to have much more far-reaching effects as, over the next decade and a half, the slave population of Philadelphia, without infusions of freshly imported Africans, wasted away from high mortality. Though the demographic experience of urban slaves was unique in Pennsylvania, the resulting decline in slaveownership in the city removed significant political support for the institution and paved the way for passage of the gradual abolition act of 1780.

Though the legislators, especially those in the city, would have been aware of high mortality among Philadelphia slaves, it remains an open question as to whether they expected to facilitate the abolition of slavery in Pennsylvania with the import law. No discussion of the bill in the Assembly minutes, which are very succinct, suggested that the lawmakers had this intent. On February 13, 1761, they received a "Remonstrance from a great Number of Inhabitants of the City of Philadelphia . . . setting forth the mischievous Consequences attending the Practice of importing Slaves into this Province, and praying a Law to prevent or discourage such Importation for the future." They tabled the petition until the next week when they appointed a committee to design the bill. The committee presented a draft on February 24, and after debate, amendment, and negotiations with Governor James Hamilton, the £10 duty on each imported slave became law on March 14, 1761. The act was renewed seven years later, having "been found by experience to be of public utility," and in 1773 the Assembly raised the duty to £20, thereby stopping the greatly reduced traffic altogether.[65]

The Assembly minutes contain no roll call vote for the 1761 law and provide no insight into the legislators' reasoning. What were the "mischievous Consequences" of the slave trade that so concerned Philadelphia's citizens and their delegates? Disease is one possibility. Samuel Foulke, who served in the Assembly at the time of the 1768 renewal but was not a member in 1761, wrote in a September 25, 1762, diary entry that "for two or three weeks past an Infectious Distemper, said to be brought in by a Vessel with Slaves from Africa, attended with an uncommon Mortallity, Spread & prevail'd in this City [Philadelphia], & Especially in the Lower parts of the Town, by which many Hundreds of the Inhabitants were carry'd off in a Short Time."[66] This episode occurred after 1761 and perhaps was more virulent than others but ships continually brought disease and death to the port city.

The petitioners and their legislators also certainly dreaded the infusion of a large number of Africans into the town's ranks. Pennsylvanians had not experienced a slave revolt, but they cowered at the news of mutinies in other places. And many of their own freshly imported slaves refused to accept their fate and rebelled by committing petty, and more serious, crimes and by running away. The number of runaways advertised in the *Pennsylvania Gazette* was higher in the early 1760s than at any time from 1730 to 1790.[67] With an increasing slave population, white Philadelphians and their assemblymen apparently feared widespread social disorder.

The composition of the 1761 Assembly further suggests that its goal was limited to stopping the slave trade, not strangling the institution altogether. Speaker Isaac Norris II was a slaveowner, as were Philadelphia County representatives Joseph Fox, John Hughes, Daniel Roberdeau, and John Baynton, city delegate Benjamin Franklin, and Chester County legislators John Morton, Joshua Ash, Joseph Gibbons, and Isaac Wayne. Fox, a gentleman who had been disowned by Friends, and Morton, a prosperous Anglican farmer, served on the committee to draw up the bill along with Philadelphians Thomas Leech, an Anglican gentleman, Quaker Samuel Rhoads, and representatives from Bucks, Lancaster, York, Berks, and Northampton counties. At least ten of the Assembly's thirty-six members were Quakers but none was known for fervent antislavery beliefs. These were Friends who chose to take places of political power while the province was at war, not reforming pacifists who eschewed involvement in military affairs.[68] Nevertheless, as we will see, the heavy import duty on slaves imposed in 1761 had an enormous effect on slavery in the city of Philadelphia.

By 1762, then, Pennsylvanians had taken several steps that, when followed through, would end slavery in the commonwealth. The Quakers had denounced the practice, forbade members from buying or selling slaves, and appointed Friends to visit slaveholders. A small number of Quakers acknowledged the evil of slavery and freed their bondswomen and men and others avoided buying them at all. Blacks themselves prepared the way for slavery's destruction by running away, and the Assembly resolved to discourage the institution's further growth. However, abolitionism was not yet ascendant in the province: nothing guaranteed that Philadelphia Yearly Meeting would eventually prohibit slaveholding or that the Assembly would renew and strengthen restrictions on imports. Manumission was not yet a broad-based "movement," and only among Quakers was there a hint that dying testators felt some obligation to liberate their slaves. It would require other events in the 1770s and 1780s—years of revolutionary turmoil, ideological ferment, and economic and demographic upheaval—to nurture among white Pennsylvanians what David Brion Davis has called "an enlightened climate of opinion, defining liberty as a natural and fundamental right."[69]

3

Slavery and Abolition in the Revolutionary Era

In 1767, when eastern Pennsylvania was emerging from the economic doldrums that followed the withdrawal of British forces fighting in America during the Seven Years' War, slaveowners held captive about 1500 Africans in Philadelphia and another 4000 in rural Pennsylvania. At the same time Philadelphia Yearly Meeting took steps against slavery and the trade and a few Friends manumitted blacks, slave importations had reached an all-time high in the years from 1757 to 1766, when about 1300 slaves, most of them fresh from Africa, marched off slave ships onto the Delaware docks. Slave trading merchants held slave auctions regularly in the city, and Philadelphians became accustomed to watching slave coffles, with blacks chained to each other, filing into the countryside to be sold. Slaveowners frequently advertised their human property for sale in the Philadelphia newspapers; and only a small number of blacks had gained their freedom in the Delaware port town or its hinterland.

In the next several decades the institution of slavery underwent a dramatic change. Importations of slaves ceased altogether; slave auctions became a thing of the past. By about 1780 the number of slaves had fallen by almost two-thirds in Philadelphia, and twenty years later only 55 slaves remained in the city. The decline lagged in rural Pennsylvania as employers continued to acquire slaves until passage of the gradual abolition act in 1780, but then slavekeeping fell in the hinterland as well—by almost one-half in just a decade and by three-fourths by 1800. At the same time, the free black population grew steadily, both in the city and surrounding counties.

How can we explain the rapid contraction of slavery in Pennsylvania in the last third of the eighteenth century? In dealing with this decline, historians have tended to focus on the humanitarianism of Pennsylvania's legislators and slaveowners. The former passed the gradual abolition act of 1780; the latter, led by members of the Society of Friends, freed many hundreds of slaves though not required to do so by law.

The reality is much more complicated and redounds considerably less to the benevolence of Pennsylvanians of the Revolutionary generation. Slavery was put on the road to extinction in Pennsylvania only as the result of a complex ⎯d interlocking set of phenomena, each with its own inner logic. First, the ⎯ population, in Philadelphia, the center of slavery in Pennsylvania during ⎯olonial period, could not sustain itself without new importations, so when ⎯ traffic in slaves ended, the number of slaves dropped sharply, as deaths ⎯eeded births. Second, the slave population declined as slaves took matters ⎯o their own hands and fled their masters, in fact, far more than has been ⎯ispected. Third, the slave population did indeed decrease through manumis-⎯ion, though not as extensively as has been thought. Few except Quakers freed ⎯laves before 1780. Thus, two sorts of factors contributed to the decline of slaveholding in Pennsylvania by 1800. One sort comprised those that influenced slaveowners to make conscious choices to release their slaves or in other ways move away from slaveholding, including economic concerns, moral or religious sentiment that slavery was wrong, and Revolutionary ideology that all people have the right to be free. The other sort included those over which slaveholders had little control: demographic attrition of the slave population after regulation of the Pennsylvania slave trade and decisions by slaves to free themselves. Finally (and of less importance), the slave population diminished as Pennsylvania slaveowners sold slaves out of state.

The account that follows divides the Revolutionary era into two parts, the first between 1763 and the outbreak of hostilities in 1775 and the second the war years from 1775 to 1780. We examine the situation in urban Philadelphia and rural Chester County for each period.

What is most striking in the sharp decline of the slave population in Philadelphia between 1763 and the eve of the Revolution is that the manumission of slaves had only limited significance: more important were the renewed supply of white workers, the £10 import duty on slaves, high mortality among city bondsmen, and slave escapes. As soon as the return of peace in 1763 allowed unobstructed passage in the Atlantic, large numbers of white indentured servants and free laborers from Germany and Ireland offered their services to Philadelphia employers, who quickly demonstrated their preference for white workers. Also influenced by the £10 import duty on slaves, producers looking for extra hands turned away from dark-skinned laborers.[1] Thomas Riche, one of the most active importers of labor, was a few years premature in asserting in 1764 that "the time is over for the sale of Negroes here."[2] But between 1764 and 1768, when thousands of Germans and Scots-Irish arrived at the Delaware docksides, slave imports fell to an average of 68 per year. From 1768 to 1770 they averaged fewer than half of that—about thirty per year—and then they virtually stopped. By 1773, Benezet reported that more slaves were exported than imported in Philadelphia, and thereafter it was only an occasional slave who was brought to Pennsylvania's capital explicitly for sale.[3] And, as discussed in Chapter 1, the Philadelphia slave population dwindled after importations dropped to a trickle, the result of the high mortality that prevailed among the large number of slaves imported directly from Africa in the late 1750s and early 1760s, high infant mortality, and reduced fertility among slaves who infrequently lived under the same roof with their marriage partners. Without new importations, the slave populations could not sustain themselves in the urban parts of northern colonies, as Benjamin Franklin, in his famous essay on population, had observed as early as 1751.[4]

Slaves themselves contributed significantly to the decline of slavery in Philadelphia. Their resistance to captivity troubled slaveholders because it was obvious that the institution could be maintained only through coercion. The sight of some resistant Africans laboring in shackles and neck irons, such as the slaves of brickmaker John Coats, was "no rarity in . . . the neighborhood of Philadelphia," recalled one resident in later years.[5] Pennsylvanians could also see that slavery bred violence within the black population, especially when men had no available marriage partners. In 1764 a huge crowd gathered in Philadelphia to witness the execution, "in the midst of the dreadful tumult," of a black man who had murdered a slave child out of jealousy, it was charged, "over females of his black, heathen race."[6]

The advertisements for runaway slaves that appeared frequently in Philadelphia's newspapers were another reminder of the troublesomeness of slaveholding. In the 1760s, when the city's slave population averaged nearly 1500 slaves, advertised runaways averaged about four per year—one of every 375 slaves. But from 1770 to 1775, when the number of Philadelphia slaves averaged about 900, about ten each year took flight—approximately one in ninety. In Chester County, the runaway rate was higher in the 1760s but then lessened in the early 1770s. About one of every 200 slaves ran away each year from Chester masters in the 1760s and about one of every 250 from 1770 to

1775. Philadelphians may have wondered why, if slavery was beginning to decline and the Quaker commitment to freeing slaves was growing, the rate of running away increased. Slaves might have responded that as the rhetoric of natural rights spread, they too were infected by it; and as the number of emancipated blacks grew, slaves more and more came to regard their situation as intolerable.[7]

In the last stages of the period of protest and turmoil that led to the outbreak of the Revolution, slaves in Philadelphia aroused new fears among their masters. In late 1774, word reached Philadelphia of the English plan, if a final rupture occurred between England and its American colonies, to offer freedom to all slaves and indentured servants who would take up arms against their masters. The printer William Bradford, himself a slaveowner, reported that the plan was discussed at a coffeehouse, so Philadelphians were well apprised of the potential enemy they held in their midst.[8] A year later, in November 1775, word of Dunmore's Proclamation, by which the royal governor of Virginia carried out the reported plan, reached Philadelphia within a week. A few days later, those who counted on docility from their slaves must have been shocked to read in the *Evening Post* that a white "gentlewoman" walking near Christ Church was insulted by a black man. When she chastised him, he shot back, "Stay you d[amne]d white bitch 'till Lord Dunmore and his black regiment come, and then we will see who is to take the wall." Hearing the commotion, two white Philadelphians chased the bold slave. But he escaped into the darkness, leaving his pursuers, and readers of the newspaper account, to wonder how many such potential rebels they were holding in their households and what such resistant slaves might do if war came to Pennsylvania.[9]

Thus, in the years leading to revolution, slavery was disintegrating in Philadelphia, sabotaged by blacks and whites alike. Urban employers, dismayed by the high mortality and resistance of slaves, showed a clear preference for free and indentured white workers, who were now in plentiful supply. Contained within this preference for white labor was an unstated desire by some Philadelphians to see slavery gradually wither in their colony. But they were still in the minority. As to those who would act to speed the process by freeing their slaves, the number proved to be even smaller.

Benjamin Rush, who was building his medical career in Philadelphia on the eve of the Revolution, was certain that Americans had been widely infected by 1773 with the contagion of humanitarianism, but he seems to have generalized too quickly from a small number of sincerely abolition-minded individuals to the populace at large. The son of a slaveowning gunsmith in the Quaker city, Rush wrote optimistically to the English abolitionist Granville Sharp that the "spirit of liberty and religion with regard to the poor Negroes spreads rapidly throughout this country." In 1774, Rush wrote again that the "cause of African freedom in America" was still gaining ground and in November of that year, when the Continental Congress banned slave importations throughout the colonies, Rush effusively predicted that "the emancipation of slaves in America will now be attended with but few difficulties except such as arise from instructions given to our Governors, not to favour laws made for that purpose." Perhaps swept away by an increasing number of pamphlets and newspaper essays that called for abandoning an institution seen as contradictory to the principles being enunciated in the colonists' confrontation with England, Rush reported to Sharp in late 1774 that the abolitionist spirit "prevails in our counsels and among all ranks in every province." Slavery, Rush predicted in a monumental miscalculation, would be totally moribund in America in forty years.[10]

Rush overestimated that abolitionist fever in 1773–74, and in fact he did not himself contract the infection, for he retained possession of his own slave, William Grubber, for many years after writing Sharp.[11] What Rush was really describing was a dramatic increase in discussions about slavery and the charges of hypocrisy thrown at colonial Americans who cried out against British tyranny at the same time they continued to hold fellow human beings by force. The rise of this abolitionist literature boosted the Quaker calls for cleansing their own society of a cancerous sore and gave eastern Pennsylvanians of all religions and classes an ennobling ideological argument that strengthened economic reasons for abandoning slavery. But before measuring the impact of this convergence of economic and ideological stimuli to abolitionism in the Revolutionary era, the nature of the abolitionist appeal itself needs consideration.

Many of the pamphleteering opponents of slavery were members of the Society of Friends, and none figured more importantly among them than Anthony Benezet, the spartan-living Quaker schoolteacher in Philadelphia. He was the premier antislavery propagandist, stitching together the writings of others in a series of pamphlets which he distributed throughout America, England, and Europe.[12] But as war approached, the peace testimony of the Quakers made them increasingly unpopular in the city they had founded nearly a century before. This unpopularity, which at some points in the late 1770s reached the point of ugly attacks on Quaker houses, subdued their advocacy of any position publicly and weakened their ability to influence those outside their circle of belief. Antislavery as a moral argument would have to be carried to non-Quakers in eastern Pennsylvania by those who were not Quakers themselves.

Advocates of abolitionism did step forward, even before the war brought Quakers into disfavor. Among the first of them was "Anti-slavetrader," an anonymous newspaper essayist who in 1768 thundered against the hypocrisy of protesting tyrannical British policies while enslaving hundreds of thousands of Africans. "The flame has spread north and south, and every breast now pants for Liberty," he wrote, and the American colonies must ban further slave importations, "emancipate the whole race" of Africans, "restoring *that* liberty we have so long unjustly detained from them," and resettle them on lands to the south or in some other land.[13]

Five years after this plea, Rush penned another powerful appeal for putting slavery on the road to extinction. Prevailed upon by Benezet in 1773 to write a pamphlet attacking the slave trade, at a time when the Pennsylvania legislature was considering a bill to raise the import duty on slaves so high as virtually to kill the trade with taxes, Rush produced *An Address to the Inhabitants of the British Settlements in America, upon Slave-Keeping.* Rush called slavery one of those "national crimes" that would "require national punishments." Like other antislavery pamphlets appearing at this time, his appeal pointed to the hypocrisy of American patriots who condemned the tyranny of England's colonial policies adopted after the Seven Years' War while keeping one-fifth of the colonial population in chains.[14]

Rush's pamphlet had been in the streets of Philadelphia for less than two years when there appeared a recent immigrant from England who was soon to write the quintessential pamphlet indicting British oppression of the Americans, but who wrote his first essay in America on the colonial oppression of Africans in the land of liberty. Hired by the printer Robert Aitken to edit his *American Magazine,* Thomas Paine looked down from his room above Aitken's shop on Market Street to witness the auctioning of slaves in the city marketplace. Shocked by the trading in human flesh in a land where he had come seeking greater liberty and opportunity than he had found in England, the 38-year-old Paine penned a biting attack on slavery in Aitken's magazine. Drawing on the philosophy of natural rights that was central to the American remonstrances against England, Paine queried "with what consistency" could American slaveholders "complain so loudly of attempts to enslave them, while they hold so many hundred thousand in slavery?"[15]

Rush and Paine were both young, radically inclined, and probably regarded by most slaveholding Pennsylvanians, especially those in the upper ranks of society, as unseasoned and strident. But even conservatives raised their voices against slavery, including the recently arrived merchant and eventual Loyalist Richard Wells. How could Americans, he asked in 1774 in the *Pennsylvania Packet,* "reconcile the *exercise of* SLAVERY with our *professions of free-*

dom?" "In vain shall we contend for *liberty,*" chided Wells, "'till this barbarous inhuman custom is driven from our borders."[16]

By the spring of 1775, slaveholding Pennsylvanians had been bombarded by a score of pamphlets and newspaper essays condemning slavery, some of them by residents of their colony and others by New Englanders, New Jerseyans, Virginians, and others.[17] If any were still oblivious to the rising spirit of emancipation, they must have been awakened by the founding of the first abolitionist society in the colonies in the spring of 1775, just a few days before gunfire erupted at Concord and Lexington. Ten Philadelphians met in early April 1775 at the Rising Sun Tavern to found the Society for the Relief of Free Negroes Unlawfully Held in Bondage. Coming to the tavern was a small group of men, mostly Quaker artisans and small retailers, who had imbibed the humanitarian messages of Woolman, Benezet, and others and had been drawn together particularly by the pathetic case of a woman of mixed ancestry—Indian and black—who with her three children was about to be sold into slavery, though she claimed she was born free. Led by the merchant Israel Pemberton and the tailor Thomas Harrison, both of whom had been quietly aiding blacks in purchasing their freedom for several years, the Society entered a suit on behalf of Dinah Nevill and her children to prevent their being taken from the city by a Virginian, Benjamin Bannerman, who had purchased them from a New Jersey man who lived across the Delaware River from Philadelphia. Nevill and her children were judged to be slaves, but in 1779 Harrison arranged for the Philadelphia brewer Samuel Moore to purchase the woman and two of her children from Bannerman. Moore then transferred ownership to Harrison, who signed their manumissions.[18]

Though not explicitly organized as an abolition society at first, the Society for the Relief of Free Negroes was abolitionist in its founding principles and in its ultimate goals. It would meet only four times in 1775 before Philadelphia became deeply entangled in the anti-British resistance movement. But it attracted attention in the city and added to the ideological momentum for abolishing slavery by showing how the presence of slavery could nefariously trap dark-hued people, even those who were born free, in its net.

With multiple motives for freeing their slaves, how many eastern Pennsylvanians actually released their slaves in the final years before the Revolution? Benjamin Rush believed in 1773 that whereas a few Quakers such as Benezet had "stood alone in opposing Negro slavery," now three-quarters of Philadelphians "cry out against it."[19] But the records show that while they might "cry out" against slavery, the number who were ready to release their slaves grew very slowly. From 1763 to 1766, only twelve Philadelphians out of some 600 slaveholders released slaves. Of the nine whose religion is identifiable, three were Quakers, three were Anglicans, and three were Presbyterians. Then, in the prewar years from 1767 to 1774 the number of those inspired to free slaves rose to 38—about one of every fifteen slaveowners (Table 3–1). Through the actions of these 38 manumitters 44 slaves were given an outright release, twelve were promised freedom within two years, and fourteen were pledged freedom at some point in the future, sometimes many years off, especially if they were children. This was hardly the outpouring of antislavery sentiment described by Rush. In the entire period from 1763 to 1774 only 87 Philadelphia slaves obtained release from bondage, and the rate of manumission—about half of one percent of all slaves per year—rose only fractionally from the pre-1760s decades (see Table 2-1). If Philadelphians were opposed to slavery, their commitment up to this point was mostly to allow the institution to die away for lack of freshly imported slaves rather than to end it at any loss to themselves. Four of every five Philadelphia slaveholders resisted the multiple challenges that had been made to coerced labor and held on to their slaves.

Among the fifty Philadelphia manumitters in the nine years from 1763 to 1774, eighteen were Quakers. Most of these manumitting masters freed their slaves without demanding compensation, but in a few cases the slave was

TABLE 3–1. Religion, Slaveholding, and Manumission in Philadelphia, 1767–80

	Slaveowners *1767*	*Manumitters** *1767–74*	*Slaveowners* *1775*	*Manumitters* *1775–79*	*Slaveowners* *1780*
Quaker	87	15	62	74	16
Anglican	227	8	188	5	132
Presbyterian	57	4	55	5	81
Methodist	3	0	0	0	3
Baptist	4	0	4	0	3
German Luth.	24	1	22	3	28
German Ref.	2	0	4	0	6
Rom. Catholic	12	2	12	0	10
Jewish	4	0	7	0	15
Free and Ex-Quaker	16	2	15	4	15
Unknown**	119	6	83	4	87
TOTAL	555	38	452	95	396
Non-Quakers	468	23	390	21	380

*Manumitters are counted only the first time they freed a slave.

**In many cases, these slaveholders were affiliated with no church.

Sources: Phila. tax assessment list, 1767; Phila. constables' returns, 1775 and 1779–80 (adjusted to include the Northern Liberties and Southwark); manumissions; church records. Information about Methodists and Roman Catholics was provided by Doris E. Andrews and Edith Jeffreys.

required to purchase his or her freedom. Thus, Benjamin Mifflin, a Quaker merchant who claimed that several people had offered him £75 for his man Cuff, allowed his slave to purchase his freedom in 1770 for £60, most of it coming from the contributions of Mifflin's fellow Quakers. Cuff himself was required to put up another £30 as an indemnification that neither Mifflin nor his heirs "shall be damaged by his becoming a publick charge."[20] The rising protests against slavery within the Society of Friends convinced many Quakers to free their slaves even before this became mandatory beginning in 1776. About one-sixth of all Quaker slaveowners had responded to the conscience reformers within the Society by the time the Second Continental Congress met in the city, and Quakers, though moving only step by step, outpaced all other religious groups in withdrawing from the peculiar institution (Table 3–1).

Compared with Quakers, members of most other religious denominations were much less responsive to the religious and secular arguments raised against slavery and did little to fulfill Rush's abolitionist expectations. By far the largest group of slaveowners in the city were the Anglicans, gathered in three churches, and their doctrinal affiliates, the Swedish Lutherans, who worshiped in the venerable Gloria Dei church near the Delaware waterfront. Together they accounted for more than 40 percent of the city's slaveowners, but only eleven of at least 227 owners in 1767 released any of their slaves from 1763 to 1774. Anglicans were only one-fourth as likely to manumit their slaves as were Quakers in this era. However, the most sensational release of slaves in this period did involve an Anglican, the staymaker William Broomwich, who in 1763 freed a woman named Minor, her daughter Phebe, and her mulatto son John. Broomwich also gave Minor and John during their lives the house and lot on Mulberry Street where he lived, along with kitchen furniture. Broomwich's daughter Anna Randolph, wife of the joiner Benjamin Randolph, was to receive the house and lot only after Minor and John died. Shocked by Broomwich's generosity to his slaves, the Randolphs contested the will, claiming that he was out of his mind when he wrote it. If not out of his mind, Broomwich was certainly out of sorts with other Philadelphians, who, like slaveholders everywhere, rarely bestowed such property on their chattel servants. The one witness to Broomwich's will who could be found testified in 1771 that the old staymaker was sane when he signed it, and the terms of it remained in force.[21]

Presbyterians and German Lutherans also held substantial numbers of slaves in 1767, at least 57 and 24 respectively. Only four Presbyterians and one German Lutheran freed their human property in these years, barely reducing the number of slaveowners in these groups (Table 3–1). Other religious groups—Catholics, Baptists, Jews, and German Reformed—held only small numbers of slaves, and the number of slaveowners in all these groups, as shown in Table 3–1, remained the same or actually increased between 1767 and 1775.

The data in Table 3–1 indicate how limited was the power of natural rights ideology, at least in the years leading up to the Revolution, to soften the hearts of more than a small fraction of slaveholders, even in the city that was becoming regarded as the capital of American abolitionism. With the exception of the Society of Friends, none of the churches took a stand on slavery in this period. Their members were thus under no religious compulsion to free their chattels. Of 468 non-Quaker slaveowners in 1767, only one in twenty (23 of 468) had manumitted a slave by 1775, demonstrating that natural rights philosophy unaccompanied by moral pressure within the religious group could accomplish little to feed the abolitionist spirit. The number of Philadelphia slaveowners was declining steadily in the pre-Revolutionary decade (from 555 in 1767 to 452 in 1775), but nearly two-thirds of the decrease was represented by men and women whose slaves had died or run away and only one-third of the decrease by owners who freed their slaves.

If the armor of economic interest protected slaveowners from ideological appeals for the most part, it is also true that the declining utility of slaves, in a disrupted and uncertain economy, convinced few of them to liberate their slaves. The growing distaste for slave labor led men with need of laboring hands to replace life-long black slaves with white indentured servants, who would serve from three to seven years, or free wage laborers, who could be hired and released as occasion dictated. But the step from deciding not to acquire additional slaves, which involved no cost, to a decision to release those already in one's possession, which amounted to a divestment of private property, proved to be very large.

Something more about the economic component in the dynamics of individual decisionmaking among slaveholders can be learned by looking at the occupations of those who freed and did not free their slaves. By the 1760s, slaveholding in Philadelphia had spread downward from merchants and professionals in the upper stratum of the city's social structure, where most slaves were held as domestic servants, through the middling ranks of master artisans, ship captains, shopkeepers, taverners, and schoolteachers, as well as farmers residing on the periphery of the town. Most of these masters held only one or two slaves; among 555 in 1767, only thirty-two held four or more. As indicated in Table 3–2, the tendency to quit the ranks of slaveholders during the years from 1767 to 1775, whether by the death, sale, or manumission of slaves, was not concentrated in any one occupational group. But artisans and

TABLE 3–2. Occupation, Slaveholding, and Manumission in Philadelphia, 1767–1780

	Slaveowners 1767	Manumitters* 1767–74	Slaveowners 1775	Manumitters 1775–79	Slaveowners 1780
Merchants	154	13	142	18	113
Artisans	175	8	129	24	97
Proprietors	47	1	38	9	45
Mariners	48	1	13	1	22
Professionals	32	3	23	4	22
Gentlemen	6	3	18	5	15
Officials	5	0	9	0	7
Women**	29	2	57	25	45
Farmers	18	4	18	1	7
Unknown	41	3	5	8	23
TOTAL	555	38	452	95	396

*Manumitters are counted only the first time they freed a slave.
**For whom no occupation is known.

Sources: Phila. tax assessment list, 1767; Phila. constables' returns, 1775 and 1779–80 (adjusted to include the Northern Liberties and Southwark); manumissions.

mariners divested themselves of slaves most rapidly, while merchants and proprietors of shops and businesses more slowly. Meanwhile, the number of slaveholders among officials, gentlemen, and women (mostly widows) increased.[22]

The reasons for these occupational differences in accepting or resisting abolitionist sentiment can only be surmised. It is not surprising that officials and gentlemen would be reluctant to give up slaves, for lifetime servants conferred status upon those whose positions required it. Among women, it might be supposed that humanitarian instincts would prevail, but this does not seem to have happened. That relatively so many artisans and mariners quit the business of slaveholding—more than one of every four artisans and almost three-fourths of the mariners, including many non-Quakers who were under no moral pressure to do so—is most likely explained by the growing recognition that in a fluctuating economy those with capital to invest in labor would be better advised to hire wage laborers who could be employed and discharged at will. Only eight artisans and one mariner manumitted slaves between 1767 and 1775 when the number of mechanic and maritime slaveowners decreased by 46 and 35 respectively, so it is apparent that most of these men got out of slavekeeping by some other means—by sale, death, or flight of their slaves.

With the exception of Quakers, the armor protecting slaveowners from abolitionist appeals proved particularly impenetrable among the city's large slaveholders, those with four or more slaves. Thirty-three non-Quaker Philadelphians held four or more slaves in 1767, including eight merchants (who might have been holding some of them for sale), five lawyers, four colonial officials, three bakers, and a variety of other persons. Within this group of those with the greatest investment in slaves, only one slaveowner liberated her slaves, the spinster Martha Higgins, who in 1771 released Isaac, Samuel, and Chloe and promised freedom to London in 1775. Among Quakers it was different. Merchant William Coleman freed Ozmior and his wife Hagar, another woman named Phillis, and four children in 1768. In the same year Jacob Duberry, a Quaker farmer, freed a slave family of man, wife, and three children. Joseph Potts, a Quaker entrepreneur, in the following year freed eight slave men, all of whom probably worked at his iron forge outside of Philadelphia. In 1775, Quaker Stephen Maxfield, a joiner, liberated Bathsheba and her four small children, although deferring the freedom date for the children until they reached adulthood.

Meanwhile, large slaveholders who were not Quaker remained resistant to the arguments of Revolutionary pamphleteers, moral reformers, and slaves themselves that slavery was incompatible with the principles upon which the American protests against British policy were founded. Such appeals did not soften the hearts of large slaveowners such as lawyers Benjamin Chew, James Tilghman, and John Dickinson, all of whom maintained large plantations in Delaware worked by numerous slaves; nor could antislavery appeals move artisans such as the baker William Hodge, who owned six slaves; the sailmaker John Malcom with five; brickmaker John Coats with six; or John Phillips, the city's largest slaveowner, whose thirteen slaves manned Philadelphia's largest ropewalk in Southwark. Even among those who were in the vanguard of the Revolutionary movement in Philadelphia, no crisis of conscience developed through the year 1775. Neither Benjamin Franklin, Benjamin Rush, Charles Willson Peale, William Bradford, James Cannon, nor Christopher Marshall would release their bondsmen and bondswomen, although King, one of Franklin's slaves, had run away after Franklin took him to England.[23]

While most Philadelphians balked at suffering an economic loss through freeing their slaves, many severed their connection with an institution that was under moral attack by selling their slaves in the last decade before the Revolution began. A lively market for slaves had always existed in Philadelphia, serving not only the port town but the surrounding countryside. In fact, slaves seem to have been much less tied to a particular master and a particular place

in the cities of the northern colonies than in the plantation South. The Philadelphia Quaker Isaac Roberts may have been somewhat unusual in becoming
the twelfth master of a slave in about 1755, but few were the slaves who had
not had at least three or four masters.[24] Some idea of the magnitude of the sale
of slaves, or transfer after death, can be inferred by comparing the tax as-
sessors' reports of 1767 and 1769. At a time when few new slaves were being
imported into the city, 125 persons who had not been assessed for slaves in
1767 appeared on the 1769 tax lists as slaveowners, indicating about a 20
percent turnover of slaves in two years.[25] By the early 1770s, Philadelphians
who wished to quit the business of slaveowning, but not at an economic loss,
had new opportunities as slave merchants from the southern colonies roamed
the city and hinterland advertising for able-bodied slaves. "House Negroes . . . when under the displeasure of their owners," wrote a deploring
Anthony Benezet, "[are] to be Sold cheaper here, than [slaves] from on board
the Guinea Ships, for which purpose the Southern people have one or more
Agents, who are frequently advertising they are ready to buy all Negroes, who
are proposed for Sale, if but able to work, their other qualities they are not
concerned about."[26]

Abolition followed a different course in rural Pennsylvania than in the city
in the pre-Revolutionary years, especially with regard to Quakers. Throughout much of the late colonial period many rural and urban Friends held
opposing views on slavery. Chester Quarterly Meeting, encompassing local
meetings in Chester and Lancaster counties, western Pennsylvania, Delaware,
and parts of Maryland and Virginia, had denounced the slave trade in the
1710s and 1729–30 and called on Friends to stop buying and selling slaves.
Philadelphia Quakers, active in the trade and dependent on imported black
labor, rebuffed Chester's plea. After 1730, however, the sides changed. As
slaveholding Philadelphia leaders died off, a generation of city reformers set
about to cleanse the Society of sin, including the practice of owning slaves.
Few rural Pennsylvania meetings joined the reform drive of the 1750s to purge
the Society of Friends of slavery. Chester Quarterly Meeting, earlier the
foremost opponent of the slave trade, now became deadlocked on the issue.
Over the years, increasing numbers of rural Quakers had acquired blacks, so
that by the late 1750s, when Philadelphia leaders and their allies pressed for
abolition, country Friends showed little enthusiasm.[27] As the supply of white
indentured servants dried up during the Seven Years' War, well-to-do farmers,
millers, artisans, and innkeepers who needed year-round additional labor
could not be deterred by urban reformers from purchasing black slaves. Thus,
while Philadelphia's slave population grew substantially between 1760 and
1765 and then began a precipitous decline, Chester County's slave population

grew even faster between 1760 and 1765, doubling in just five years, and then began a slow decline that was very much outstripped by Philadelphia's (Table 1–8).

Though most rural meetings of Friends were not in the forefront of the 1750s Quaker abolitionist movement in Pennsylvania, by the early 1760s they did proceed to discipline errant Friends who bought or sold slaves. For example, Chester Monthly Meeting dealt with two men in 1760 who traded in slaves. Davis Bevan acknowledged that he "inadvertently" bought and sold a black but now agreed that the practice was wrong and promised to avoid it in the future. The meeting accepted his written statement and allowed him to participate fully in meeting affairs. Jonathan Copeland, however, vindicated his action and purchased at least one more slave while under scrutiny for the first offense. Chester Meeting agreed to bar him from meeting business as directed by the Yearly Meeting. Concord Monthly Meeting made the same decision a few years later when Robert Chamberlin purchased and subsequently sold a slave, and then refused to acknowledge his wrongdoing.[28]

Individual rural Friends continued to manumit slaves in their wills, and several of them liberated blacks before their deaths, but the pace of emancipation among Friends in Chester County did not quicken even slightly until after 1774. Only 27 Chester County residents, almost all of them Quakers, are known to have freed slaves before 1763. In the years 1763 to 1765, as the slave trade was winding down, only three more slaveholders released their bondspeople. Though 51 Friends on the Chester County tax list of 1765 owned blacks, only seven of them freed slaves between 1766 and 1774—a rate of manumission unchanged from what rural Friends had maintained since the mid-1740s (Tables 3–3, 2–1). These were the years when John Woolman and other Quaker abolitionists were criss-crossing the Delaware Valley visiting families, and the issue of slavery often came up for discussion at monthly, quarterly, and yearly meetings. But rural Quakers, like other residents of the countryside, showed themselves to be largely impervious to the message, although the few who decided to release their slaves were more likely than earlier manumitters to grant immediate freedom. Before 1766, most Quaker manumitters freed their slaves by will, that is, only at their deaths, when they themselves had no further need of their slaves' labor. Even then, the testators often encumbered the slaves with additional terms of service to heirs or payments to be made annually or in lump sum. In the late 1760s and early 1770s, several country Friends moved closer to the guidelines the Society would insist upon after 1774: immediate and unconditional freedom for adults and release at maturity for children (18 years for girls and 21 for boys). In 1766, John Minshall, a Chester County farmer, posted £30 bond with the

TABLE 3–3. Religion, Slaveholding, and Manumission in Chester County, 1765–1780

	Slaveowners 1765	Manumitters* 1766–1774	Slaveowners 1774	Manumitters 1775–1779	Slaveowners 1780
Quaker	51	7	33**	45	3
Ex-Quaker	14	4	12	3	19
Anglican	43	2	42	3	41
Presbyterian	26	0	24	0	43
Baptist	1	0	2	0	7
Rom. Catholic	1	0	1	0	2
German Reformed	0	0	1	0	0
Unknown***	72	0	44	2	86
TOTAL	208	13	159	53	201

*Manumitters are counted only the first time they freed a slave.

**A number of Quakers who manumitted adult blacks just a few years later were not taxed for slaves in 1774, perhaps because they had promised them freedom.

***In many cases, these slaveholders were affiliated with no church.

Sources: Chester Co. tax assessment lists, 1765 and 1774, Chester County Archives; Chester County slave registration list, 1780, Pennsylvania Abolition Society Papers, Reel 24, Historical Society of Pennsylvania; manumissions; church records.

Court of Quarter Sessions for his black man Oran Hazard, also a farmer. The next year Daniel Sharpless of Nether Providence township posted bond for his slave Phillis Menereau, who was Hazard's wife. John Knowles of Ridley released his slave James Funney in 1770 by the same method.[29]

If the high-toned rhetoric of natural rights and moral rectitude that accompanied the onset of the Revolution had only a limited power to soften the hearts of eastern Pennsylvania's slavemasters, what about the effects of the tumultuous war years on those who held slaves? The data for answering that question are unusually good for Philadelphia because two household censuses conducted in 1775 and the winter of 1779–80 have survived, and for Chester County because tax lists in the late colonial period and a registration list of all slaves recorded in 1780 give an accurate picture of how slaveholding changed. These data raise serious doubts about the impact of Revolutionary Whig ideology on attitudes toward slavery.

In 1775, when the city constables conducted a household enumeration of families, they listed 452 slaveowners holding 728 slaves remaining in the city.[30] Five years later, after the most economically volatile and politically tumultuous years in the city's history, the constables returned to the streets to conduct another enumeration. This time they found 396 slaveowners in possession of 539 slaves. Thus the war years reduced the number of Philadelphia slaveowners by 56 (12 percent) and the number of slaves by 189 (26 percent). At first glance, this seems a creditable display of abolitionist sentiment for such a short period of time.

Yet by combining these census data with records showing the release of slaves, by will or through individual acts of manumission, it becomes apparent that except among Quakers the abolitionist spirit that Benjamin Rush spoke so optimistically about on the eve of war had quickly dissipated by the time the Continental Congress issued the Declaration of Independence and never revived significantly during the years of fighting. Slavery was dying in Pennsylvania, to be sure; but it was dying mostly through the manumissions of Quaker slaveowners, who made a dramatic move to cleanse themselves of holding fellow humans in bondage in 1776, and otherwise only because slaves themselves were taking matters into their own hands when their masters stubbornly clung to the institution in spite of appeals to their conscience and to the consistency of their Whiggish principles.

The decision of Philadelphia Quakers to move from a ban on buying slaves in 1755 to prohibiting slave ownership took twenty years—until 1774. By this time most of the slaveowners in the monthly meetings who had earlier led the opposition to such action had died or left the meeting.[31] The Philadelphia Yearly Meeting decision in 1774 provided that committees would visit and begin "a speedy & close Labour" with all slaveowners. Masters should promptly free their slaves, and if they refused, meetings should bar them from participating in meeting business or from contributing funds (the same punishment slave buyers and sellers faced after 1758).[32] This committee work proceeded apace in late 1774 and through 1775. Committeemen must have sometimes felt that the process resembled that of breaking the will of a stubborn child, for only seven Philadelphia Quakers freed slaves in 1774 and five in 1775, leaving a large number of the city's Friends in noncompliance at the end of the latter year. Even among Quakers, the loss of an investment of £50-100—equivalent to the annual income of many artisans, and a sum that would have paid the annual rent on all but the largest houses in Philadelphia—was not easy to swallow. Some of them, such as the tanner Joseph Marriott, buffered the loss by deferring the freedom date of his slaves, James and Judith, but most simply chalked up the loss to their original error in acquiring slaves.

The Yearly Meeting that convened in September 1775, took some satisfaction in the "considerable Number" of slaves who had been freed in eastern Pennsylvania as a result of committee pleadings with masters, but they warned that Friends must "manifest a Concern for further proceeding in this weighty Service. . . ."[33] In the year of independence committees continued to visit foot-dragging Friends and probably took a more insistent approach to judge by a report by Philadelphia Quarterly Meeting in August 1776 that much greater success had been achieved. Scores of slaveowners had promised the release of their chattel property, although many more masters and mistresses withheld freedom for slave children until they reached the age of 21 for males and 18 for females. This was a way of preserving some of the labor value of young slaves; but Friends also regarded it as a method of preparing young slaves for freedom.[34] Then at the Yearly Meeting in September 1776 the Society's leaders agreed to disown slaveowners completely and urged local meetings to step up their efforts to obtain manumissions. Committees repeated their visits until they obtained manumissions or lost hope of doing so.[35]

The appeal to conscience had extraordinary effects among a few Quakers. Perhaps most notable was Joshua Fisher, who had arrived from Lewes, Delaware, in 1745 and become one of Philadelphia's wealthiest merchants and a weighty Quaker in the years before the Revolution. Fisher had owned a number of slaves in Delaware and had sold several of them when he moved north to Philadelphia. He acquired other slaves after arriving in the city. In the 1760s, for example, Fisher purchased 12-year-old Jim from the printer David Hall, and after keeping him six years sold him to another man. Jim passed from owner to owner until Fisher "apprehended it to be his duty as a Christian" in 1776 to buy Jim back and free him. Now 69 years old, the old Quaker spent the last eight years of his life tracking down the slaves he had owned in the past, along with all their offspring, and trying to buy them out of thralldom. Some searches proved futile; others succeeded. Fisher located the son of Jim (now James Freeman), paid £100 for him, and manumitted him in December 1776. He inquired about Sal and her two children, Scipio and Cyrus, who had served him for ten years and then had been sold to Fisher's cousin in Delaware. All were now dead, Fisher learned. Sue had been sold in Delaware 31 years before and had died about 1755, but Fisher was determined to find her children, all of whom had been born into slavery after he had sold her. Spread through Delaware, the five children, all in their twenties, were located one by one and purchased by Fisher. All took the surname Freedom— Glasgow, Paris, Sabina, Moses, and Diana.[36]

Despite such inspiring successes as Joshua Fisher, the Quaker visiting committees in Philadelphia still met with resistance among a substantial number of slaveowners. The Quarterly Meeting reported a few months after independence had been declared that Friends had dealt with members "who notwithstanding our repeated Labour continue to withhold from them their just, & natural Right to Liberty, and we have not at present a Prospect that our further Visits will be acceptable, or useful to them, tho most of them acknowledge themselves to be convinced of the Injustice of the Practice of dealing in Slaves. . . ."[37] At this point, after two years of moral cudgeling, the Yearly Meeting called for its monthly meetings to "testify their disunion" with any Friend who from "views of temporal Gain, & Self Interest" refused to comply with a final entreaty to free his or her slaves.[38] Even this attempt to force those caught in the conflict between economic interest and moral compunction to order their priorities, was not completely successful, for monthly meetings proved extremely reluctant to banish recalcitrant slaveowners. As late as 1780, after six years of moral pressure, some slaveholders still remained members of the Society of Friends.

Nonetheless, all but about eight Quakers of Philadelphia Monthly Meeting eventually complied, these eight choosing to leave the Society of Friends rather than set their slaves free.[39] Forty-four Quakers freed 80 slaves in 1776. Twenty-eight owners freed 56 slaves in 1777 and 1778, although the date of freedom of fifteen of these, all under age, was deferred from one to 21 years. Nine more Quakers reluctantly released their slaves in 1779 and 1780 so that by the latter year the Meeting for Sufferings could report to London Friends that members of Philadelphia Yearly Meeting were now "nearly clear" of holding slaves.[40] One of the last to comply was the prominent Quaker minister Samuel Emlen, who freed his house slave Dinah in 1779. Some younger slaves were kept thereafter in the houses of their masters, to be freed when they reached maturity, and several other slaves remained in families where the wife but not the husband was a Quaker. These instances, however, were relatively rare. Among the vast majority of Friends, religious and natural rights principles had triumphed over pecuniary interest.

The decision of the leaders of the Society of Friends in the 1770s to erase the moral blot of slavekeeping, and the actions of hundreds of individual Quakers in abiding by this decision, were belittled by many commentators at the time and in later years. Hearing the news in England while he was finishing his epic book, *An Inquiry into the Nature and Causes of the Wealth of Nations,* Adam Smith oddly twisted the Quaker divestment of slaves into an additional proof of his argument that economic self-interest ruled human affairs. Man's pride "makes him love to domineer," wrote Smith, and because he hates to condescend to extract labor from those he has hired, "he will generally prefer the service of slaves to that of free men," whenever the law permitted it and the nature of the work "can afford it." The fact that the Quakers of Pennsylvania had decided to free their slaves, Smith continued, proved that their investment in human property could not have been "very great," for if the economic interest in slaves "made up a considerable part of their property, such a resolution could never have been agreed to."[41] Convinced that economic interest always outweighed moral principle, Smith could interpret the decision of many Quakers who gave up their slaves rather than sacrifice membership in the Society of Friends in no other way.

Other commentators were even less convinced of Quaker magnanimity than Smith. Whereas the Scottish philosopher argued that Quakers released their slaves only because their investment in human property was slight, Charles Varley, an English writer who arrived in Philadelphia in 1784 and made an extensive tour of the Northeast and upper South, was convinced that the Quakers had freed their slaves because it provided an absolute economic benefit. "The most shrewd" people in Pennsylvania, he wrote, had come to see that their slaves "were of little use, but to stock [their masters] with a swarm of helpless children, and big-bellied women, which in time would eat them out of house and home." Hence, "in order to get quit of them, they preached up a doctrine, making it a matter of conscience not to keep a slave; but in fact it was a matter of frugal state policy, to get quit of them." Varley claimed that he had been told this "by some of their own principal brethren."[42]

The difficulty that Quaker leaders had in implementing their policy against slaveholding tells us that even when the economic stake in slaveholding was relatively small, most of those who had invested in human property were reluctant to dispose of it without compensation, even when deeply held religious allegiances were involved. This might be taken as confirmation of Adam Smith's proposition, although his law of human nature could hardly be applied to the south of Pennsylvania, where many Delaware Quaker farmers gave up much larger holdings in slaves in a victory of conscience over economic self-interest. But the resistance of most Philadelphians who were *not* Quaker in the Revolutionary years to releasing their slaves shows either that Quakers were more skilled in determining their economic interest than non-Quakers or that Smith and Varley's cynical belief that morality could never transcend economic interest was not justified. In the midst of the final decision for independence, and then through five years of war and the greatest internal strife that Philadelphians and eastern Pennsylvanians had ever experienced, hundreds of slaveowners who were not Quaker also had to make decisions about whether to free their slaves. In the main, they decided in ways that contrast sharply with the Quakers and demonstrate that most Philadelphia slaveowners still believed in the absolute benefits of slave-owning.

In Philadelphia such non-Quaker slavemasters numbered about 390 in 1775. Of these, only 21, a paltry 5 percent, are known to have released any of their slaves from 1775 to 1779, and the total number of non-Quaker slaveowners decreased from 390 to 380 (Table 3–1). Whether it was the uncertainties of war or some other factor that had dampened the abolitionist impulse, it is apparent that the high hopes of Benjamin Rush had been dashed and that the decision of Quakers to divest themselves of human property had only a puny effect on those who were members of other religious groups. In fact, among Philadelphians who were not Quakers, the tendency to manumit slaves increased only slightly during the years from 1775 to 1779. Between 1767 and 1774, only twenty-three of 468 non-Quaker slaveholders (4.9 percent) had liberated at least one slave; this percentage of beneficent owners rose to 5.4 during the war years from 1775 to 1779. Though only five Anglicans freed slaves, the number of Anglican slaveowners declined by 30 percent, partly the result of Loyalists fleeing the city. Among Presbyterians, Jews, German Lutherans, and German Reformed, the number of slaveowners actually grew during the war, in the case of the Presbyterians by a whopping 47 percent (Table 3–1). While Quakers were completing the process of ending their involvement with slavery, other Philadelphians were becoming only slightly less reluctant to end theirs or were increasing their participation in what Quakers were calling by 1783 a "crying iniquity."[43] Successful among their co-religionists, reformers such as Anthony Benezet and the members of the Quaker visiting committees must have despaired at their lack of influence among other city dwellers.

From an examination of the occupations of non-Quaker slaveholders during the years of Revolutionary turmoil in Philadelphia, it is clear that artisans continued to be the most likely to end their connection with coerced labor. With so many artisans serving in the militia and with the war years disrupting their businesses, the preference for hired labor could only have increased. Among most occupational groups the impulse to free slaves, not to replace them when they died or ran away, or even to allow them to buy their freedom, had weakened during the difficult years of war, and in some groups, such as mariners and proprietors, the number of slaveowners had even grown slightly.

While the great majority of slaveowners who were not Quaker proved to be impervious to the abolitionist message, large numbers of them detached themselves from the institution by means other than manumission. These cases demonstrate how slaveholders who had lost confidence in the economic viability of compelled labor, or had suffered wartime reverses that reduced their need for labor, withdrew from the system of bondage only by the death or escape of their chattel or by transferring ownership to someone else with no such doubts about the economic benefits and obviously no moral qualms. Nearly three of every five slavemasters reported by the constables in 1775 owned no slaves five years later when the constables returned. Some of the slaveholders in 1775 had no doubt died or left Philadelphia during the war, accounting for some of this rapid turnover; but many others, as advertisements for the sale of slaves in the city newspapers show, were eager to quit the business of holding property in human beings if they could find someone to make good their investment.

Buyers were not lacking, and sometimes the circumstances were shabby, showing that high-minded Revolutionary principles had nothing to do with everyday life. While intoxicated, John Hanna, a Philadelphia brushmaker sold Romeo to the horse jockey William Ryan for £60, but when Ryan would not complete the payment, Hanna reclaimed his slave and signed him over to James Durant for £70.[44] For some Philadelphians the war offered lucrative war contracts, and with white labor in short supply because of the military drain on manpower, slaves became the only available source. With the war creating a heavy demand for leather, Jonathan Meredith's tanning business flourished. Meredith had purchased one slave in 1773 and before the war ended he had bought six others to work in his tannery.[45] Stephen Girard, who settled in the city in 1777, was another who capitalized on the risky but sometimes highly profitable shipping business. Girard, by purchasing Abraham from his Virginia master, added his name to the list of new city slaveowners and initiated a long and troubled period of owning slaves who ran away chronically from the difficult Girard.[46]

Other Philadelphians became slaveowners by purchasing at public auction slaves from British ships captured by privateers sailing out of the city. The state ship *General Greene* brought a 300-ton prize into port in the summer of 1779, loaded with sugar, coffee, molasses, and slaves—all of which were disposed of at public auction.[47] Other slaves entered the city workforce when they were confiscated as the property of Loyalist masters. Such was the case of the eight slaves of Oxford Township resident Isaac Snowden, who lost his bondsmen and bondswomen in 1778.[48] Wartime Philadelphia was a city where for every Quaker withdrawing from the sordid business of slavekeeping there was a non-Quaker ready to acquire the lifetime labor of a black man or woman.

While Quakers and a few others were freeing their slaves, other slaves were freeing themselves. Slaves were privy to the talk about universal rights and to the specific calls for the abolition of slavery, and of course they were living in a city where the number of free blacks was growing substantially because of Quaker manumissions. Hence, their tolerance for serving dutifully must have dropped greatly during the war years. The occupation of Philadelphia by the British army from September 1777 to June 1778 offered slaves whose masters had decided not to flee the city as the British approached or had withdrawn to nearby rural areas a special opportunity to gain their freedom by joining the British ranks. For some male slaves the presence in Philadelphia of the Black Guides and Pioneers, a black regiment with Scottish officers formed by Cornwallis from escaped slaves in Virginia, must have been appealing. By joining the British they gained their freedom, and by fighting against the Americans, blacks understood they struck a blow against slavery. The belief was "almost universal" among blacks, wrote Philadelphia's German Lutheran minister, Henry Muhlenberg, that the British would liberate all American slaves after defeating the upstart colonies.[49]

How many slaves fled to the British or ran away to pass as free blacks cannot be ascertained exactly, but the number was substantial. Dozens of advertisements for runaway slaves appeared in the Philadelphia newspapers during the war years. Whereas fewer than ten Philadelphia slaves fled annually from 1770 to 1775 (about one of every 90 slaves each year), the number, among a substantially diminished slave population, rose to nearly 24 per year from 1776 to 1780—a runaway rate of one of every 26 slaves per year.[50] Scores of slaves from the region fled their masters when the British occupied the city in September 1777, and still more when the British evacuation began in June 1778. Probably at least one hundred were crowded onto the ships, along with several thousand Loyalists from eastern Pennsylvania and western New Jersey, that embarked from the Delaware docks with the British army. Eighteen months later, a Philadelphia newspaper reminded readers that "by the invasion of this state, and the possession the enemy obtained of this city, and neighbourhood, [a] great part of the slaves hereabouts, were enticed away by the British army."[51] This may have overstated the case, but it appears that more than one hundred slaves in the city and its environs achieved personal independence by joining the British. Five years later, at the end of the war, when the British evacuated about 3000 former American slaves from their New York City headquarters, sixty-seven of them were listed as having fled from masters in the Philadelphia region. Many others who fled must have died in the interim or made the decision, as the English fleet prepared to embark for Nova Scotia, to remain in America as free persons.[52]

While many Pennsylvania slaves understandably cast their lot with the British, since they and not the Revolutionary governments offered personal freedom to bondsmen and bondswomen willing to fight, a few blacks chose to support the American side. Black patriots included free-born James Forten, later one of the most respected and wealthiest men in Philadelphia, who at age 15 signed on Stephen Decatur's privateer the *Royal Louis*. Another black Philadelphian, who remained anonymous, in 1782 published a sermon in

support of American independence. He excoriated the British policy of arm-
ing "domestics to fight against their masters," but did not neglect to remind
his readers of the broader meaning of liberty. "And now my virtuous fellow
citizens," he wrote, "let me intreat you, that, after you have rid yourselves of
the British yoke, that you will also emancipate those who have been all their
life subject to bondage."[53]

Rural Pennsylvanians, to judge by the record of those living in Chester
County, became even more reluctant abolitionists in the early years of the
Revolution. Most country Friends eventually gave up their slaves rather than
suffer disownment from the Society, but from 1775 to 1779 only eight of 126
(6 percent) slaveowners of other persuasions succumbed to the moral preach-
ments of the Quakers or the natural rights ideology of the Revolution.

The Chester County monthly meetings followed the instructions of the
Yearly Meeting in 1774 to set up committees to visit all slaveholders and
persuade them to release their bondsmen and bondswomen. Goshen Monthly
Meeting, for example, appointed Amos Yarnell and Isaac Thomas in 1774 to
visit members of their meeting who held slaves. Yarnell and Thomas found
that a few Friends still owned slaves, but they were "well used" and some had
been taught to read. By 1776, the meeting, with a higher consciousness of the
issue, reported to Philadelphia Yearly Meeting that there were few slaves
"amongst us but we cannot say they are well used while they are kept in
slavery."[54] In December 1776, Goshen promptly followed the Yearly Meeting's instruction to appoint Friends to visit slaveholders again and this time
hold the threat of disownment over them. For over a year this committee and
others attempted to obtain manumissions from obdurate slaveholders. By
February 1778, Goshen Friends believed they had expended enough effort and
agreed to bring the case of John Morris of Marple before the meeting. Morris
agreed in principle to manumit his slaves but would not set a date. He was
therefore disowned in November 1778. The following year, the meeting dealt
with John and Ann Kerlin, who refused to free their two slaves. John would
not manumit and Ann said she must follow her husband's decision, so Friends
testified against them both. Goshen also had several cases in the late 1770s in
which members bought and sold slaves. When two of these offenders, husband and wife, refused or were unable to secure freedom for the black woman
they had sold, the meeting disowned them.[55]

Thus Friends throughout Pennsylvaniá, as in other parts of the Philadelphia
Yearly Meeting area, eradicated slaveholding within their membership within
a period of six or seven years after 1776. Forty-five Chester County Friends
signed manumissions from 1775 to 1779 (Table 3–3), and six more freed
slaves by 1783. Only three people who registered slaves in 1780 can be

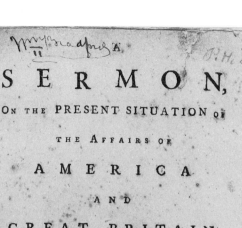

SERMON,

On the PRESENT SITUATION of

THE AFFAIRS OF

AMERICA

AND

GREAT-BRITAIN.

WRITTEN BY A BLACK,

And printed at the Requeſt of ſeveral Perſons of

diſtinguiſhed CHARACTERS.

PHILADELPHIA:

PRINTED BY T. BRADFORD AND P. HALL.

M, DCC, LXXXII.

Title page of a tract published in 1782 by an anonymous black patriot. The sermon, which called for prompt emancipation of slaves following American victory, is the earliest known publication by an African-American in Philadelphia. Courtesy of The Library Company of Philadelphia.

identified as Friends. Three years later, no Chester County Quakers still held slaves for life. Among ex-Quakers, however, a considerable number registered slaves in 1780. Some had accepted disownment rather than give up their human property, but others had been testified against for other reasons such as marrying a non-Quaker, joining the army, or taking an oath of allegiance during the Revolution. Like members of other churches, former Friends were under no direct pressure to give up their slaves.

The other major groups of Chester County slaveholders were Anglicans/Episcopalians (including Swedish Lutherans) and Presbyterians. Both groups contracted little of the abolitionist fever that Rush had described in 1773. From 1775 to 1779, when the antislavery stance of the Society of Friends impelled 45 Chester County Quakers to free slaves, only three Anglicans and no Presbyterians were moved to do likewise (Table 3–3). Anglican emancipators, though few in number, could be generous to the slaves they freed. William Grantham of Ridley, in his will probated in 1774, not only freed his men Caesar and William, but gave them part of his plantation on Crum Creek and all profits from it during their lives, a house and lot, all grain sown on the land, and £40.[56] Other Anglican manumitters were less munificent, requiring their slaves to serve terms beyond the testator's demise. John Gronow of Tredyffrin in his will freed Phillis, one of his two slaves, and gave her bed and bedding and wearing apparel but required her to work for her mistress, the widow, for six additional months. John Bryan of Ridley expected Pamela to work for his wife until the slave reached age 31, while John Salkeld of Chester delayed freedom for Peg and her child until after the death of his wife.[57] Whether more or less generous in their provision for the freed women and men, all these Anglicans agreed to manumission only after their deaths, when they could no longer use their slaves' labor.

Like the wartime currency of the Continental Congress, the value of benevolent rhetoric depreciated rapidly in the late 1770s. The Society of Friends, following religious precepts more than natural rights philosophy, had boldly broken through the resistance to freeing slaves in the early stages of the war and had almost completely purged themselves of the ownership of other human beings by the time the cannons were spiked. But slaveholders of other religious persuasions, or no religious commitment at all, were overwhelmingly oblivious to the antislavery message. If the economic advantages of using free labor obliged many artisans and mariners in Philadelphia to quit slavekeeping, most of them separated themselves from the institution by selling their slaves to others or not replacing them when they died or ran away. Men in other occupations, with a continuing need for labor, in both the city and country, stood ready to buy slaves offered for sale.

4

Dismantling Slavery: Institutions

Although Pennsylvanians who were not members of the Society of Friends had proved remarkably impervious to the Revolutionary rhetoric of natural rights, as well as to the humanitarian appeals of Quakers to cleanse the new republic from the sin of bondage, they changed remarkably in the decade after hostilities with Great Britain ceased. On two levels—one institutional and the other personal—a new commitment to withdrawing from the system of compelled labor emerged that set Pennsylvania off from neighboring states. In this chapter we analyze how the state's leaders, in the legislature and in organizations such as the Pennsylvania Abolition Society and the Society of Friends, groped for ways to excise slavery from the body politic. In the next chapter we examine how individuals, slaves as well as slaveowners, extricated themselves from the roles of victim and oppressor in the business of human bondage.

From 1780 to 1790 two events combined to deal slavery in Pennsylvania a crippling, though not mortal, blow. The first was the passage of a gradual abolition act by the state legislature in 1780, and event much celebrated in the history of antislavery because never before had any polity, in America or elsewhere, abolished racial slavery by legislative act. The second was the revival of the Pennsylvania Abolition Society in 1784, an institution that would prove indispensable in maintaining the law of 1780 when it fell under attack and in assisting thousands of blacks freed under the provisions of the 1780 law or entering the state in search of a new life as free persons. Both

events provide opportunities to examine the intersecting influence of economic interest, religious affiliation, and ideology in the growth of antislavery
sentiment among many Pennsylvanians and the resistance to it among others.
Neither the law of 1780 nor the re-founding of the abolition society has been
subjected to the close scrutiny that is necessary to reveal how ideological and
material factors intermingled as the Revolutionary generation confronted the
contradiction between the natural rights principles of the revolt against England and their social and economic system that was built to a considerable
extent upon coerced labor.

The move to abolish slavery by legislation began well before 1780 and in
fact was in process from the beginning of the Revolution. In 1775 the Chester
County Committee of Correspondence had petitioned the provincial legislature to pass a gradual abolition act.[1] In the summer of 1776 a group of
Philadelphia radicals and democratic backcountry Scots-Irish Presbyterians,
elected to write a constitution for the state, produced a document that embod-
ied "the most radical ideas about politics and constitutional authority voiced
in the Revolution."[2] In the first article of the "Declaration of Rights" in the
constitution they set forth the memorable notion "that all Men are born
equally free and independent, and that they have certain natural, inherent, and
unalienable rights, among which are the enjoying and defending Life and
Liberty. . . ."[3] In the following years, legislators would lean heavily on these
words in arguing for abolition. But at the time the more important matter was
the reform of Pennsylvania's government. No evidence survives that any of
the small number of fervent antislavery proponents faulted the drafters of the
constitution for failing to confront directly the issue of human bondage.
Benjamin Rush's main thought, for example, was that the convention had
been swept away with overly democratic notions and had "substituted a mob
government for one of the happiest governments in the world."[4] But while
finding the new constitution "absurd," the antislavery doctor did not utter a
word of criticism that the document never mentioned slavery.

Although the Constitution of 1776 sidestepped the issue of slavery, some of
those who attended the convention appear to have been biding their time.[5]
Only two years passed (which included the 9-month occupation of Phila-
delphia when the military situation in eastern Pennsylvania preoccupied polit-
ical leaders) before one of the constitution's principal promoters, George
Bryan, took the lead in fashioning a gradual abolition bill. An immigrant from
Ireland in the 1750s, Bryan had established himself as a small merchant in
Philadelphia and, after his business failed in 1769, devoted himself to politics.
An important member of the Scots-Irish Presbyterian bloc that took control of
Pennsylvania politics during the war, Bryan had risen to prominence at the

state constitutional convention.[6] Three months after becoming acting president of the Supreme Executive Council, in May 1778, Bryan pressed the idea of an abolition bill on the legislature.[7] An Assembly member introduced such a bill in August 1778, but it was tabled, indicating that opposition to the idea existed from the beginning.[8]

Three months later, the Executive Council, under Bryan's leadership, raised the issue again and even offered a draft of an abolition bill that Bryan may have prepared. "No period seems more happy for the attempt than the present," it advised the legislature, to extinguish slavery, "as the number of [slaves] . . . has been much reduced by the practices & plunder of our late invaders." If they abolished slavery, Pennsylvanians would erase from within their borders the "opprobrium of America" and would regain the respect of "all Europe, who are astonished to see a people eager for Liberty holding Negroes in Bondage."[9] It was not proposed, however, that freedom be extended to any of those who were slaves. In language that revealed the limitations of Bryan's thinking, or, alternatively, his sense of what was politically possible, this was justified on the basis that most of "the present Slaves . . . are scarcely competent of freedom" and thus should not "be meddled with."[10]

Bryan's gradual abolition bill, offered to the Assembly in November 1778, aroused jealousy in that body regarding its sole right to initiate laws. Nonetheless, the Council pressed the issue again in February 1779, arguing slavery was "disgraceful to any people, and more especially to those who have been contending in the great cause of liberty themselves." Offering to provide another abolition bill for the Assembly's consideration, the Executive Council declared: "Honored will that State be in the Annals of History, which shall first abolish this violation of the rights of mankind, & the memories of those will be held in grateful and everlasting remembrance, who shall pass the Law to restore & establish the rights of Human nature in Pennsylvania."[11]

By this time the Assembly needed little urging. They quickly established a committee to draft their own law in 1779, and in two weeks a prepared bill was ordered printed for public discussion.[12] The authorship of the bill is disputed with everyone from Thomas Paine to Benjamin Franklin receiving credit retrospectively. George Bryan is generally cited as the author, and his tombstone claims as much. However, the first historian of the Philadelphia bar, Horace Binney, noted that William Lewis, a Quaker lawyer in Philadelphia, was known during his lifetime as the draftsman of the abolition law.[13] It seems likely that the drafting committee, which included George Clymer of Philadelphia, an Anglican leader of the Revolutionary movement but a man who cut his ties with Philadelphia radicals over the Constitution of

1776, and Robert Knox of Philadelphia County, as well as two representatives from Berks County, in the heart of Pennsylvania's iron-forging region, turned to William Lewis for help and that Bryan was chiefly responsible for shepherding the bill through the legislature.[14] The poignant preamble contained language suggesting that Anthony Benezet was also involved in an advisory capacity. In a pointed history lesson, it called attention to the tragic retrogression of human progress in the New World where "the practice of domestic slavery, so highly detrimental to morality, industry, and the arts, has been, in the instance of the natives of Africa and their descendants, in modern ages revived among christians." Thus America had been "made the scene of this new Invasion of the rights of mankind after the spirit of Christianity had abolished it from the greater part of Europe."[15]

From the very beginning, not a single legislator proposed freeing a single slave, for this would be tampering with property and would raise treacherous problems regarding compensation for slaveowners. When the 1780 law was first proposed in 1778, it called only for the emancipation of all children born to slaves after the act took effect, and it required them to serve, in the manner of indentured servants, until age 18 if they were female and age 21 if male. Every slaveowner in the state must register his or her slaves so a legal record would exist for determining whether a child had been born before or after the effective date of the law and hence was entitled to freedom upon reaching adulthood. Unregistered slaves would be automatically entitled to freedom, following the legal principle that title to unregistered property was deemed void.[16] Congressmen and foreign ministers entering Pennsylvania with slaves were to be exempt from the law, but any other persons arriving with slaves must release them within six months, although they might be indentured until 28 years if a minor or for seven years if an adult. The bill also prohibited slave importations and repealed the slave code in effect since 1726, while retaining the former legal prohibition of mixed marriages and the old practice of binding out free blacks if they were unable to maintain themselves.

How much public discussion occurred regarding the proposed bill is difficult to ascertain, but it is certain that opinion varied widely, especially regarding the economic sacrifice that slaveowners should have to make. Though few owned slaves, most Pennsylvania Germans from Lutheran and Reformed backgrounds, who dominated Lancaster, York, Berks, and Northampton counties in an arc sweeping west and north of Philadelphia, were staunchly opposed.[17] Equally set against any abolition act was a group that did hold numerous slaves—Scots and Scots-Irish Presbyterians, centered in Chester County, who argued in a petition in September 1779 that freeing slaves would saddle the state with a group of people who were inveterately lazy and would never work without compulsion.[18] Less extreme views were rendered by "A Citizen," writing in the *Pennsylvania Packet,* who argued that children born to slaves after the bill passed should be required to serve until at least 28 to 30 years of age because only then would their masters have recovered the expenses involved in rearing them.[19]

The Assembly of 1778–79 never voted on the abolition bill because the Revolution was swirling around their heads, embroiling them in controversies over runaway inflation, food shortages, and price fixing. Then violence broke out in Philadelphia in late 1778 in the Fort Wilson riot that pitted patriot against patriot. Amid such turmoil, the bill was carried over to the next legislature, which turned out to be one of the most radical ever elected in eighteenth-century America. Among the Philadelphians elected was George Bryan. Serving as chairman of the committee to redraft the abolition bill in October 1779, along with Joseph McClean of Philadelphia County and David Thomas of Chester County, he pushed the measure forward as the first bill to be considered by the new Assembly.[20] A new preamble to the bill elaborated on the spirit of liberality that had allegedly overtaken Pennsylvanians because of their firsthand experience with tyranny during the British occupation of Philadelphia from September 1777 to June 1778. "We conceive that it is our duty," wrote Bryan, "and we rejoice that it is in our power, to extend a portion of that freedom to others, which hath been extended to us; and to release from a state of thraldom, to which we ourselves were tyrannically doomed, and from which we have now every prospect of being delivered."[21]

Despite the eloquent language of the preamble, which spoke of the "sorrows of those who have lived in undeserved bondage," Bryan's drafting committee brought in a bill that made a major concession on the issue of when children born of slaves would be released. Rather than free female children born to slaves when they reached the age of eighteen and male children when they reached twenty-one, as the earlier bill had provided, all children of slave mothers were to be required to serve their mother's master until age 28. Under this clause the first Pennsylvania slave would not have walked in freedom until 1808. Such a concession may have been required to obtain the votes of many who had opposed the earlier bill; Bryan candidly stated that the age of 28 was agreed upon "to recompence the charge of nurture."[22] But whether or not this compromise was vital to achieving a majority vote, it added ten years of bound labor for females and seven for males in the prime of their lives. By this extension of the years of servitude the costs of gradual emancipation were transferred from slaveowners to the children of slaves. Given the life expectancy of laboring people—one commentator, "Phileleutheros," believed that most people "used to hard labour without doors begin to fail soon after thirty"—this provision offered Pennsylvania slaveowners who had been affected by natural rights philosophy and appeals to Christian duty what two historians have called "the opportunity to engage in philanthropy at bargain prices."[23]

While the revised abolition bill doubled the number of productive years the children of slaves owed their mothers' masters, it also made two concessions to former slaves and those with white spouses. The provision for binding out free blacks if they could not maintain themselves was dropped and so was the ban on interracial marriage.

Placed before the public, the proposed gradual abolition sparked a spirited debate. Some, such as "Phileleutheros," regarded the law as badly blemished because it ignored all those already enslaved and set "innocent children not yet in being, at liberty, at so late a time as twenty-eight years of age."[24] Others opposed any kind of abolition, and resistance of this kind came from various quarters: from Presbyterians in western Chester County, those who lived just north of neighboring Maryland and Virginia, from Pennsylvania's iron-making region—Berks, Northampton, and Westmoreland counties—where slaves were frequently used, and from the heavily German areas in Philadelphia's immediate hinterland.[25]

In the first recorded vote on the bill, in November 1779, only eight of 46 voting members opposed printing it for public discussion, and all of the delegates from the city and county of Philadelphia gave their assent.[26] Opposition gathered thereafter. Attempting to overcome growing resistance to gradual abolition, the 66-year-old Anthony Benezet visited every member of the legislature, and Bryan published a set of anonymous newspaper articles in December 1779. Directing himself to Chester County Presbyterians, Bryan defended the bill and drew on the language of the 1776 state constitution, with its ringing pronouncement that "all men are born equally free and independent, and . . . have certain natural, inherent, and unalienable rights." Bryan pointed out that, living under a government erected on this principle, any member of the legislature "must feel himself to be but awkwardly employed in opposing such a design." Appealing to the idea of a redeemer nation in the making, he argued that the blot of slavery must be wiped from the national escutcheon, for "this new Aera of founding a new empire in America seems to be designed by Providence, for the extinction of so savage a practice, inconsistent with civilization, morality and the true spirit of Christianity."[27] In Bryan's mind slavery was an historical anomaly that the progressive character of the American Revolution ought to obliterate. Thus, he aligned himself with an ideological position that heretofore had been taken mainly by members of the Society of Friends.[28]

Bryan's appeals to religion, morality, and patriotism seemed to have swayed few of those opposed to gradual abolition, for on a second vote in February the opposition grew to 18 votes. Three additional dissenters could not prevent the bill from passing the third reading on March 1, 1780, by a vote of 34 to 21.[29] By this time three of Philadelphia County's representatives had joined the opposition, although the city delegates remained solidly in favor of gradual abolition. It has been suggested that the mounting opposition included both those who thought the bill too liberal and those who wanted a more thoroughgoing abolition measure;[30] but the fact that all but one of the legislators who voted against it signed a "dissention" indicates otherwise. The dissenters, probably seeking public support for a repeal of the law at the next session, argued that the abolition act would encourage southern slaves "to demand an immediate and intire freedom," thus weakening the war effort. Moreover, they found it objectionable to allow free blacks to vote and hold public office, serve as witnesses and jurors, and marry whites.[31]

A variety of circumstances influenced the decisions legislators made on the gradual abolition act. No doubt each weighed Bryan's natural rights rhetoric

TABLE 4-1. Support for the Gradual Abolition Act of 1780

Delegation	Number of Representatives	Percentage Supporting Law*
Philadelphia City	5	100
Bucks	5	100
Bedford	2	100
Cumberland	6	83
Northumberland	3	67
Chester	8	63
York	5	60
Philadelphia County	7	57
Berks	5	40
Northampton	5	40
Lancaster	11	27
Westmoreland	2	0
TOTAL	64	59

*Supporters of the law include assemblymen who voted favorably on three roll calls taken in November 1779, February and March 1780, or who changed their votes to support the law in March 1780. The votes are recorded in *Journals of the House,* pp. 399, 425.

against his own religious and ideological views on the issue, his personal interest in slavery, and the demands of his constituents. Of sixty-four legislators who participated in the three roll calls on the 1780 act, thirty-six supported the bill on every vote in which they took part (two voted only once), and fourteen consistently voted nay (four voted only once). While only two changed their positions from disapproval to support between the first roll call and the third, twelve initially approved it and then reversed themselves.

In his analysis of ten roll-call votes on the abolition act and subsequent efforts to amend it from 1779 to 1788, Owen S. Ireland concludes that the most strenuous opposition to abolition came from German Lutherans and Reformed representatives. Ireland argues that members of these churches, but not German sectarians, who were pro-abolition, were concerned about their own status in Pennsylvania society and feared the social change that might result from emancipation.[32] As shown in Table 4.2, on votes on the 1780 act itself German Lutheran and Reformed lawmakers were the most unified in attempting to thwart passage of the law, but significant antagonism also came from Presbyterians and Episcopalians, whose status was presumably not threatened. Indeed, over one-half of the anti-abolition representatives whose religions have been identified were Presbyterian and thus were members of

TABLE 4–2. Religion and the Gradual Abolition Act of 1780

Religion of Assemblymen	Number	Supporting Bill	Opposing Bill
Presbyterian	30	19 (63%)	11 (37%)
German Lutheran	5	1 (20%)	4 (80%)
German Reformed	4	1 (25%)	3 (75%)
Episcopalian	5	3 (60%)	2 (40%)
Ex-Quaker	4	4 (100%)	0
Baptist	2	2 (100%)	0
French Huguenot	1	1 (100%)	0
Unknown	13	7 (54%)	6 (46%)

Sources: Owen Ireland identifies the religious affiliation of many of the 1779–80 legislators in "The Ratification of the Federal Constitution in Pennsylvania" (Ph. D. diss., University of Pittsburgh, 1966), appendices; and "Religion, Sectionalism, and Wealth: Constitutionalists and Republicans in the Pennsylvania General Assembly, 1778–1789" (Paper presented at the Tricentennial Interdisciplinary Conference on Immigration and Its Impact on Pennsylvania, Delaware County Campus of the Pennsylvania State University, Media, Pa., 1982), appendix. We supplemented this information with evidence from *Pa. Archives*, 2nd ser., 8 and 9; and numerous county histories and published and unpublished church records in the Genealogical Society of Pennsylvania collections, HSP.

the same church as the principal sponsors of the bill. While clear differences between German Lutherans and Reformed on the one side and former Quakers and Baptists on the other suggest that religious affiliation influenced some legislators' positions on slavery, the split among Presbyterians and Episcopalians demonstrates that neither religion nor concern about status can fully explain the positions assemblymen took on this issue.

Personal involvement in slavery and the interests of constituents seem to have been the determining factors for many representatives. Philip Marsteller of Lebanon, then located in Lancaster County, who was not a representative, summed up for George Bryan the attitudes on slavery of his neighbors in 1780. "The Law for Freeing of Negroes hereafter Born," he wrote, "in my opinion does Honor to your House, but perhaps I only think so because I have no Slaves, and incline never to keep any, but Such who have them think otherwise. Self Interest is a Partial Judge of things."[33] Overall, nearly half (28 of 58) of the assemblymen for whom we have evidence owned slaves. Antiabolition legislators were twice as likely to own slaves as those who voted for the bill, and Presbyterians who opposed abolition were more than twice as likely to be slaveowners as those who supported it (Table 4–3). German Reformed legislators also split along the lines of slave ownership, with all three of those holding slaves voting against the act; but two German Lutherans who apparently held no slaves opposed gradual abolition. The actions of

TABLE 4–3. Slave Ownership of Pennsylvania Assemblymen, 1779–1780

Religion	Pro-abolition		Anti-abolition	
	Number*	% Owning Slaves	Number*	% Owning Slaves
Presbyterian	18	39%	9	89%
German Lutheran	1	0	3	33%
German Reformed	1	0	3	100%
Episcopalian	3	67%	2	100%
Ex-Quaker	3	0	0	—
Baptist	2	50%	0	—
French Huguenot	1	0	0	—
Unknown	6	33%	6	33%
TOTAL	35	34%	23	70%

*Number for whom information is available on slave ownership.

Sources: Slave ownership of Philadelphia and Chester County legislators is taken from our master lists of slaveowners and manumitters for these areas. Evidence on other assemblymen was obtained from tax and census records published in *Pa. Archives*, 3rd ser., 13, 16–18, 20–22.

former Quakers and the single French Huguenot were consistent: they owned no slaves and supported abolition.

Although the 1780 law freed no slaves born prior to enactment so long as owners promptly registered their blacks, the positions of twelve assemblymen who owned slaves but still favored the law deserve attention. Several had already been convinced that slavery was unjust while others were in the process of coming to that conclusion. William Harris, for example, had owned a slave in 1765, and John Fulton had held one black as recently as 1774, but neither of these western Chester County farmers registered slaves in 1780. Frederick Watts of Cumberland was taxed for a black in 1779 but not in 1780, and he had no slaves in his household in 1790. All approved the gradual abolition act, as did Robert Knox, a Southwark lumber merchant who freed his slave Harry in his 1784 will, and the painter Charles Willson Peale of Philadelphia, who still owned two slaves in 1790 but in 1786 had agreed to free two-year-old John Williams at age 21. Five other supporters of the bill, including Arthur Watts of Bucks County, still had slaves in 1790. Evidently they accepted the law as the compromise that it was and gave their consent only because it would allow them to retain their slaves. Their actions were much like those of manumitters who freed slaves in their wills. They held on to the benefits of slaveholding while voicing discontent with the institution. Of the ten known slaveowners who voted for the act whose religion has been identified, seven were Presbyterian, two were Episcopalian, and one was a Baptist. In the early 1780s, Presbyterians and Episcopalians especially were confronting the issue of slavery, just as Quakers had done a quarter of a century earlier. Influenced by the Revolutionary ideology and the Quaker commitment to abolitionism, Pennsylvania's political leaders, even some of those who owned slaves, determined to bring about the eventual death of slavery. In the tradition of most early manumitters, who delayed freedom for slaves in one way or another, and of the Society of Friends, which took 22 years to move from its 1754 statement that slavery was a sin to its 1776 ban on slavekeeping, the Pennsylvania Assembly chose a gradual approach.

At the same time, looking at another group whose voting behavior appears inconsistent with their personal decision on slavery, we find that of the six assemblymen who apparently owned no slaves but opposed abolition anyway, three were from Lancaster County and one each from Berks, Northampton, and Westmoreland. One was Presbyterian, two were German Lutheran, and the religions, if any, of the others cannot be determined. Four of the representatives, those from Lancaster and Westmoreland counties, seem to have yielded to constituent pressure. The three Lancaster delegates voted on the November 1779 roll call to publish the bill for public discussion, but by the

Charles Willson Peale, painter and Assemblyman, voted for the gradual abolition law in 1780, but still owned slaves a decade later. Portrait by Rembrandt Peale (1812). Courtesy of The Historical Society of Pennsylvania.

next February they had joined five other Lancaster members in rejecting the act. Over the winter, they heard from their neighbors what Marsteller reported to Bryan in March 1780—that the county's slaveowners bitterly opposed the law. Immediately before passage of the act on March 1, the House received an anti-abolition petition from "divers inhabitants" of Lancaster County phrased so intemperately that the Assembly dismissed it indignantly "on account of its indecency." In 1780, Lancaster residents registered 830 slaves with the county clerk. The primary slaveholding areas were around Donegal and Salisbury townships and Lancaster borough, which incorporated the area from which six of the county's eight anti-abolition delegates came.[34] In 1790, Lancaster County (and Dauphin, which separated from Lancaster in 1785) had the fourth largest slave population in proportion to total population in the state (Table 1–1). The two delegates from Westmoreland County in western Pennsylvania, where slavery also remained relatively strong as late as 1790, similarly yielded to their constituents. After approving the bill on February 15, 1780, Isaac Mason, who owned no slaves, and John Proctor, for whom we have no information on slaveholding around 1780, voted nay on March 1 and signed the dissent.

Clearly, no neat, single-factor explanation can account for voting behavior on the gradual abolition act of 1780. The Philadelphia city delegation had support from Bucks, Bedford, Cumberland, eastern Chester, and most of the representatives from Northumberland, York, and Philadelphia counties. Proponents included two-thirds of Presbyterians, three-fifths of Episcopalians, and all Baptists, former Quakers, and a single French Huguenot. At least twelve supporters owned slaves but several of them had already decided to release them or were considering manumission; others wanted to retain their slaves but could support the 1780 bill with the knowledge that it obliged no master to free a registered slave born before 1780. Opposition to the act came primarily from delegates of western Chester County, Lancaster, Berks, Northampton, and Westmoreland counties. Anti-abolition legislators were Presbyterians, German Reformed and Lutheran, and Episcopalian; a large percentage owned slaves themselves; and, in the cases of western Chester, Lancaster, and Westmoreland counties they represented slaveholding constituencies who strongly opposed any move toward emancipation. But overall, it is apparent that conditions conducive to the acceptance of abolitionist ideology had brought many Pennsylvania leaders into a camp almost solely occupied by Quakers only five years earlier.

The abolition bill of 1780 warrants notice as the first passed in America, and it has drawn effusive praise as exemplifying the spirit of enlightened reform in the Revolutionary era. The first historian of the Pennsylvania Abolition Society, writing in 1847, called it a law "which for justice, humanity, and philanthropy, has seldom been equalled, and which raised the State of Pennsylvania to a high position amongst the nations of the earth."[35]

Somewhat less enthusiasm is warranted in historical hindsight. Support for the proposed law waned after it was put before the public for debate, and it was in fact the most restrictive of the five gradual abolition laws enacted by northern states from 1780 to 1804.[36] The law freed not a single slave; it held in lifelong bondage all children born before the law became effective; and it consigned to 28 years of servitude every child born of a slave after March 1, 1780. Thus, it was possible for a female child, born of a slave on the last day of February in 1780 to live out her life in slavery and, if she gave birth to children up to her fortieth year, to be bringing into the world in 1820 children who would not be free until 1848. Total abolition of slavery would not come to Pennsylvania, in fact, until 1847. If the 1780 law was a death sentence for slavery in the state, it was a sentence with a two-generation grace period and one meant both to avoid an abrupt or disruptive end of slavery and to accomplish abolition at little cost to those who claimed ownership over other human beings. Pennsylvania's legislators had found a way to satisfy the ideological objections of those who saw slavery as inconsistent with the principles undergirding the revolutionary struggle while touching nobody's chattel property and depriving them of future human property only on a cost-free basis.

Even at the time, the 1780 law drew sharp criticism. Some, like Quaker David Cooper, were far from satisfied. "If we keep our present slaves in bondage," he wrote to a New Jersey newspaper that circulated in Philadelphia, "and only enact laws that their posterity shall be free, we save that part of our tyranny and gain of oppression, which to us, the present generation, is of the most value." In effect, Cooper charged, Pennsylvanians were saying to their slaves: "we will not do justice unto you, but our posterity shall do justice unto your posterity."[37] The French reformer Brissot de Warville reached the same conclusion after visiting Philadelphia in 1788. Why, he asked, did the legislature not "extend at least the hopes of freedom to those who were slaves at the time of the passing the . . . act?" Because slaves were property, the Frenchman was told, "and all property is sacred." Yet what is property, Brissot retorted, "founded on robbery and plunder?" At the least, he believed, Pennsylvania's legislators should be willing to limit slavery "to a certain number of years, in order to give at least the cheap consolation of hope" and to grant the slave the "right of purchasing his freedom." Under the Pennsylvania law, Brissot concluded, "the son is favoured and the father is consigned to despair."[38]

Yet Pennsylvania had taken an important step that neighboring states would not. Moreover, the stage had been set for further action. The language of the law itself had condemned slavery, admitting that it deprived blacks of "common blessings that they were by nature entitled to." Furthermore, it had expressed a belief in the unitary nature of humankind—a "universal civilization." "It is not for us to enquire why, in the creation of mankind," the preamble stated, "the inhabitants of the several parts of the world were distinguished by a difference in feature or complexion. It is sufficient to know that all are the work of an Almighty Hand . . . who placed them in their various situations [and] hath extended equally his care and protection to all. . . ."[39]

Watered down though it was, the 1780 law continued to draw fire. Some slaveowners refused to register their slaves, and their opposition to the law became one factor in the political revolt of October 1780 that swept 60 percent of the previous assemblymen from their seats and replaced them with more conservative representatives.[40] The new assemblymen read petitions for repealing the law and others for extending the registration date and reenslaving blacks whom the courts had set free because their masters, many of whom claimed ignorance of the law, had failed to register them.[41] A bill for extending the registration deadline to January 1, 1782, and for recommitting to slavery those who had used their master's noncompliance to gain their freedom through the courts passed a first reading in March 1781, despite the appeals of "Philotheuros," writing in the *Pennsylvania Packet*.[42]

The prospect that the hard-fought partial victory might be so quickly lost and that the legislature would actually pass a law for enslaving men and women who had been declared free by the courts brought a flurry of petitions and newspaper appeals against the proposed bill. It also inspired a full-scale defense of slavery in a three-part series published in the *Pennsylvania Journal* early in 1781 in which an anonymous writer proclaimed sanctions for slavery in the Bible and denied that "all mankind are born alike free."[43] Free blacks, engaging in one of their first political acts, also penned petitions and newspaper appeals. "Cato," writing in *Freedom's Journal*, beseeched the legislature to defeat the proposed bill allowing the reenslavement of many blacks. "To make a law to hang us all would be merciful, when compared to this law," he pleaded, "for many of our masters would treat us with unheard of barbarity, for daring to take advantage (as we have done) of the law made in our favour." Since the preamble of the 1780 abolition law unequivocally declared that all men were entitled to freedom from birth, how could the present legislature, he asked, turn its back on that principle one year later?[44]

Another group of free blacks in Philadelphia drew similarly on the language of the 1780 law, pointing to the phrase that slaves had "lived in undeserved bondage" and declaring that they believed that "this honourable house, possessed of such sentiments of humanity and benevolence" would not "pass an act to make slaves of those who they have freed by law, and to whom they have restored 'the common blessings they were by nature entitled to.' "[45] On the same day that the Assembly received this petition it voted 27 to 21, with only a single supporting vote from Chester or Philadelphia, against repealing or revising the 1780 law. Five days later, pro-abolitionist legislators repulsed a final attempt to reenslave those who had gained their freedom.[46] The idea of gradual abolition had survived a strenuous challenge and would now be accepted without question in the state.[47]

The declining economic viability of slave labor in Philadelphia, the spread of natural-rights ideology and religious moralism, the actions of hundreds of blacks who fled to the British, and the determination of a small group of reformers to set slavery on the road to extinction, all help to account for the partial victory of 1780. But for the most dedicated antislavery advocates, who in the early 1780s were Quakers in Philadelphia and the outlying regions, the half-victory was insufficient since immorality and un-Christian behavior could not, in their view, be half-corrected. Anthony Benezet carried the burden at first when others rested content with the progress already made. Benezet kept peppering the public with appeals to end slavery and the slave trade, which had reopened as the war drew to an end throughout the now independent states. In June 1782 the *Pennsylvania Evening Post* published his letter to Abbé Raynal, the aristocratic French reformer, calling for an abolition of slavery, along with Raynal's approving reply. It was probably Benezet who wrote the moving plea to abolish slavery throughout the land that appeared in the *Pennsylvania Packet* two months later, where the author called for the end of "the galling chains, the cruel stripes, the dying groan" of slavery, lest America lose its soul. Certainly it was Benezet who at that very time had placed an essay on the "state & grievous Effect of Slavery" before the Philadelphia Meeting for Sufferings and who convinced the Philadelphia Yearly Meeting the next year to petition the Continental Congress to end the slave trade.[48]

How effective were Benezet's appeals among eastern Pennsylvanians? Benjamin Rush claimed late in 1783 that "advocates for the poor Africans" were regarded before the Revolution as fanatics, but "at present they are considered as the benefactors of mankind and the man who dares say a word in favor of reducing our black brethren to slavery is listened to with horror, and his company avoided by every body."[49] Bryan, in arguing for the abolition bill in 1779, claimed that pro-slavery Pennsylvanians were ashamed to admit their position.[50] But only members of the Society of Friends signed petitions that publicly attacked slavery, and even among the Quakers it took Benezet's ceaseless prodding to produce results. For most Pennsylvanians the main work at hand was the reconstruction of their war-torn economy, and the most controversial political issue remained the functioning of government under the radical constitution of 1776, which conservatives were eager to revise. For many Quakers, the reclamation of rights trampled during the war and the rehabilitation of the Society's reputation, much maligned because of its wartime pacifism, were the most important issues.

Yet Benezet and a handful of other antislavery Quaker reformers could build upon the momentous shift within the Society of Friends in continuing the struggle against slavery. For a generation before the Revolution, Quaker reformers had preached a return to the old asceticism of Friends, warning that material indulgence and moral backsliding would be punished. The war fulfilled the darkest prophecies of suffering, and many Friends emerged from it convinced of the rectitude of the reformers' position and filled with a new vision of the road they must travel. That road led to plain living and abstinence from worldly power; but it also led to a renewed concern for wrongs perpetrated in the world around them.[51]

In particular, the matter of slavery and the condition of liberated slaves commanded the attention of Friends. Many Quakers were driven by the severity of their wartime experience to an emotional identification with oppressed blacks, a sympathy intensified by the fact that Friends had recently and publicly cleansed themselves of slaveholding, while acknowledging an obligation to assist those released in reordering their lives.[52] Such sympathy manifested itself at Philadelphia Yearly Meeting in 1783 when more than 500 Friends from eastern Pennsylvania, as well as from Delaware and New Jersey, exhibiting "a sense of the remarkable weight" in regard to "the case of the oppressed Africans," signed a ringing petition to the Continental Congress to prohibit the slave trade from being reopened by those "prompted from avaricious motives" in contradiction of "the solemn declarations often repeated in favour of universal liberty."[53]

With an abolition law on the books and Quakers beginning to reassert themselves in public life, it was a logical step to revive the abolition society that had disbanded during the war years. Why such efforts, led by Benezet, were unsuccessful at first is not clear, "though its objects," it was written in 1787, "were styled dear to many."[54] Certainly the need was great, especially for legal assistance to blacks whose masters were eager to evade the 1780 act by various stratagems—selling their slaves out of the state, shipping pregnant women across the border to Virginia or Maryland where their children would be born into slavery, and in other ways circumventing the law. Benezet described how blacks in Philadelphia came to him "almost daily and sometimes more" seeking help. But it took two dramatic cases of suicide by blacks facing reenslavement to galvanize reform-minded Philadelphians into following Benezet's imprecations to reorganize the Society for the Relief of Free Negroes (in 1787 renamed the Pennsylvania Society for Promoting the Abolition of Slavery, and hereafter PAS). One "sensible" black, Benezet related, "who from the most clear evidence was a freeman," but was denied a writ of *habeas corpus* to prevent his forced departure from the city despite Benezet's request to the court, "hung himself to the great regret of all who knew him." Another, "having pressingly, on his knees, solicited a friend, without success, to prevent his being sent away to the southward" from his family, threw himself from the deck of a ship into the Delaware River as it departed the city and drowned.[55] Even after these two sorrowful cases, four months elapsed before a group of Philadelphians, including six survivors of the short-lived Society launched in 1775, revived the organization in February 1784.

The initial group of eighteen that met in February 1784, just a few months before Benezet's death, was almost entirely composed of Quakers. The only exceptions were William Lippincott, a free Quaker, and Lambert Wilmore, a Methodist. Ten of the eighteen lived in four adjacent wards—Middle, North, Chestnut, and High Street—not far from Friends Bank meeting house and close to the Middle Ward home of Thomas Harrison, the unassuming Quaker tailor who kept the idea, and apparently the work, of the Society alive over the Revolutionary years.[56] However, this core group took only a few meetings to recognize the advantages of building a cross-denominational organization. Accordingly they began to reach out for additional members to every neighborhood and church in the city and in the outlying rural areas as well. Within six weeks they had recruited 28 additional members, and nearly half of these were not Quakers. Then in the next 21 months, from April 1784 to December 1785, another 37 men joined of whom only thirteen were Quakers. This left the organization at the end of its second year with a bare majority of Quaker members.

What is notable about the PAS in its first few years after reorganization, along with the rapid dilution of its Quaker composition, are the occupations of its members. The core group that reestablished the Society in February 1784 was conspicuous for the absence of Philadelphia's great overseas merchants and rentiers, as well as the city's prominent doctors and lawyers. No Pembertons, Norrises, Emlens, Drinkers, Reynells, Fishers, or Bringhursts chose to involve themselves. Instead, the founding members were mostly firmly established artisans, shopkeepers, manufacturers, and lesser merchants. Three hat-

ters, three shoemakers, and two tailors joined the initial group; so did a
soapboiler, grocer, board merchant, flour dealer, tallow chandler, ironmonger,
and grazier, along with two small merchants. The second set of recruits,
almost equally divided between Quakers and members of other churches or
none, included 14 artisans, 4 retailers, 6 small merchants, and a schoolmaster.
In the third group, who joined between April 1784 and December 1785, were
15 artisans, 3 doctors, 2 schoolteachers, 2 printers, 6 retailers, a miller, and a
shipbuilder, but only two merchants and one "gentleman."

The PAS founders were not, so far as can be determined, members of an
economic elite who sought, consciously or unconsciously, to further their own
class interests by opposing slavery, although their abolitionist stance, as we
will see, can be partially explained by their positioning in the economic
structure of the city.[57] The lengths to which many went to win freedom for
individual slaves suggests that their motives were often genuinely altruistic.
Of the eighteen men who met in February 1784 to reestablish the Society,
eight had estates assessed in the upper 10 percent of Philadelphia's taxpayers
but none was enormously rich. While in 1782 Philadelphians such as John
Stamper, Thomas Willing, Robert Morris, Samuel Rhoads, Jr., and Tench
Francis were assessed at over £4000, the most affluent of the initial 1784
group had less than £2000 assessed wealth (Table 4–4). Over one-quarter of
the founders for whom a 1782 tax assessment can be found ranked below the
wealthiest third of Philadelphians, with less than £200 assessment. Though
the second group of Society members, those who joined within six weeks of
the February meeting, included a merchant, Joseph Russell, whose assessment

TABLE 4–4. Wealth of Early Members of the Pennsylvania Abolition Society

	Group I Feb. 1784	Group II Feb.–March 1784	Group III April 1784–Dec. 1785	Groups I–III
£900+	8 (53%)	9 (41%)	12 (48%)	29 (47%)
£400–899	2 (13%)	6 (27%)	5 (20%)	13 (21%)
£200–399	1 (7%)	3 (14%)	0	4 (6%)
£199 and under	4 (27%)	4 (18%)	8 (32%)	16 (26%)
Unknown	3	6	12	21

Note: The first wealth category comprised those in 90th–100th percentile; those in second category the 78th to
89th percentile; those in third category the 65th to 78th percentile; and those in fourth category in the bottom 65
percent of taxpayers. Group I includes 18 men who reestablished the society in February 1784; Group II
comprises 28 men who joined within six weeks; Group III is composed of 37 men who became members during
the remainder of 1784 and 1785.

Sources: PAS Minutes; 1782 Effective Supply Tax, *Pa. Archives*, 3rd ser., 16. This tax list is difficult to use
because rental properties are listed under the name of the tenant rather than the landlord. Although we
took considerable care in determining assessments, the rankings should be considered approximations.

exceeded £3000, and those who became members in 1785 included the ship-builder Thomas Penrose, with an estate in excess of £9000, for the most part the economic composition of the membership remained much the same through 1785. Slightly under one-half of those with 1782 assessments ranked in the top 10 percent, about one-fifth were in the second decile, and one-fourth fell in the bottom 65 percent.

That these early abolitionists were thoroughly respectable but generally not drawn from the economic elite is confirmed by identifying the positions they occupied in the Society of Friends. Just under half of the 45 Quakers who joined the PAS in 1784–85 were representatives from their respective monthly meetings to Philadelphia Quarterly Meeting, the coordinating body for monthly meetings in the city and county of Philadelphia. This is a sure sign of the respect in which they were held by their fellow Quakers. Of all the monthly meetings' representatives to the Quarterly Meeting from 1780 to 1785, one-sixth (21 of 122) joined the PAS in its first two years. By contrast, only three of the 99 representatives of the Quarterly Meeting to the Yearly Meeting, the highest body of Friends that supervised Quaker life in a broad area encompassing Pennsylvania, New Jersey, Delaware, eastern Maryland, and Virginia, joined the PAS in these years. The Quaker elite proved notably reticent about involving themselves in the work of abolition in these years, while those who did join were about equally divided between the second rank of Quakers who held positions of authority within the Society of Friends and those in the common membership.

Recruited largely from the ranks of successful artisans and retailers, with artisans outnumbering merchants and professionals by three to one, the PAS was led, after the first election of officers in April 1784, by Quaker shoemaker Samuel Richards. Previously, Thomas Meredith, an Anglican shopkeeper, had served briefly, but he resigned for unknown reasons. Elected as treasurer and secretary were shoemaker James Starr and Quaker schoolteacher John Todd. On the first standing committee, which played the primary role in investigating cases brought before the Society, were lawyer Benjamin Miers, flour dealer Lambert Wilmore, merchant John Thomas, tailors William Lippincott and Thomas Harrison, and shoemaker James Whiteall. Among these, Thomas, Harrison, and Whiteall were Quakers. In May 1784, Miers and Thomas were replaced on the standing committee by hatter John Evans and carpenter Israel Hallowell, both Quakers.[58] These early Society officers were securely situated in Philadelphia's social order but were not among the city's economic elite, who resided in large houses, maintained coaches, and lived in affluence. Members of the first standing committee were Harrison, whose £496 assessment placed him in the second decile of the 1782 tax list; Lippincott and Whiteall, whose assessments were each about £1000; Wilmore and Miers, each assessed at less than £200; and Thomas, whose wealth in 1782 cannot be ascertained. President Richards had an assessment of £385, treasurer Starr ranked in the top 10 percent, and secretary Todd owned very little property.

What impelled these men to intervene on behalf of beleaguered slaves in their city and to shoulder the responsibility for aiding the growing free black population? These were men who had established themselves successfully in their city and not suffered a decline of status, as some historians have characterized the abolitionists of the pre-Civil War era. Why was it mostly artisans and retailers, shoemakers and tailors foremost among them, who at last answered Benezet's pleas rather than wealthy merchants, lawyers, and urban entrepreneurs—the nascent capitalists whom David Brion Davis has found at the heart of the English abolitionist movement in the late eighteenth century?[59]

To diagnose group motivation is a perilous enterprise, and various early members of the PAS doubtless acted out of inner compulsions that can never be fathomed. What can be reckoned is the changing conditions of labor in late eighteenth-century Philadelphia and the prior connections with slavery experienced by these reformers.[60] Like all Philadelphians, they had seen their city increase its dependence on indentured servants and slaves until by 1750 almost half the labor force was composed of bound laborers. They had also lived through the rapid decline of bound labor after the Seven Years' War, when violent economic fluctuations reduced the capital available for investment in slaves and servants and convinced many employers that wage laborers, who could be hired and let go as the situation demanded, were better suited to an unstable economic climate. They had witnessed the flight from bound labor that proceeded so rapidly that by the eve of the Revolution indentured servants and slaves composed only one-sixth of the city's labor force, a decline that continued after the war. Master artisans, men like themselves, were prominent among those who shed their dependence on bound labor. In 1767 they had owned nearly half the city's indentured servants and slaves; by 1791 they held barely one-eighth of those who remained.[61]

An ancient resentment of slave labor among young artisans trying to negotiate the rise from journeyman to master also contributed to the decline of bound labor. As early as 1707, city journeymen had complained that master artisans who purchased slaves or others who hired them out for day labor drove down wages and caused unemployment. These complaints from young white leather-apron men continued throughout the colonial era, especially during downswings in the economy. Among the journeymen who became masters, some quickly forgot their former scruples when they reached a position to invest in slaves and servants; but others retained the old feeling that bound labor cheapened the labor of free craftsmen.[62] It was from this master artisan group that most of the early members of the PAS were drawn. Those who were Quakers were subject to the moral strictures of the Society of Friends, of course, and non-Quaker craftsmen and retailers may also have been influenced by the spreading abolitionist sentiment inspired by natural-rights philosophy after the Revolution. But these early abolitionists were also convinced, it appears, that slave labor was offensive to the health and dignity of the crafts. Even after achieving the status of master, most of them had avoided slave labor. Of the 83 persons who joined the PAS in 1784–85, only twelve are known to have owned slaves, a much lower rate than prevailed among Philadelphians at large of their economic bracket. Very few of the city folk who had been involved in slavery had anything to do with abolitionism, while those who had steered clear of perpetual servitude, even when few townspeople regarded it as immoral, were the first to become involved.[63]

Once reestablished, the PAS was flooded with cases because more than most laws the 1780 act was susceptible of various interpretations and open to challenge. Slaves eagerly sought the assistance of the Society, hoping that they might secure their freedom or that of their children. Other blacks, who claimed to have been wrongfully enslaved at some time in the past, also began to avail themselves of this powerful new ally. Foremost among the Society's assets, as blacks quickly recognized, was a small group of dedicated men, several of them lawyers, who were recruited to determine the merits of particular cases and press forward in the courts with those regarded as viable. For the first few years the legal burdens were carried mainly by William Lewis, a birthright Quaker who apparently left the Society of Friends in the Revolutionary era. Then others became involved. Miers Fisher, Quaker son of Joshua Fisher, who during the war had repurchased slaves he had sold years before and all their children in order to free them, gave his time liberally. Four young lawyers who would later be pillars of the Philadelphia bar joined in—William Jackson, Benjamin Miers, Jonathan Sergeant, and William Rawle, the latter three not Quakers.

The Society's lawyers were always on the lookout for ways to broaden the scope of the 1780 law, but the organization showed its moderate approach in not attempting to achieve the abolition of slavery by judicial decree. They might have done so, for less than a year before the Society was reestablished the chief justice of Massachusetts ruled in the Quok Walker case that no law existed sanctioning slavery in that state and declared that slavery was incompatible with the declaration of rights in the state constitution that affirmed all men free and equal. Pennsylvania's constitution included almost exactly parallel language; thus, it appears that the Society's leaders consciously chose not to pursue a similar judicial result.

Agreeing that a legal foundation for slavery existed in Pennsylvania, the PAS devoted itself to rescuing slaves from bondage one by one. Some of the intricacies of the process can be seen in the case of Christopher Elliott's slaves. Elliott used slave labor extensively on a large farm on the edge of the city, in Kingsessing, which he had inherited from his father. Three of his male slaves had fled to the British during the war.[64] In May 1784 the Society learned that he was holding in slavery a large number of persons, including many children of several slave women he had inherited before the Revolution from his father and uncle. The wills had provided that these slave women should be held only until thirty years of age and then released. Between them they had given birth to nine children, all born between 1768 and 1780. Elliott had sold four of the children away from their parents to Chester County farmers and had duly registered the other five in 1780 as the law required. Elliott regarded the children as slaves for life since they were born before 1780 and while their mothers were still enslaved. But the PAS, seeing the possibility for securing the freedom of many children born in similar circumstances, reasoned that the mothers had been promised freedom when they reached age 30 by their original masters in their wills, and therefore from the time of their masters' deaths, when the wills promising freedom were executed, these women "could only be considered as servants until they respectively arrived at the age of thirty." Therefore, their offspring were born "altogether free."

Threatened by the PAS with costly litigation, Elliott and three Chester County farmers to whom he had earlier sold four of the children came to terms. Three of the older children were released outright to their parents, and the other six, with their parents' consent, were indentured to their purported slavemasters until eighteen years in the case of the girls and twenty-one in the case of the boys. It took seventeen months for attorneys working without pay for the Society to complete this case, but they had rescued from perpetual servitude nine black children.[65]

Shortly after the PAS addressed the Elliott case, another opportunity to broaden the scope of the 1780 law presented itself, but it was a case that showed the limitations as well as the strengths of the organization. In late 1784, a very light-skinned boy of sixteen, who had been brought to the city as a slave by his Virginia master, came to the notice of the Society. Named Francis Belt, the boy "presented so pure a complexion," as the subsequent lawsuit put it, "that the attention of the society was excited," even though the master had left the state before six months expired, and thus was not obliged by the 1780 law to free his slave.[66] What also commanded the attention of the Society was the fact that the boy was illegitimate—the offspring of a mulatto slave woman and a white man. William Lewis, arguing for the Society, and joined by William Bradford, attorney general of Pennsylvania, did not base their case on the fact that there "was no positive law for slavery" in the state. They conceded that certain state laws that made reference to slaves amounted "to an express toleration" of the institution. Choosing more restricted ground, they argued on the basis of skin color and Belt's illegitimate birth. Because he was indistinguishable in color from whites, Lewis and Bradford pleaded, he was neither mulatto nor Negro. Further, they reasoned, illegitimate children could not "be the property of the master of the mother and less so if possible when there is a greater share of white than black." Lewis and Bradford based the former part of this contention on the English legal principle that "he who can gain nothing by inheritance, ought to lose no part of his natural freedom, by relation to his progenitors," and they probably had in mind the possibility of rescuing from slavery many black children whose parents were not legally married.[67]

The Society may have been encouraged in pressing this case by the fact that George Bryan was now sitting on the state supreme court. If so, they were disappointed because the court accepted the slavemaster's argument that he had not resided in the state with his slave for six months and therefore interstate comity should protect his slave property, born in Maryland and resident in Virginia.[68] The case demonstrated that while the Society attempted to narrow the legal definition of slave property, even to the point of skin color, they were not ready to challenge the legal foundation for slavery itself in Pennsylvania.

The Society was more successful in securing freedom for slaves whose masters had not registered them as required by the 1780 gradual abolition act. Once it became apparent that the courts would not excuse slaveowners' purported ignorance of the law, many masters who had not complied tried to cut their losses by selling their slaves, usually in neighboring New Jersey, Delaware, or Maryland. For many years, as word spread among blacks of their entitlement to freedom in such cases, they got word to the PAS or fled their masters and appeared personally before the organization in Philadelphia seeking assistance. Such was the case with the slave of John Steele, a farmer outside of Philadelphia. When the court ordered his female slave freed in the early 1780s because he had failed to register her, he quickly sold her to a man who in turn sold her to a certain Mr. Levy in Easttown, New Jersey. When Levy found that his title to the woman was defective, he sold her to a certain

Jonas Philips, while recovering his money from the previous owner. When the PAS applied to Philips he refused to release her, but the Society's lawyers quickly won a writ of *habeas corpus* from the local court and she was freed.[69]

In another case, the Society heard a pathetic tale of Abraham Butter, who years before had been sold to a New Englander and then resold to Joseph Mitchell in Warm Springs, Virginia. Mitchell sold Butter to Robert Ellison, a mariner, who, upon going to sea, passed him along to James Crawford at Christiana Bridge, Delaware. His fourth owner sold him to George Hess, a miller in Lancaster County, Pennsylvania, who promptly deeded him to his brother, who sold him to John Whitmore, an innkeeper near Philadelphia. When Butter was marketed a seventh time, in 1784, to John Keen, an innkeeper in Philadelphia, his luck turned because he was now in a position to seek the aid of the PAS. Suspecting that he had never been registered after the 1780 law passed, the Society challenged Keen, who returned the slave to the previous owner who in turn tried to pass him back along the line of former masters. With the Society's support, Butter gained his freedom.[70]

The Society also dealt with many cases involving slaveowners arriving in Pennsylvania after 1780 who tried to evade the provision of the law that declared any slave brought into the state free after six months. Surrounded by slave states, rural Pennsylvania received a steady flow of slaveowning migrants seeking to establish themselves in the state; and Philadelphia, one of the busiest commercial seaports of the western Atlantic, was always full of merchants and others who arrived with slaves in tow from the Caribbean and the South, some there for extended business and some investigating the possibilities for reestablishing themselves. Many of these sojourners, scarcely able to do without their house slaves, arrived with a retinue of black servants; but they soon had to deal with the six-month clause of the 1780 law. For example, Robert Fagan arrived with his family and several slaves from St. Croix in 1785. Ten months later, learning that his slaves understood their entitlement to freedom under Pennsylvania law, Fagan arranged to ship them back to St. Croix. Sam Browne and Venus fled their master, claiming their freedom, but Fagan forced the third slave, Nancy, aboard a brig about to depart for the Caribbean. The Society's lawyers intervened and obtained a writ of *habeas corpus* from the court, which in due course discharged Nancy as a free woman.[71]

In other cases, the Society interceded between runaway slaves and their masters in other states. Philadelphia's lines of commerce to the hinterland carried news of the Society's work and the growing free black community throughout a wide orbit. Runaways from Virginia, Maryland, Delaware, New Jersey, and more distant points showed up regularly in Philadelphia, and in many cases the PAS was able to work out a compromise whereby the slave was bound until age 28 to a Philadelphia master who would pay the owner for a number of years of the fleeing slave's labor. In this way, the Society brokered a three-way contract with advantages to all three parties: the slave was promised eventual freedom; the master recouped his investment; and a Philadelphian obtained a set of hands at a relatively cheap cost.[72]

The aggressive litigation strategy of the Society troubled some Philadelphians and more outsiders, who protested that it strained interstate harmony in a nation struggling to establish itself. George Washington, arguing on behalf of a fellow Virginian, put the case strongly. When his acquaintance had entered the state with a slave, the Society sued on behalf of the bondsman's freedom, and when the case came to trial two years later, the Virginian was obliged to return to defend himself. Writing Robert Morris, the wealthy merchant slaveholder and treasurer of the Continental Congress, Washington pleaded on behalf of slaveowners whose assets for litigation could not match those of the PAS. "When slaves who are happy and contented with their present masters are tampered with and seduced to leave them," and when practices of this kind "fall on a man, whose purse will not measure with that of the Society, and he loses his property for want of means to defend it; it is oppression . . . and not humanity . . . because it introduces more evils than it can cure."[73]

The argument that any slaves were content to be living in a perpetual bondage that was passed to their children or that slaveowners ought to be protected from litigation because they were too poor to defend themselves must have seemed laughable to PAS members, not to mention the slaves. Whether Morris attempted to alter their strategy is not known, but if he did he was unsuccessful. The Society continued to press cases and in 1786 was on the verge of reorganizing and broadening its scope. Moreover, as word circulated of its frequently successful interventions on behalf of slaves, blacks brought to the city as slaves and those held in bondage throughout Philadelphia's hinterland sought the Society's aid. In the first year of its reestablishment the Society investigated at least twenty-two cases. Thereafter the caseload increased. Through such actions the work of a small number of men "restored to liberty," as the Society's secretary phrased it, "upwards of one hundred persons" between 1784 and 1787.[74]

At the center of the Society's activities stood the tailor Thomas Harrison. His shop on Third Street near Walnut became the listening post, information center, and place of temporary refuge for blacks fleeing their masters. Born in 1739, Harrison had emigrated from England to Philadelphia in 1763. A year later he married Sarah Richards, a Chester County Quaker who was to become a minister in 1781. The young couple knew pain enough of their own. Nine times Sarah Harrison gave birth between 1765 and 1778, and seven times they buried children—five of them in a two-year period from 1771 to 1773.[75] But Harrison was irrepressible. Described by a contemporary as "a lively, bustling man, with a roguish twinkle in his eye," Harrison involved himself more than any other member of the Society in the day-by-day work of listening to the stories of blacks, assigning their cases to members of the Acting Committee, posting security with the courts in particular cases, and negotiating with individual masters and mistresses in the attempt to avoid court action.[76]

In late 1786, before the end of its third year of operation, Harrison and other active members of the Society were ready to expand their scope of operations. Led by their successes to a sense of greater possibilities, and knowing that a Constitutional Convention would be meeting in the city the next May, the Society's leaders seem to have adopted the view that this was the time to attack slavery directly rather than rescuing individuals one by one from its snares. Early in 1787, the Society reorganized. Benjamin Rush, Thomas Harrison, William Jackson, shipbuilder Jonathan Penrose, and Tench Coxe, the last having recently joined the Society, were charged as a committee to revise the Society's constitution. Seven weeks later the reorganization was effected.

In reorganizing, the Society adopted a new name—the Pennsylvania Society for Promoting the Abolition of Slavery, and the Relief of Free Negroes, Unlawfully Held in Bondage. This signaled a new direction, for the abolition of slavery had never before been mentioned in its title, although many of its members were abolitionists at heart. The preamble reiterated the belief that was fundamental to abolitionism, that humankind was indivisible, "it having pleased the Creator of the world, to make of one flesh all the children of men." The new direction being taken was also indicated in the election of thirty-six new members and a new set of officers on April 23, 1787, just three weeks before the first delegates to the Constitutional Convention arrived. As a group, these men were wealthier and of higher status than the artisans, retailers, and lesser merchants who had revived the organization and carried its work forward after 1784. Among them were James Pemberton, a wealthy Quaker merchant and philanthropist; Hilary Baker, soon to be mayor of Philadelphia; the city's most eminent citizen, Benjamin Franklin, recently returned from France; internationalist Thomas Paine; the wealthy and well-known lawyer and officeholder Richard Peters; and prosperous merchants Caspar Wistar, John Keighn, and Caspar Haines. Elected as president was the aged Benjamin Franklin, now so crippled with gout that he had to be carried in a sedan chair to the opening of the Constitutional Convention. As first vice president, the Society chose James Pemberton. A second vice president, shipbuilder Jonathan Penrose, had been involved since 1785, as had one of the secretaries, Benjamin Rush. But the other secretary, Tench Coxe, also a wealthy and influential merchant, had only recently been recruited.[77]

It seems clear that the old membership of the PAS had decided that the time had come to attack slavery overtly, and they knew that men of high political visibility would be needed to do this. They must have been encouraged that weighty Philadelphians like Pemberton, Coxe, and Franklin, who had chosen not to involve themselves before this, now decided to weigh in with the lesser men who had carried on the Society's work since 1784.

New work began immediately. Coordinating their efforts with those of the Quaker Meeting of Sufferings and with opponents of the slave trade in England and France, the PAS began circulating abolitionist literature and placing it in magazines, such as the *American Museum,* that were reaching out to a widening middle- and upper-class audience. One sardonic letter to the printer that tried to convey the dehumanizing effects of slavery commented on a newspaper advertisement of a Maryland plantation to be sold for "negroes, merchandize, or cash." Since it appeared that "negroes are to be introduced in that state instead of paper money as a medium of commerce," the writer offered a table of the value of "this new black flesh coin" with prices listed for black males and females of various ages; and, "as change will be necessary in this species of money," he compiled a list of values for an arm, a leg, a hand and foot, a thumb and great toe. "To prevent any inconvenience from the smell of this species of change when it is first emitted," the writer continued, "it is proposed to harden it by exposing it to salt and smoke, before it is taken from the mint." Thus, under this new form of species, estates would soon be measured by thousands of dried hands and great toes. "The fortunes of young ladies will likewise be estimated in the same manner; and instead of saying miss _____ of the Western Shore is worth six thousand guineas, it will be common to say, she is worth near three thousand negroes arms well smoked and salted."[78]

The Society also appointed a committee to convince the city's newspaper publishers to shun advertisements for slave sales—a campaign that achieved partial success. They began circulating petitions advocating the abolition of the slave trade and, eight days after it convened, remonstrated with the Constitutional Convention to outlaw the nefarious traffic.[79]

While the PAS mounted campaigns to fight slavery and the slave trade on a broad political front, its Acting Committee continued the day-to-day work involving individual cases. Hardly a week passed without the Society learning

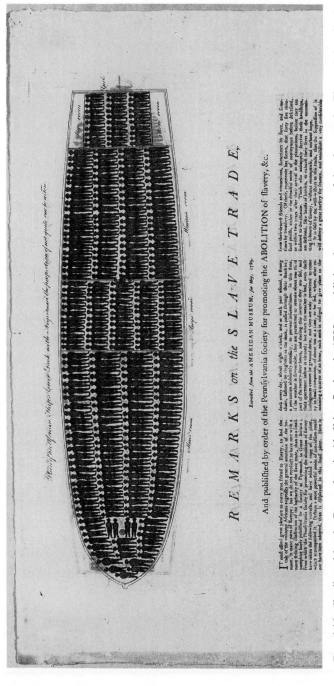

Broadside distributed by the Pennsylvania Abolition Society in 1789 to publicize the excesses of the slave trade. The text described the plight of enslaved Africans, "packed, side by side, almost like herrings in a barrel, and reduced nearly to the state of being buried alive." Courtesy of The Library Company of Philadelphia. (Detail)

of a possibility of obtaining the release of someone caught in slavery's net. When Michael Cainer, a coachmaker, sold his slave Mary to a visiting North Carolinian in 1788, the Society joined with Richard Allen, the young black Methodist preacher who had recently come to Philadelphia, to bring suit against Cainer for illegally selling a slave out of the state.[80] In the same year an 18-year-old East Indian lad, tagged Joe, arrived aboard a ship captained by a Rhode Islander named Green. Hearing of the Abolition Society, Joe made his way to one of its members and told of being kidnapped from his father's house, in the vicinity of Calcutta, ten years before. Sold as a slave to a Portuguese ship captain, Joe recounted, he was later purchased by a Dutch mariner, who sold him to Green in Rhode Island in 1784. Understanding from Joe that he had never been legally bound to Green but simply given to him in an informal transaction, perhaps to satisfy a debt, the PAS challenged his purported owner. When Green backed down, lacking proof of his ownership, the Society placed Joe with a Bucks County farmer on a three-year indenture, after which he was to be a free citizen of Pennsylvania.[81]

While pursuing individual cases, the Society looked for broader fronts on which to fight. With the Constitutional Convention still in its first month of deliberation, the arrival in the city of two Englishmen who commissioned one of Philadelphia's shipyards to fit out their vessel for the African slave trade gave occasion for a campaign to strengthen the 1780 gradual abolition act. A Society committee decided on a series of proposed changes supported by a petition campaign later in 1787 to show that public opinion was widespread for "humanity & justice to the oppressed Africans."[82] Gathering more than 2000 signatures, the PAS called upon the legislature to outlaw the outfitting of vessels for the slave trade, prevent the separation of slave families, prohibit masters from sending pregnant slaves out of state so their children would be born as slaves, and impose severe punishment for kidnappers of free blacks, who sold their victims into slavery in the South.[83] Important Philadelphia Quakers, many of them members of the PAS, attended the legislative session considering the bill and presented an official address from the Society of Friends calling for a "more extensive and effectual law."[84] Also contained in the law, which passed with a large majority in the legislature in March 1788, was a provision strengthening the six-months provision of the 1780 law. Under the new law any slave brought into the state by persons intending to reside there was immediately free.

Under the 1788 law the question of what constituted residence and precisely how six months were calculated became important issues. PAS lawyers fought cases in the court from 1788 to 1821 to get the strictest possible construction of intended residence as being simply the renting of a house or doing business in the state. When a French refugee from St. Domingue tried to beat the deadline by taking her slaves across the river to Burlington, New Jersey, after five months and three weeks, the slaves fled back to Philadelphia, and the Society argued that they had lived for six lunar months of 28 days each in the state and were therefore entitled to freedom.[85] Society members also kept close watch on the comings and goings of visitors who did not establish residence. When six months expired, they flew into action. In the case of a French visitor from Hispaniola, who carelessly allowed the six months to pass, the PAS aided his slaves who claimed their freedom and even maintained a street watch as the Frenchman prepared to depart so that he could not seize his former slaves and hustle them down the Delaware River.[86]

Even before the nation began to operate under the federal Constitution, the PAS reorganized a second time in order to increase its effectiveness in aiding free blacks and campaigning against the slave trade and slavery. Drawing up articles of incorporation in 1789, the Society became a legal entity that could raise money and receive bequests. In the same year it approved a "Plan for Improving the Condition of the Free Blacks." Reflecting the common understanding that recently freed blacks needed much assistance in transiting the dangerous waters between bondage and freedom, the Society began to function as the nation's first freedmen's bureau. It intervened in the job market to secure positions for former slaves, created schools and promoted education, offered moral advice in broadsides and home visitations, and tendered legal assistance to those in need. A Committee to Improve the Condition of Free Blacks (CICFB), or the Committee of Twenty-four as it was known, became the operational center of the Society. The committee was divided into four subcommittees which were charged with carrying out a variety of tasks. The Committee of Inspection was to "superintend the morals, general conduct, and ordinary situation of the Free Negroes, and afford them advice and instruction, protection from wrongs, and other friendly offices." A Committee of Guardians would bind out children for apprenticeships with suitable families, using "persuasive influence on parents" to place their children in white familial environments where moral tutelage as well as apprenticeship training were available to prepare black children for life as free persons. A Committee of Education would persuade parents to send their children to already established schools for black youth and establish others for this purpose. Finally, a Committee of Employment would serve as an employment bureau, locating jobs for blacks and encouraging white artisans to take black apprentices.[87]

To launch their work the Committee of Twenty-four distributed 500 handbills among black families explaining the new system and listing the subcommittee members' names and printed notices in the newspapers. At the same time, they invited the city's free blacks to a general meeting where the plan was explained. "The Blacks behaved with great decorum," the Committee

The Pennſylvania Society for the Abolition of Slavery, &c. agreeable to a Plan for im- ⟩
proving the condition of the Free Blacks, previouſly agreed upon by them, at their
meeting in April laſt, 1790, appointed a committee of twenty-four of their members to
carry the ſaid Plan into execution, who have ſince met together and divided themſelves
into the ſeveral ſub-committees, as follows, viz.

COMMITTEE of INSPECTION.

Nicholas Collin,	Nathan Boys,
John Evans,	John M'Crea,
Thomas Harriſon,	Amos Gregg.

Who ſhall ſuperintend the morals, general conduct, and ordinary ſituation of the Free Negroes, and afford them advice and inſtruction, protection from wrongs, and other friendly offices.

COMMITTEE of GUARDIANS.

Thomas Armat,	Joſeph P. Norris,
Joſeph Crukſhank,	Abraham Liddon,
William M'Illhenny,	Benjamin Say.

Who ſhall place out children and young people with ſuitable perſons, that they may (during a moderate time of apprenticeſhip, or ſervitude) learn ſome trade or other buſineſs of ſubſiſtence.

COMMITTEE of EDUCATION.

James Pemberton,	Caleb Lownes,
John Todd,	Richard Wells,
Samuel P. Griffitts,	William Rogers.

Who ſhall ſuperintend the ſchool-inſtruction of the children, and youth of the Free Blacks.

COMMITTEE of EMPLOY.

Richard Jones,	John Bleakley,
Thomas Rogers,	Matthew Hale,
Samuel Coates,	William Lippencott.

Who ſhall endeavour to procure conſtant employment for thoſe Free Negroes who are able to work.

Pennsylvania Abolition Society broadside (1790) identifying subcommittees of the Committee of Twenty-four. Thomas Harrison, here listed as a member of the Committee of Inspection, was the linchpin of the PAS through the 1780s and 1790s. Courtesy of The Pennsylvania Abolition Society Papers, Historical Society of Pennsylvania.

noted approvingly. "Well satisfied," the free blacks appointed a large committee of their own to work with the CICFB.[88]

Throughout the last decade of the eighteenth century the PAS distributed advice literature to free blacks, as did the American Convention for the Abolition of Slavery, an interstate organization founded by the PAS that met almost annually in Philadelphia for many years. Black leaders read such advice, often entitled "To the free Africans and other free people of colour," aloud in black churches and special meetings convened for the purpose, and broadcast printed copies in neighborhoods where blacks resided.[89]

After first reorganizing in 1787, the PAS continued for a few years to attract the new kind of men with higher status and wealth than the shopkeepers and artisans who had composed most of the membership in the mid-1780s. In 1789, a list of members showed that among nearly one hundred new recruits to the PAS since 1787 there were 33 merchants, 4 shopkeepers, 6 officials, 22 professionals, 19 artisans, 5 printers, and 8 men whose occupations are unknown. With this influx of new members the PAS became briefly a body of entrepreneurial and professional men of the sort that David Brion Davis has characterized as being concerned not only with the inhumanity of slavery but also the development of a disciplined free-labor system that would function smoothly in a new era of capitalist development.[90] But some of them were of another stripe, such as James Pemberton, who despite his wealth, followed the old Quaker precepts of plain living. "His coat was threadbare but spotless," reported one impressed visitor to Philadelphia; "he prefers to clothe the poor than please the wanton."[91]

As it happened, however, the interest of many wealthy men in the ongoing work of the PAS was fleeting. By 1795, the wealthy and well-known members of the PAS who had joined in the late 1780s had died or quietly withdrawn, leaving the organization in the hands of a dedicated band of men who were drawn mostly from the ranks of Quaker craftsmen and small shopkeepers. Thus, the PAS, after several phases of recruitment, returned to the kind of unswerving antislavery devotees who had founded the organization two decades before. About eighteen stalwarts accepted most of the assignments on the Acting Committee and the committees of education, guardians, inspection, and employment in the years between 1795 and 1803, when the Society reorganized once again. These were men who were engaged in the day-by-day work of aiding the city's newly freed blacks and finding ways of wresting freedom for slaves who found their way to the tailor shop of Thomas Harrison or to the shop of another Quaker tailor, Isaac T. Hopper, who was becoming Harrison's successor as the prime contact person for beleaguered blacks. Of these men at least fourteen were Quakers, two were Anglican, and two cannot be identified by religion. Eleven of the eighteen were artisans (four of them Windsor chair makers) and among the other seven were two teachers, an accountant, a shipmaster, a single merchant, and two whose occupations are unknown. These were mostly ordinary Quakers, only a few of them representing their monthly meetings at the Friends quarterly meetings and only one serving as representative at the Yearly Meeting. The unswerving Thomas Harrison, who by the mid-1790s was almost the only remaining figure from the core group that had reestablished the PAS a decade before, continued to function at the center of Society activities. He occupied the position of secretary of the Acting Committee that did most of the casework in rescuing or protecting blacks from slavery and also served from 1798 to 1803 on the Committee of Guardians and for several years on the Committee of Inspection. Accountant Samuel Lippincott, the son of a founding member of the PAS; ship captain Mordecai Churchman; teachers Benjamin Tucker and Benjamin Kite; and chair and cabinet makers Jacob Johnson, John Letchworth, Abraham Garrigues, Gilbert Gaw, and John Ackley also served for many terms on several committees.

Emerging as the new dynamic figure was Isaac Hopper, a young Quaker tailor born on a New Jersey farm just before the Revolution. Coming to Philadelphia as a young man in the late 1780s, Hopper had been converted to Quakerism by the preacher-tanner William Savery in 1793. A few years later he threw himself into the work of the PAS and began teaching at nights in the Quaker school established years before by Anthony Benezet for black Philadelphians. While he and his wife raised a family of sixteen children, Hopper busied himself with service to the oppressed blacks. Virtually no runaway slave from the South or free black threatened by kidnappers failed to find his or her way to his door from the late 1790s well into the nineteenth century. Writing the story of his life the year after he died in 1852, the abolitionist L. Maria Child had no difficulty filling a large volume with moving stories of the distressed African-Americans he had helped.[92]

By the mid-1790s the flagging interest of well-situated Philadelphians of various religious persuasions and the rise of a new generation of Quakers typified by Isaac Hopper had returned the PAS to its original social and religious origins. Thomas Harrison was virtually the only figure who bridged the Revolutionary abolitionists and the new Quaker men who dedicated themselves to helping free blacks when Philadelphians of other religious affiliations withdrew from the organization.

While stalwarts like Harrison and Hopper extricated individuals from slavery one by one, the PAS attempted in the 1790s to end slavery altogether in the state. Their first attempt, in 1792, was inspired by the reaction of the state legislature to a petition from French slaveowners who were pouring into Philadelphia from St. Domingue, as black rebellion there drove them from the sugar island. Among the assets that the French colonials escaped with, their slaves figured importantly, and scores of these slaves took flight soon after reaching Philadelphia. French masters and mistresses quickly asked for exemption from the 1780 and 1788 gradual abolition acts, by which their slaves would have become free no more than six months after arrival. The French refugees excited considerable sympathy in Philadelphia, where donations of $12,000 were made in a few days to alleviate their plight, but the PAS put before the legislature a vigorous argument to reject the refugees' plea. To the surprise of the PAS the legislative committee appointed to consider the petition not only recommended against amending the abolition act but asserted that slavery was "obviously contrary to the . . . Constitution of this state."[93]

Armed with this opinion, which was based on the language in Pennsylvania's new constitution of 1790 that "all men are born equally free and independent, and have inherent and indefeasible rights, among which are those of enjoying and defending life and liberty," and fortified with a petition from Philadelphia Quakers to the state Senate to abolish slavery, Representative John Shoemaker of Montgomery County introduced a bill in 1793 to release all children from slavery at age 21.[94] A committee appointed to consider Shoemaker's proposal went even farther. Declaring that "slavery is . . . repugnant to the spirit and express letter of the Constitution of this commonwealth," it recommended immediate and total abolition, the first such proposal from a publicly elected body.[95]

A devastating yellow fever epidemic late in the summer of 1793 drove the legislature out of Philadelphia before it could consider the abolition bill, and the succeeding legislature, for reasons that are not clear, did not take up the issue. It seems probable that the proposers of the new abolition bill recognized that the votes were not available for passage because the PAS switched tactics in 1794, attempting to obtain the judicial rather than legislative abolition of slavery. Picking Flora, the slave of the Philadelphia Anglican tailor Joseph Graisberry, as a test case, they sued the slavemaster for holding Flora in bondage and asked the court to uphold their contention that slavery was inconsistent with the state's constitution. When the case became stalled in the lower courts, the PAS, "with a view to obtaining a speedy decision and to give the utmost solemnity and weight to a subject of so much importance," was able to get the case removed to the High Court of Errors and Appeals in 1798.[96] But the high court took another four years to proffer a decision, finally deciding in 1802 that slavery was not illegal since it had existed legally in Pennsylvania before the adoption of the state constitution and was not specifically abolished in that document.[97]

While the case of *Flora v. Graisberry* bogged down before a judiciary torn between defending property rights and human rights, the PAS and the Society of Friends renewed their efforts to legislate slavery out of existence. Appealing annually for a total abolition law, they had the prospect of success in 1797, when the lower house reported a bill that declared slavery unconstitutional, ordered its complete abolition [or at age 21?], and authorized slaveholders to obtain compensation for releasing their slaves from their county treasury in an amount to be decided by appraisers appointed by county courts of quarter sessions. This was the first time that compensated emancipation was mentioned in the mid-Atlantic states.[98] Spreading the cost of emancipating about 2000 slaves remaining in the state at this time among some 110,000 Pennsylvania families would have ended slavery at the price of a few dollars per family. But even at this modest price the votes for passage could not be secured, and the bill consequently stalled in the House for two years.

For the PAS, this must have been a discouraging defeat. Yet the rapidly declining number of slaves in the state, which would drop to 1,706 by the time of the second federal census in 1800, offered the possibility that opposition to complete abolition would gradually wither. In 1799 the PAS tried again, organizing a petition campaign in the city and county of Philadelphia and also in Lancaster, Delaware, and Chester counties, all in the eastern part of the state. Following this, a committee of the PAS traveled to Lancaster to lobby for the bill with the legislature in January 1800.[99]

While the PAS delegation was lobbying for the legislative abolition of slavery, a petition arrived from free blacks in Philadelphia that changed the complexion of the debate and ironically scuttled the PAS efforts. Eager to break the prolonged legislative resistance to the abolition bill and apparently convinced that the main stumbling block was the compensation of slave-masters from county tax coffers—a way of distributing the cost of abolition among all Pennsylvanians—the free blacks made a startling offer. Let the legislature abolish slavery completely and lay a special tax for the compensation of slave masters on the free black citizens of the state. In this way white Pennsylvanians, both slaveholders and nonslaveholders, could cleanse their polity of slaveholding without a penny's expense; slaveholders would receive full compensation for their property and nonslaveholders would not have their taxes applied to compensate those who released their slaves.

Presented with this generous offer from Pennsylvania's free blacks, the House of Representatives gladly revised the abolition bill to shift the cost of compensating some 1500 slaveowners from all taxpayers to free blacks. Approving an amendment to tax each free black person entering the state ten dollars for this purpose, it passed the abolition act in March 1800 by a vote of 55 to 15, with every representative from Philadelphia and the eastern counties but one voting for it.[100]

In the eyes of the PAS the offer to subsidize abolition, though well intended, was a strategic mistake on the part of Philadelphia's free blacks because to offer compensation to slaveowners was implicitly to recognize the legality of slavery and thus to compromise the case of *Flora v. Graisberry* still before the Court of Appeals. No record of deliberation within the Society has survived to tell us how they must have agonized over sacrificing a bill they had struggled to obtain for a decade in order to preserve the consistency of their argument that slavery was unconstitutional. In making this decision, they deprived some 1700 slaves of the opportunity to become free men and women. But PAS leaders, arguing that the abolition bill "tacitly admits the propriety of an adverse construction of the constitution," that is, that slavery is constitutional, could not swallow their objections. They declared that the PAS could not be "instrumental in paying for that which they believe incapable of purchase or sale." A second objection, equally serious, was that the bill postponed the freedom of those still remaining in slavery for some years. A third objection was that a tax levied only on the black part of the population, if not unconstitutional, created a dangerous precedent, opening the door to untold discriminatory legislation in the future.[101]

Although the House of Representatives had passed the abolition bill, the Senate agreed with the PAS's position that laying a tax on one part of the population violated "the principles of equal liberty, dispensed to all men by the . . . constitution." The Senate took no note of the irony that so long as any persons remained in slavery "equal liberty" did not exist in Pennsylvania.[102] For now, the issue of complete abolition was dead.

While the PAS could not achieve the goal of total abolition as the eighteenth century drew to a close, it continued to devote itself to rescuing individual blacks from slavery. Much as in the 1780s, the PAS wasted no opportunities to obtain from the courts the broadest possible interpretation of the 1788 law amending the gradual abolition act of 1780. In requiring a very strict procedure for registering the children born of slaves, the 1788 law provided opportunities to negotiate the freedom of some slaves whose masters avoided or complied carelessly with the registration procedure. The first case, in 1789, involved a young woman named Betsey, whose parents were released from slavery because their owner had not registered them. Trying to minimize his loss, the master claimed Betsey's labor until she was 28, but he lost his case when the Supreme Court of the state indicated that it would favor liberty over property even on the most technical grounds of noncompliance with the 1788 registration requirement.[103] In other cases, the high court ordered immediate freedom for the children of slaves whose masters had registered them with an incorrect name or even recorded the date of birth imprecisely, such as "born in May last, or beginning of June."[104] The PAS involved itself in cases of this sort throughout the 1790s and into the early nineteenth century, obtaining freedom for individual slaves or their children who were bound servants for 28 years.[105]

As the number of slaves in Pennsylvania declined, most of the cases litigated by the PAS involved black Pennsylvanians who had strayed or been taken beyond the state's borders into slave territory where no laws prohibited their sale to the South. In 1798, for example, Samuel Allen applied for assistance in the case of his son John, a 12-year-old who had been apprenticed to the black master chimneysweeper Doras Jennings. Near the end of his apprenticeship, the lad's master had taken him to New Jersey and left him there without giving him his freedom dues. Arrested as a vagrant in New Brunswick, New Jersey, John Allen was then sold by the sheriff at public auction to a local doctor, who resold him to another man. Fearing that his son would become a slave for life, in a state where no abolition law had been passed and where such youths were frequently sold to visiting southerners, Samuel Allen asked the PAS to intervene. The PAS spent five years attempting to obtain the boy's freedom but had not succeeded by 1803 when the case disappeared from the Society's minute books.[106]

In another case in 1801, the PAS became involved in intricate negotiations to secure the freedom of Jane Bladen and her children. Bladen and her son Aaron were formerly the slaves of an East Nottingham, Chester County, farmer, Timothy Kirk, whose son inherited them upon his death in 1788. The son, Roger Kirk, signed articles of agreement freeing Jane Bladen in four years and then sold her and her son to a relative, Abner Kirk, in Cecil County, Maryland. Abner Kirk promptly sold the woman and boy to a neighboring Marylander, Benjamin Mitchell, and during her four years of service to him she bore two other children, both of whom Mitchell claimed as slaves for life. It took Jane Bladen seven years after completing her term of servitude to make contact with the PAS, but when she did in 1801, claiming that her two youngest children were illegally held in slavery, the PAS intervened. Hearing that Mitchell might sell his farm in Maryland and carry her children further south, Bladen and her husband traveled to Cecil County and secreted the children away to Philadelphia. Mitchell's son, a Philadelphia resident, promptly countered by obtaining a warrant to seize the mother and children. The PAS met this action by obtaining a writ of *habeas corpus* for all three on the grounds that the children had been born after Jane Bladen's manumission and therefore were born free. Eventually the PAS obtained a compromise with Mitchell, who agreed to bind the two young children to farmers outside Philadelphia until they reached the age of 20 and 23 and to manumit the older boy, born a slave, while retaining his labor as an indentured servant until age 23. Mitchell tried to renege on the contract, but it was finally enforced in June 1803, nineteen months after the PAS entered the case.[107]

In a case that acquired national significance, Ben came to the PAS in 1804 seeking help. Born a slave in the family of Pierce Butler in South Carolina, Ben had resided in Philadelphia, where Butler maintained a house because he was a Senator in the U. S. Congress, which met in Philadelphia from 1790 to 1800. Butler had taken Ben back to South Carolina annually and in any event was immune from the six-months clause of the 1780 gradual abolition act as a member of Congress. Ben had married in Philadelphia. In 1804, when Butler resided in Philadelphia with him for more than six months and then prepared to take him to Georgia, Ben sought the help of the PAS in order not to be separated from his wife and to gain his freedom. The Society obtained a writ of *habeas corpus* and won its suit in the Philadelphia Court of Common Pleas, which accepted the argument that Butler had held Ben in Pennsylvania for more than six months and that the immunity of Congressmen from the 1780 law no longer applied because the seat of government had now moved to Washington. A year later Butler became the first slaveowner in the United States to ask a federal court to protect his claim to slave property; the federal court, however, saw little merit in Butler's claim that the Fugitive Slave Act of 1793 should be invoked to protect his property. Ben's freedom was secured, and the law permitting a free state to emancipate slaves brought into its territory was upheld by a federal court.[108]

While the PAS became largely the domain of young Quaker men by the end of the eighteenth century, other Philadelphians evinced less and less interest in the issue of slavery or in assisting former slaves as they strove to find a place for themselves in Philadelphia society. Most of the young Quakers became Federalists as the two-party system developed in the 1790s and early 1800s, and among the rising urban Jeffersonians it was almost an oddity to find a man who interested himself in the PAS. Among several hundred members of the Democratic-Republican Society of Philadelphia, which attracted the radically democratic element in the city in the years of the French Revolution, for example, only two belonged to the PAS. The Jeffersonian newspapers, William Duane's *Aurora* and John Binns's *Democratic Press,* were among the few that continued to run advertisements for slave sales in the city. The party of the city's Irish immigrants, who competed with blacks for jobs at the lower end of the scale, the Democratic-Republicans not only eschewed PAS activities but included in their ranks many who were becoming overtly hostile to the city's growing black population. If the antislavery impulse had weakened, after a generation of cautious strategies but solid accomplishments in the city, what remained of it lay in the hands of those who subscribed to a failing Federalist political persuasion and a religious group that represented an ever-more minuscule fraction of the growing city's populace.

5

Dismantling Slavery: People

As Pennsylvanians took part in fashioning a new nation, they ordained, through their legislators, that slavery would have no long-term existence in their state. The gradual abolition act of 1780 was a cautious document that protected the property rights of slaveholders and freed no slaves. But by prohibiting all slave importation and consigning children to servitude rather than perpetual slavery, the law and its amendments mandated that the institution would cease to expand and eventually expire. With this act the legislature implicitly adopted the abolitionist message that slavery was sin. The cancer of slavery, threatening the moral life of the body politic, would slowly atrophy rather than grow. In the heat of Revolution, the state took steps against slavery similar to those Philadelphia Yearly Meeting had taken during its reformation in the 1750s, when Friends first declared slavery unrighteous in the *Epistle of Caution and Advice* of 1754 and then forbade members from importing or buying blacks in 1758.

The sequential drives against slavery—the Quaker reform that culminated in the 1774 ban on slaveholding and subsequent manumission by Friends of hundreds of slaves, and emancipation by Pennsylvanians of other religions following the 1780 act—shared a common characteristic. Both groups were more interested in purging the evil of slavery from their midst than in relieving the oppression of black Pennsylvanians. Though Friends and others, including members of the Pennsylvania Abolition Society, worked to provide basic education and protect the freedom and rights of blacks, they accepted and

137

abetted, often without perceptible hesitation, the system of black servitude and the limited employment opportunity that succeeded slavery.

In other ways, however, the eradication of slavery in Pennsylvania society as a whole was quite different from the Quaker crusade. Within the Society of Friends, abolitionists like Woolman and Benezet had worked tirelessly to convince members that slaveholding was inconsistent with basic tenets of their faith. Over the course of two decades they built up a momentum that enabled Philadelphia Yearly Meeting to ban slaveholding absolutely and establish stringent rules mandating specific ages at which slaves must be freed, 21 years for men and 18 for women, and eliminating most loopholes by way of which unenthusiastic Quakers might attempt to retain their slaves. Friends could not avoid manumission by sale, will, or gift, and were obligated to free any slaves they inherited.

In contrast, Pennsylvanians of other religions had fewer limits on their actions. After 1780, they could not import slaves into the state, but they could purchase any slaves who had been registered as mandated by law. They could sell bondsmen and bondswomen to their neighbors or out of state, with the exception that after 1788 pregnant women could not be taken away from Pennsylvania with the purpose of having their children born in slavery. If non-Quaker slaveowners chose to manumit their slaves, they could free them at any age they wished and require payments or long periods of additional service. Though several churches other than the Friends encouraged their members to consider emancipation, none made opposition to slavery an article of faith. Nevertheless, slavery withered in Pennsylvania in just a few decades because individuals freed their slaves, blacks escaped their bonds, and, as discussed in the preceding chapter, abolitionists kept pressure on officials to enforce the abolition act and protect free blacks from reenslavement. Though Pennsylvania courts and the legislature consistently refused to adopt total abolition until the Assembly acted in 1847, slavery had nearly vanished in eastern Pennsylvania by 1800, dismantled piece by piece through individual action, both black and white.

In 1780, approximately 400 Philadelphians owned 539 slaves and 201 Chester County residents held 493 slaves. Slavery had been on the decline in Philadelphia since the 1760s. Artisans had abandoned bound labor as they discovered an abundant supply of wage workers who could be hired and fired as economic conditions dictated. High import duties on slaves levied since 1761 had discouraged importation with the result that, in combination with dismal mortality and fertility rates among slaves, the city's black population plummeted. More than one hundred enslaved men and women had escaped in the confusion of war and Quakers emancipated scores more. Between 1767 and 1780 the number of Philadelphia slaves dropped by nearly two-thirds.

Elsewhere in Pennsylvania slavery emerged from the Revolutionary decade in much better condition and was even expanding in places when the 1780 act stopped its growth. In Chester County, where there had been few slaves before the 1750s, wealthy farmers turned to coerced labor when the Seven Years' War cut off European immigration, and in the more wholesome environment of the country the black population grew. The proximity of the Delaware and Maryland borders undoubtedly allowed some Chester County residents, like those in Lancaster, York, and Cumberland counties, to circumvent the ban on imports.[1] Thus, the number of slaves in Chester County decreased by only 11 percent between 1765 and 1780, from 552 to 493, though county residents, mostly Quakers, had freed at least 131 blacks during that time. Slaveholding was never widespread in Chester County, but those who owned slaves were influential and well-to-do. They did not view slavery as a dying institution. Rather, they saw its success in nearby Maryland and conceived that their labor needs and those of their descendants could be filled by generations of slaves. The gradual abolition act seemingly ended those dreams by banning slave importation and freeing the children of slaves at age 28 years.

Completely invisible to us is the role that slaves themselves played through cajoling or even tormenting their masters and mistresses to release them. No doubt the emotional dynamics between master and slave played some role in many cases as rural and urban slaveowners weighed the productive and reproductive value of their blacks in making decisions on whether to release, sell, or hold on to their slaves. Masters who were untouched by antislavery sentiment but who no longer needed their labor could recoup their investment through sale. Between 1767 and 1780 many artisans, mariners, and merchants had disposed of their slaves, but few except for Quakers had freed them. Craftsmen and seamen, especially, found wage labor plentiful, economical, and suited to their needs in the unpredictable post-1760 business climate. In the 1780s, artisans, mariners, and merchants continued to withdraw from slaveholding in large numbers, but not by manumitting their slaves. While about three-quarters of merchants and craftsmen and 60 percent of mariners left slaveholding, only one-quarter to one-third freed their slaves (Table 5–1). Some sold their blacks, while many others lost them through death or flight. We cannot be sure that slave sales contributed to the decrease in the number of slaves in Philadelphia and Chester County between 1780 and 1800 because we can identify only some sellers and few buyers, but it is clear that many slaves changed hands within these areas. Of 127 slaveowners who lived in the city proper in 1790,[2] only 35 percent had appeared on the 1780 list. Just five of 27

TABLE 5–1. Occupation, Slaveholding, and Manumission in Philadelphia, 1780–1800

| | Slaveowners 1780 | Manumitters* 1780–90 | | Slaveowners 1790 | Manumitters 1791–1800 | |
	A	B	(B ÷ A)	C	D	(D ÷ C)
Merchants	113	36	(32%)	30	38	(127%)
Artisans	97	27	(28)	20	19	(95)
Proprietors	45	18	(40)	23	16	(69)
Mariners	22	5	(23)	9	1	(11)
Profess'ls	22	9	(41)	10	9	(90)
Gentlemen	15	8	(53)	18	11	(61)
Officials	7	4	(57)	7	3	(43)
Women**	45	24	(53)	24	10	(42)
Farmers	7	5	(71)	2	0	(0)
Unknown	23	24	(104)	31	39	(126)
TOTAL	396	160	(40)	174	146	(84)

*Manumitters are counted only the first time they freed a slave.
**For whom no occupation is known.

Sources: Phila. constables' return, 1779–80 (adjusted to include the Northern Liberties and Southwark); U.S. Bureau of the Census, *Heads of Families*, 199–245; city directories; manumissions.

owners on the 1800 federal census for Philadelphia were listed as slaveholders in 1790.[3] In Chester County only one-third of slaveowners in 1780 had been taxed for slaves in 1765 or 1774, and only one-half of slaveholders on the 1800 census had registered slaves in 1780 or appeared on the 1790 census as a master.[4]

While many slaveowners washed their hands of the system of perpetual servitude by selling their slaves, others were turned into nonslaveholders by blacks who refused to wait for their owner's heart to soften. All over eastern Pennsylvania in the 1780s and 1790s, and especially in Philadelphia, slavery was declining and the free black population was growing. Along with the climate of freedom and equality nourished during the Revolution, the sight of so many slaves being freed must have made all the more intolerable the condition of those still held in bonds. The early 1780s marked a sharp upturn in the flight of slaves from Philadelphia masters. Blacks were enraged that the abolition act left them enslaved. From 1780 to 1784, at least 122 slaves ran away, four-fifths (97 of 122) of them males. In a slave population that had declined to 420 in 1785, this amounted to one in every seventeen slaves (including those of all ages and conditions) running away each year, and among young able-bodied males the rate may have been as high as one in seven. Another forty-five slaves took flight from 1785 to 1789, so that for the entire decade, when about 222 slaves were manumitted in the city, runaways reached three-fourths of that number. Included in these personal attempts to speed the death of slavery were the bondsmen of some famous Philadelphia revolutionaries: Punch, the 23-year-old slave of Benedict Arnold; Joe, the 27-year-old slave of Haym Solomon; Will, the slave of Tench Coxe; and Jack, the 19-year-old slave of Joseph Wharton. Merchant John Duffield was particularly beset by his recalcitrant slaves. Nineteen-year-old Tom had fled in March 1777 and after being captured had escaped again in September. Three years later, 34-year-old Amorita fled with her 4-year-old daughter; taken up, she ran away again in January 1781 and once again in December of that year.[5]

Almost two-thirds of those who fled were young men in their late teens and twenties—in the prime of their working lives. Slaves as young as the 9-year-old boy Mag, who escaped in August 1784, and as old as 60-year-old Jack, who fled his master in 1782, were exceptions among runaways advertised in the Philadelphia newspapers.[6] Thirty-five percent of the runaways in the 1780s were 16 to 20 years old, and another 43 percent were 21 to 30; only 9 percent were younger than sixteen and 13 percent over thirty. It appears that at least one-half and as many as three-fourths of the young slave men whose masters had shown no inclination to free them took matters into their own hands in the 1780s, thus depriving the house of bondage of many of its most serviceable timbers. For example, Adam, the 21-year-old slave of baker Simon Fishbaugh, ran away in September 1786, asserting that he was freeborn, a claim his master refuted in advertising for him. Bacchus, the American-born slave of a recent immigrant, the broker B. Nories, fled in January 1789, shortly after finding out how few of Philadelphia's blacks remained in slavery.[7]

Such frequent challenges to the already declining institution of coerced labor by its most valuable workers probably convinced many masters that holding slaves had become a bootless proposition. The merchant entrepreneur Stephen Girard, a French West Indian who was impervious to abolitionist pleadings, switched to European indentured servants after three of his slaves, Rosette, Abraham, and Sam, ran away recurrently after the war, Abraham taking to his heels four times between 1785 and 1787.[8]

Philadelphia slaveowners who held on to their slaves most persistently or who replaced those who died or escaped were largely masters whose slaves were domestic servants. Most of these domestic slaves were women, often with children, and less likely than men to run away. In 1780, occupational groups that were most likely to employ slaves in their homes, stables, stores, and shops—merchants, professionals, gentlemen, officials, widows, and proprietors of shops, taverns, and inns—composed two-thirds of slaveowners whose occupations are known (Table 5–1). By 1790 they made up almost 80 percent of the city's slaveholders, largely because artisans, mariners, and farmers, who were more likely to employ their bondsmen in crafts, on board ships, or in fields, had left slavekeeping in considerable numbers during the intervening years. Many merchants had also given up their slaves during the 1780s but they remained the largest group of masters, and the degree to which they and gentlemen, officials, and widows held slaves in 1790 was highly disproportionate to their numbers among household heads (Table 5–2). The number of gentlemen who owned slaves actually increased between 1780 and 1790, despite manumissions, and the number of public officials who held slaves remained unchanged. Thus the majority of Philadelphians who resisted emancipation most strenuously stood in the upper social strata. They needed a steady source of labor to maintain their homes, clothing, carriages, and horses, care for their children, cook and serve their meals, and deliver and pick up messages and parcels. Lower-class Philadelphians, including most artisans, lacked the resources to support household retainers, and as wage labor proved more efficient and economical to fill openings in their shops, they turned their backs on bound labor, both white and black. In 1790 craftsmen were over one-half of all household heads in Philadelphia but only 14 percent of slaveowners (Table 5–2).

Among the twenty-seven holdouts who had not freed their slaves by 1800 were a handful of wealthy gentlemen and their widows who had held slaves all their lives: four merchants, a surveyor, and an innkeeper. All but six of these recalcitrants kept only a single slave, but still they clung to a labor system that their fellow citizens in the city had rejected. Judith McCall retained one of the many slaves she and her late husband, merchant Archibald McCall, who died the preceding year, had owned over the course of their lives. Following their marriage in 1762 they resided in a large mansion on the corner of Union and Second streets, in 1772 were one of the eighty-four families in the city keeping equipages, and were pewholders at St. Peter's Episcopal Church, where Archibald was a vestryman. They had eighteen children between the years 1763 and 1788.[9] Archibald had entered a successful mercantile partnership with his elder brother Samuel McCall, Jr., and with him imported Africans on at least one occasion, in October 1761. They were among the twenty-four merchants and firms who signed the petition challenging passage of the 1761 law placing an importation duty of £10 on each slave, arguing that "an Advantage may be gained by the Importation of Slaves, which will Likewise

TABLE 5–2. Slaveholding and Occupation in Philadelphia, 1775 and 1790

	Slaveowners 1775 (% of known)		Taxables 1772	Slaveowners 1790 (% of known)		Household Heads, 1790
Merchants	142	(32%)	10%	30	(21%)	10%
Artisans	129	(29)	59	20	(14)	53
Proprietors	38	(8)	8	23	(16)	14
Mariners	13	(3)	11	9	(6)	5
Professionals	23	(5)	4	10	(7)	6
Gentlemen	18	(4)	1	18	(13)	2
Officials	9	(2)	2	7	(5)	2
Women*	57	(13)	4	24	(17)	7
Farmers	18	(4)	1	2	(1)	0.4
Unknown	[5	(1)]	[0]	[31	(18)]	[17]
TOTAL	452			174		
Known	447 (100%)			143 (100%)		

*For whom no occupation is known.

Sources: Phila. constables' return, 1775 (adjusted to include the Northern Liberties and Southwark); Gary B. Nash, *The Urban Crucible: Social Change, Political Consciousness, and the Origins of the American Revolution* (Cambridge, Mass., 1979), 387–91; U.S. Bureau of the Census, *Heads of Families*, 199–245; unpublished data from 1789 tax list and 1790 census provided by Mary M. Schweitzer.

be a means of reducing the exorbitant price of Labour." Archibald McCall held at least five slaves in 1775 and still had three in 1790. He signed manumissions in 1792 for a girl Amelia, a boy Isaac, and James, whose age is unknown, and in 1794 and 1795 released four children who had been born in the early 1780s instead of requiring them to serve for 28 years. He held on to a fifth child, Elizabeth, however, until she reached age 28, and his son Archibald, Jr., signed papers in 1800 providing for freedom for 38-year-old Molly Nealy and 41-year-old Mabel in 1807. These women undoubtedly helped to raise the large McCall family and were released only after the youngest child reached age 18.[10]

Others who still had slaves in 1800 were members of the Philadelphia elite. John Nixon, another elderly merchant and stalwart of St. Peter's, had also signed the 1761 petition against the import duty. He is best known as the first person to read the Declaration of Independence publicly. Though he lived next to his pastor the Rev. Robert Blackwell, who freed 18-year-old Pompey in 1782 and 28-year-old Richard in 1795, Nixon remained unmoved on the issue of slavery. As did merchants George Emlen and Benjamin Gibbs, merchant and city councilman Francis Gurney, or Frances Clifton, who owned six slaves in 1790 and 1800.[11]

A number of the 1800 slaveowners had plantations or other connections in Delaware and Maryland and were thus caught between two labor systems and their attendant ideologies. They included surveyor Andrew Ellicott, Williamina Cadwalader, widow of General John Cadwalader, Philemon Dickinson, brother of John Dickinson, Benjamin Chew, his son Benjamin Chew, Jr., and John Beale Bordley. Ellicott was a Bucks County native who joined his father's settlement near Baltimore soon after his marriage in 1775. Though of Quaker origin, he fought in the Continental army. During his career he surveyed the boundary between Virginia and Pennsylvania west of the Mason-Dixon line, Pennsylvania's western and northern boundaries, the ten-mile square for the District of Columbia, and the southern boundary of the United States from the Atlantic to the Mississippi. He settled in Philadelphia in 1789 with his wife and nine children. Apparently he purchased, or otherwise obtained from within the state, the slave he owned in 1800, because migrants into Pennsylvania could not by law keep slaves longer than six months.[12]

Philemon Dickinson, who retained three slaves in 1800, was the younger brother of John Dickinson, author of the protest pamphlet *Letters from a Farmer in Pennsylvania* (1768). They were raised by Quaker parents, Samuel and Mary Cadwalader Dickinson, first on the Eastern Shore of Maryland and then at Poplar Hall in Kent County, Delaware. Samuel had extensive landholdings in both provinces and owned seventy-two slaves when he died in 1760. Samuel stopped attending Friends meeting in 1739 when he was censured (but not disowned) for allowing his daughter Elizabeth to marry an Anglican, and neither Philemon nor John remained within the Quaker fold. John studied law at the Middle Temple, set up practice in Philadelphia, and became involved in the politics of both Delaware and Pennsylvania. Philemon attended the College of Philadelphia and clerked with his brother, but decided the law did not suit him. Nor did he want to manage the family estates, so the family leased its lands to tenants, hired out many of the slaves, and Philemon moved to an estate near Trenton, New Jersey, with his wife (and first cousin) Mary Cadwalader and his mother. He commanded the New Jersey militia during the Revolution and subsequently returned to Philadelphia.[13]

Slavery caused greater moral anguish for John than Philemon. In 1772, John purchased back several women and children who had been owned by the family and sold by Philemon. Then in 1777, at the Dover plantation, he manumitted twelve men, ten women, fifteen boys, and ten girls, but immediately indentured each of them to 21 years' additional service, promising that

John Dickinson, lawyer and pamphleteer, manumitted more than fifty slaves during the Revolution, but immediately indentured them to long terms on his Dover (Delaware) plantation or nearby farms. Portrait by Charles Willson Peale (1770). Courtesy of The Historical Society of Pennsylvania.

any children born to the women and girls would be free from birth. In 1781, he freed six more slaves, this time indenturing four for terms of seven, thirteen, and fifteen years. The other two remained in Dickinson's service. The long terms mandated for the blacks freed in 1777 dictated that the adults would spend most of their lives in bonds and ensured him of a continuing income until his mid-sixties. Thus John Dickinson, convinced that "the recording Angel stood ready to make Record against him in Heaven had he neglected it," believed he removed the stain of slaveholding from himself while keeping the profits of his blacks' labor.[14]

Philemon, meanwhile, refused to entertain the notion of emancipating his slaves without substantial remuneration. In 1793, when John urged him to make the move, he answered indignantly,

> I endeavor to regulate my conduct by the principle of justice and humanity and am strongly inclined to believe you are not acquainted with my conduct towards those persons you deem so unhappy. I am far from being friendly to perpetual slavery—yet I am of opinion that people should have an Education suited to freedom—under this impression (but not viewing it in a criminal light) I would willingly subscribe to a general act for the *gradual* abolition of slavery.
>
> Not being influenced by the same motives that you are, and my situation not permitting me to make so great a sacrifice as you request, I hope I shall stand excused, even in your mind.

He argued further that he had offered his slaves the opportunity to purchase their freedom but they had done little toward that goal. Philemon did sign a conditional manumission for 17-year-old Betty in 1795.[15] Clearly, both brothers struggled with the issue of slavery, John before Philemon, but were held back from freeing their slaves immediately because a considerable part of their family fortune rested on human chattel.

Benjamin Chew, Sr., was another Philadelawarean of Quaker background who resisted freeing his slaves. He was born and raised on the western shore of Maryland until his father, Dr. Samuel Chew, moved the family first to Philadelphia, where he set up a medical practice, and then to a farm near Dover. Benjamin Chew studied law at the Middle Temple but returned home before finishing his studies when his father died in 1744. He practiced in both Delaware and Pennsylvania and in 1754 moved to Philadelphia, retaining the plantation and a house in Dover. Chew joined Christ Church, was appointed attorney-general and a provincial councilor of Pennsylvania in 1755, and became a leader of the proprietary party. After the Revolution he served as president of the High Court of Errors and Appeals.[16]

Chew held slaves in both Delaware and Philadelphia and apparently man-umitted none. They were valuable property and a source of income: spotty records show that he purchased five blacks in 1752 from a Kent County cordwainer for £150 and a boy Will in 1772 for £85, and in the 1770s received £14 plus interest annually for hiring out his black man Sharper. When the Pennsylvania Assembly required owners to register their slaves in 1780, Chew first reported Will, a woman Rachel, and four children, Sal, Bet, Harry, and Jesse; then a few days before the November 1 deadline he submitted a supplementary return registering three women, a girl, two men, and two boys. One of these slaves was George, aged 21 or 22, probably the slave of the same name who had been indentured 18 years before to farmer Lawrence Garrits of Blockley Township, Philadelphia County.[17]

When he authorized his son Benjamin in 1796 "to sell & dispose of such of my Slaves in the State of Delaware or to manumit & set them free for such Prices & on such Terms & Conditions as he may think proper & expedient," Chew left the door open for some slaves to obtain freedom, but only at a price. On the whole he was impervious to abolitionism. In 1789 he registered two children born since 1780 and the same year advertised for a well-dressed man, apparently Will, who ran away that year in the company of a white woman. In 1796 and 1797 he assisted his half-brother Samuel Chew of Chestertown, Maryland, in retrieving slaves who fled to the Philadelphia area.[18]

Benjamin Chew, Jr., was somewhat more yielding to antislavery argu-ments, for under the influence of Quaker and PAS member Isaac T. Hopper he freed his man William Sewell in 1811, requiring seven years' additional service. If Sewell was the Will who absconded in 1789, however, and it is likely that he was, he was 64 years old before he achieved freedom and therefore no longer profitable for Chew to keep. Inasmuch as the younger Chew retained slaves in Maryland, issued a notice for the return of a runaway in 1819, and profited from the labor of his slave Samuel Chambers as late as 1831, his manumission of Sewell seems more like a belated and begrudged concession to the antislavery society than any genuine conversion to aboli-tion.[19]

A particularly intriguing case was that of Marylander John Beale Bordley, a lawyer and agricultural reformer, who inherited through his first wife Mar-garet Chew, a relative of Benjamin, a 1600-acre plantation on Wye Island on Maryland's Eastern Shore. He wrote a number of works on agricultural meth-ods, including *Crop-Rotations* (1784) and *Essays and Notes on Husbandry and Rural Affairs* (1799; 2nd ed., 1801), and conducted experiments in his fields. After his first wife died, Bordley in 1776 married Sarah Fishbourne Mifflin, stepmother of Thomas Mifflin, and in 1785, after Eastern Shore planters indicated little interest, he used his Philadelphia connections to found the Philadelphia Society for Promoting Agriculture. Charter members included Thomas Willing, Robert Morris, John Nixon, General John Cadwalader, Philemon Dickinson, and Benjamin Rush, influential Philadelphians who like Bordley owned slaves and faced the challenge of whether to liberate them. In 1762, Bordley had signed manumissions for a black woman Mariah, who was to be free in five years, and three children, who would be free at age 28. In 1792, after settling in Philadelphia, he released, as required by the gradual abolition act, a woman Betty and two girls whom he brought with him from Maryland. Like many other new residents, however, he bound them to the longest terms allowable by law. Betty would serve seven years and Nelly and Peggy would remain in bondage until they reached age 28, in 1813 and 1816 respectively. In 1800, Bordley did free outright a man, James Sewell, and in his will written the next year he manumitted his "Family slaves" Moses, Charles, and Jemmy. Yet Bordley had many other blacks in Maryland whom he bequeathed to his heirs. In his *Essays and Notes on Husbandry and Rural Affairs* he recognized that the system of agricultural labor had changed in Pennsylvania and thought it likely that the same would occur in Maryland, but except for manumitting, rather half-heartedly, a few favored slaves, he remained enmeshed in the business of human bondage.[20]

These Philadelphians with ties in Maryland and Delaware were less susceptible to antislavery sentiment than most of their neighbors in the city. To admit that slavery was wrong meant they should liberate all their blacks, and the income generated by employing them or hiring them out in Maryland and Delaware weighed heavily against that. Besides, their slaves in Philadelphia performed useful service, primarily as domestic servants. Chew's man Will, nattily clad when he fled in 1789, was apparently the old gentleman's personal slave. The McCalls' slaves provided continuous service to their huge family for many years. But even such Philadelphians as these, who resisted the belief that slavery was immoral, could not hold out much longer. Either their slaves died or escaped, or they set them free in the early years of the Jeffersonian era, for by 1810 the census takers counted only three slaves in Pennsylvania's capital and its environs.

Evidence from manumissions also suggests that most late eighteenth-century Philadelphia slaves worked as domestic servants. Unfortunately, information provided by the 1780 constables' return and the 1790 and 1800 federal censuses on the sex and age of slaves does not enable us to compare slaves who were freed with those who remained in bonds. Since many men had freed themselves in the early 1780s by running away, however, the remaining slaves must have been disproportionately female. In the years from

1780 to 1785 blacks freed by Philadelphians were divided almost evenly by sex (Table 5–3). Artisans and merchants freed somewhat more females than males, and proprietors manumitted a highly disproportionate number of women and girls. Widows freed an even number of males and females while professionals, gentlemen, and farmers freed more men and boys. In the late 1780s and 1790s the sex ratio became skewed, with more males than females

TABLE 5–3. Philadelphia Manumissions and Occupation, 1780–1800

Occupation of Manumitter	1780–1785		1786–1790	
	No. of Blacks* Manumitted	Sex Ratio Male/Female	No. of Blacks Manumitted	Sex Ratio Male/Female
Merchants	44	.9	20	2.2
Artisans	21	.9	12	1.0
Proprietors	11	.2	10	.7
Mariners	3	.5	2	1.0
Profess'ls	6	5.0	6	1.0
Gentlemen	6	3.0	5	4.0
Officials	0	0	5	.7
Women**	34	1.0	14	2.5
Farmers	3	3/0	2	1.0
Unknown	19	1.1	16	2.8
TOTAL	147	1.0	92	1.6
	1791–1795		1796–1800	
Merchants	35	.7	22	2.5
Artisans	21	2.5	4	1.0
Proprietors	10	.5	11	.8
Mariners	1	0/1	0	0
Profess'ls	9	3.5	2	1.0
Gentlemen	12	3.0	2	1.0
Officials	4	1.0	0	0
Women**	7	1.3	3	0/3
Farmers	0	0	0	0
Unknown	32	1.5	15	4.0
TOTAL	131	1.3	59	1.6

*Does not include blacks whose sex is unknown.
**For whom no occupation is known.

Sources: Manumissions; Philadelphia City directories.

being freed. After 1785 proprietors still manumitted more women and girls, but artisans, merchants, and widows now released more men and boys. Though males predominated in number among slaves manumitted in Philadelphia during the 1780s and 1790s, and among those who fled, many more bondsmen and bondswomen worked in households than in trades, on ships, or on the few farms located in the western Northern Liberties. Of 421 blacks freed whose sex is known, 57 percent were women, girls, and boys under age 16 years, who would not have been employed in crafts. Men over age 16 and males whose age is unknown (including an indeterminable number of boys) totaled 183, of whom only 30 had artisans, mariners, and farmers as masters. The remaining 153 of these black males were owned by merchants, proprietors, professionals, gentlemen, women, officials, and men whose occupation cannot be identified. Some were probably hired out or indentured as craftsmen, longshoremen, or laborers, but others served their owners in personal or domestic duties. For these mostly wealthy slaveholders black men drove carriages, attended their masters, performed heavy jobs around the house, store, or shop, and performed a variety of other chores, especially if the owner had no other household help. If one-half of slave men owned by these occupational groups worked as domestics, which is a reasonable (and probably low) estimate, then three-fourths of blacks freed in Philadelphia during the 1780s and 1790s were working as personal or domestic servants at the time of manumission. Their masters and mistresses had held on to them long after most artisans had looked to other sources of labor because they could employ them full-time and had the resources to provide subsistence.

In Chester County (including Delaware County, which split off from Chester in 1789) also, slaveholding persisted longest among residents who could use full-time labor year-round. After 1780, slaveholding declined among all occupational categories in this rural area, but it fell faster within some groups than others. Over the last two decades of the century, slave-ownership decreased to a greater extent among farmers who had no additional enterprises such as mills, inns, or specialized crafts than among entrepreneurs who owned mills, distilleries, taverns, and forges (Table 5–4). Thus slaveholders who did more than farm were more likely to hold on to their slaves, presumably because they had no trouble keeping them busy from one season to another and because they did not relish losing workers with special skills. Increasingly, farmers could find landless wage laborers who were familiar with harvesting and sowing, having worked for their parents and neighbors since childhood,[21] but experienced millers, forgemen, and distillers were harder to find. In addition, rich farmers, proprietors, and rural entrepreneurs were as dependent on domestic servants as Philadelphia merchants

TABLE 5–4. Occupation, Slaveholding, and Manumission in Chester County,* 1780–1800

	Slaveowners 1780	Manumitters** 1780–90	Slaveowners 1790	Manumitters 1791–1800	Slaveowners 1800
Farmers (only)	120	17	42	12	18
Farmers w/mills, distilleries, forges	14	4	11	4	8
Proprietors	15	4	2	0	5
Artisans	27	2	5	0	3
Professionals	11	3	7	1	0
Gentlemen	3	0	2	1	0
Officials	0	0	0	0	0
Women***	5	1	6	0	2
Unknown	6	0	38	0	3
TOTAL	201	31	113	18	39

*Includes Delaware County after 1789.

**Manumitters are counted only the first time they freed a slave.

***For whom no occupation is known.

Sources: Chester Co. slave register, 1780; U.S. Bureau of the Census, *Heads of Families,* 59–75, 98–104; Chester Co. tax assessment lists, 1783, 1789, 1800; U.S., manuscript census, 1800; manumissions.

and gentlemen. Affluent Chester County households had much to keep slave women and teenagers busy.

Further, slavery remained strongest in western Chester County, among Scots-Irish and Scots Presbyterians who had invested in slaves only in the decade before 1780, when Quakers had set their blacks free. These belated slaveowners were primarily from families who emigrated from northern Ireland and Scotland during the 1720s through 1750s and took up lands to the west of the Swedish and Quaker areas closer to the Delaware River. When the gradual abolition act was passed in 1780 they had only recently amassed sufficient capital to purchase slaves.[22] Just 35 percent of Presbyterians on the 1780 slave registration list were taxed for slaves in 1765 or 1774, in contrast to Episcopalian slaveowners, of whom 56 percent were on earlier lists. Thus the western Scots-Irish Presbyterians rejected the reformers' efforts, petitioned the Assembly against abolition in 1779 and 1780, and—when the act was passed despite their opposition—carefully registered their slaves and retained them for a decade or more. While slaveholding was evenly divided between eastern and western Chester County in 1780, by 1790 it was centered more in the west, with 65 percent of slaveholders in the west and 55 percent in just eleven western and southwestern townships, East and West Nantmeal,

Honeybrook, Uwchlan, Sadsbury, West Fallowfield, Oxford, Londonderry, London Grove, New London, and London Britain. In 1800, 60 percent of slaveholders lived in the even more concentrated area of Upper and Lower Oxford (formerly Oxford), Londonderry, London Grove, East Marlborough, New London, and East Nottingham townships. John Finney, a Londonderry farmer and cooper, for example, appeared on neither the 1765 or 1774 tax lists as a slaveowner, but registered a 42-year-old man in 1780 and still owned a slave in 1800. Abel Hodgson, a farmer of East Nottingham who registered two men and a woman in their twenties in 1780 but had not been taxed for slaves earlier, also had a slave twenty years later. Others included George McIlhenny of Coventry, John Menough of New London, James McDowell of Upper Oxford, and John Ross of London Grove. These western Chester County slaveowners had acquired slaves for the first time shortly before 1780 and, protecting their investment, opposed the act and kept their slaves for many years.

In both Philadelphia and Chester County, then, occupation, wealth, or the desire to benefit fully from a recent investment influenced decisions of slaveowners on whether to hold on to their slaves or sell them, or to replace those who died or ran away. Financial pressure rarely, if ever, induced a slaveholder to manumit, for those who abandoned slaveholding for financial reasons would more logically sell their slaves than release them. Philadelphia artisans, who had the lowest status among slaveholders and who continued to quit slavery in the 1780s, were among the least likely to manumit. Merchants, some of whom were battered by the ravages of the Revolution and the economic dislocation that followed, also continued to move away from slaveholding in significant numbers but freed their blacks at a relatively low rate. Ironically, manumission was most frequent among the same groups in Philadelphia and Chester County who tended to retain their slaves the longest. Gentlemen, officials, successful merchants, and well-to-do widows in the city had the means both to keep full-time household laborers and release them when touched by antislavery sentiment. We see this further by tracing those Philadelphians who freed slaves in the 1780s in the tax lists of the decade and comparing their wealth with that of city dwellers who did not manumit their slaves. About one-third of slaveowners remaining in 1790 could be located on the tax lists for 1785 and 1789, and about 45 percent of the manumitters (some of whom freed their slaves at death and therefore do not appear on the tax lists) have been located.[23] Persons in both groups who were sufficiently affluent to appear on the tax lists and who remained in the city long enough to be traced could be found in roughly equivalent proportions throughout the hierarchy of wealth (Table 5–5). In Chester County, also, the occupational

TABLE 5–5. Wealth of Manumitters
and Non-Manumitters in Philadelphia,
1781–1790

Taxable Wealth (£)	Manumitters (1781–90)		Slaveowners (1790)	
1–10	8	(12%)	3	(5%)
11–20	7	(10)	5	(9)
21–50	12	(18)	10	(18)
51–100	12	(18)	15	(27)
101–250	16	(23)	15	(27)
251+	13	(19)	7	(13)
TOTAL	68	(100)	55	(100)

Sources: U.S. Bureau of the Census, *Heads of Families,* 199–245; Phila. tax assessment lists, 1785 and 1789; manumissions.

group that held on to slaves most tenaciously, residents who had mills, distilleries, or forges in addition to large farms, had a better record for freeing blacks in the 1780s and 1790s than any other group. Artisans were the least likely to manumit. As in Philadelphia, craftsmen abandoned slaveholding in significant numbers during the 1780s but few freed their slaves.

Economic calculations obliged many slaveholders to abandon slavery but only religious and moral beliefs compelled Pennsylvanians to free their slaves outright. While the ways in which they employed slaves, their financial condition, and how recently they had purchased blacks could increase or lessen their resistance to abolitionism, only the realization that slavery was wrong could induce slaveholders to liberate, rather than sell, their bondswomen and bondsmen. By the end of the Revolution the Quaker disavowal of slaveholding as immoral was spreading throughout Philadelphia's population. Though no church other than the Society of Friends had as yet officially taken a position against slaveowning, many Philadelphians began to subscribe to the view that slavery was wrong and that responsible Christians ought to cleanse themselves of this evil. In the war years from 1775 to 1779, seventy-four Philadelphia Quakers, under religious obligation, had released their slaves, and twenty-one other Philadelphians, under no religious compulsion, had done so. Then in the early 1780s, when Quakers were completing their release of slaves, the number of other Philadelphia manumitters began to climb. The gradual abolition act and the example of Quakers prompted no immediate mass movement toward emancipation, but an upward trend was clear. At least forty-six non-Friends released slaves from 1780 to 1783, and an additional twenty-three signed documents of manumission in 1784, the year the PAS was reestablished. For the rest of the 1780s about a dozen non-Quaker slaveowners a year freed blacks (Table 5–6). From 1780 to 1790 at least 145 non-Quakers freed slaves, almost twice as many as in all the preceding decades.

The response to abolitionism varied considerably among slaveowners of different religious groups. By 1780 few Philadelphia Friends still owned slaves; those who retained them were either disowned or convinced the meeting that they would free them if they had the power. Between 1780 and 1786 fifteen Friends freed slaves for the first time, including five women who manumitted slaves after the death of their husbands. Rebecca Jervis and Sarah Johnson freed slaves in 1786, a year after their husbands died. Elizabeth Allen's husband was not a Quaker and thus apparently rejected her monthly meeting's demand that he sign a manumission for their slave girl. When he died, Allen signed a document that 14-year-old Jude would be free at age 18.[24] Philadelphia Yearly Meeting in 1778 had considered the question of

TABLE 5–6. Religion, Slaveholding, and Manumission in Philadelphia, 1780–1800

	Slaveowners *1780*	*Manumitters** *1780–90*	*Slaveowners* *1790*	*Manumitters* *1791–1800*	*Slaveowners* *1800*
Quaker	16	15	0	1	0
Presbyterian	81	23	21	15	2
Episcopalian	132	53	75	36	8
Methodist	3	1	0	0	0
Baptist	3	0	0	4	0
German Luth.	28	6	7	3	1
German Ref.	6	4	3	3	0
Rom. Catholic	10	10	8	6	2
Jewish	15	2	6	1	0
Free and Ex-Quaker	15	4	8	3	1
Unknown**	87	42	46	74	13
TOTAL	396	160	174	146	27
Non-Quakers	380	145	174	145	27

*Manumitters are counted only the first time they freed a slave.

**In many cases, these slaveholders were affiliated with no church.

Sources: Phila. constables' return, 1779–80 (adjusted to include the Northern Liberties and Southwark); U.S. Bureau of the Census, *Heads of Families*, 199–245; manumissions; church records, U.S., manuscript census, 1800. Information about Methodists and Roman Catholics was provided by Doris E. Andrews and Edith Jeffreys.

how to deal with women who had slaves in their households but whose husbands were not members of the Society. Under common law only the husband owned the slave and had the power to manumit even if the black person had been part of the wife's dowry or a gift from her family. The Yearly Meeting decided that women whose husbands refused to free slaves could retain membership if they convinced their monthly meetings that they would free their slaves if they had the power.[25]

Other late Quaker manumitters included those who had freed some of their slaves a few years earlier and now completed the divestiture required by the Society. Widow Rachel Moore had released seven slaves in 1777 and now signed manumissions for seven women she had brought from Maryland in 1770 and nine others still living there. Some of the women in Pennsylvania had been bound out to area farmers and would not be free for four years or more. She pledged that any money paid by their masters would go for their benefit when free. Several other tardy Quakers had special circumstances that affected their cases. Owen Biddle, a gentleman, had been disowned in 1775 for "promoting warlike preparation & instructing in the art of war." He freed his man Plug in 1781 and the Society reinstated him in 1783. His wife Sarah and children had remained members throughout the period. Thomas Shute and Samuel Wallace were two other late manumitters. Philadelphia Monthly Meeting had already condemned (but not disowned) them for marrying out of unity, and it seems likely that their strained relations with the Society made them less amenable to its will. It is also possible that their non-Quaker wives or in-laws objected to manumission.[26]

As the Quaker drive for emancipation reached its conclusion, Philadelphia slaveholders of other religions began to free their slaves with greater frequency. Among manumitters who were not Quakers, Episcopalians were most numerous, yet the tendency to hold on to slaves was also more pronounced among this religious group than any other. Since 1760, Episcopalians had manumitted slaves on an average of about one per year, but beginning in 1780 their number rose to five per annum. Fifty-three released at least some of their slaves between 1780 and 1790, but others purchased or sold slaves, willed their slaves at death, or retained some or all of their bondspeople. By 1790, seventy-five Episcopalians still held slaves, and the number of Episcopalian slaveowners had decreased from 1780 to 1790 by only 43 percent, the lowest rate of divestment in slaves of any of the major denominations (Table 5–6). While Episcopalians were only about 14 percent of Philadelphia's population in 1790, they comprised 43 percent of slaveholders (Table 5–7). For Episcopalians, to free slaves or hold on to them remained an individual decision. The church made no effort to encourage manumission, though it had baptized,

TABLE 5–7. Slaveholding and Religion in Philadelphia, 1775 and 1790

	Slaveowners 1775	Mortality Statistics 1761–75	Slaveowners 1790	Mortality Statistics 1788–1801
Quaker	62 (14%)	12%	0	9%
Presbyterian	55 (12)	11	21 (12%)	10
Anglican	188 (42)	18	75 (43)	14
Methodist	0	0.3	0	1
Baptist	4 (1)	2	0	2
German Luth.	22 (5)	15	7 (4)	15
German Ref.	4 (1)	5	3 (2)	6
Rom. Catholic	12 (3)	4	8 (5)	11
Jewish	7 (1)		6 (3)	0.1
Free and Ex-Quaker	15 (3)		8 (5)	
Unknown	83 (18)	23	46 (26)	23
TOTAL	452		174	

Sources: Phila. constables' return, 1775 (adjusted to include the Northern Liberties and Southwark); Billy G. Smith, "Death and Life in a Colonial Immigrant City: A Demographic Analysis of Philadelphia," *Journal of Economic History* 37 (1977): 868; U.S. Bureau of the Census, *Heads of Families,* 199–245; Susan E. Klepp, "The Demographic Characteristics of Philadelphia, 1788–1801: Zachariah Poulson's Bills of Mortality," *Pennsylvania History* 53 (1986): 215.

married, and educated free blacks and slaves well before the Revolution and was the church with which many of Philadelphia's leading blacks had affinity. The Rev. Robert Blackwell served as an example to some of his parishioners, perhaps, when he freed his 18-year-old man Pompey immediately in 1782 but waited until 1788 to agree that 21-year-old Richard should be free at age 28.[27] Anglicans had freed blacks idiosyncratically in earlier decades, and they tended still to place conditions on freedom.[28]

Some who clung to the system of bondage, like the painter and wartime radical Charles Willson Peale, an Episcopalian, were in theory convinced of the humanity of freeing their slaves but in practice willing to release them only if they could recapture their investment. Peale had supported the gradual abolition act in 1780 for both its ideals and its protection of property rights in slaves. Caught between humanitarian ideology and self-interest, Peale, after listening to PAS appeals, freed a boy who had been born after 1780 when he reached age 21. He calculated the value of his servitude between age 21 and 28 at £15. But Peale would not release Phyllis, perhaps the boy's mother. Instead, he wrote a subscription paper in 1787 in an attempt to get contributions for the £50 he thought she was worth. Following a practice established earlier, he sent Phyllis into the streets herself to appeal for money. Some of those she solicited, she related, were "cross and Ill natured" when approached because "her master was active in the War & Politics in the late revolution"; others thought Peale "was rich enough to free her" himself. Claiming deep indebtedness, Peale asked the PAS for contributions. Though rebuffed, he is supposed to have released his slave woman a few years later.[29]

Other Episcopalians absorbed more abolitionist spirit. When Thomas Saltar, a Northern Liberties merchant, wrote his will in 1785, he directed his executors to pay fifty Spanish silver dollars each year to his boy Tom, who was already free. Widow Martha Dagworthy, sister of Philemon Dickinson's wife Mary, liberated her three black men Bristol, Abner, and Belfast in her will dated 1786 and added that if she could not legally manumit her slaves (presumably because she was a woman), then she gave them to her brother Lambert Cadwalader who should free them. In 1780, the heirs of Ann Rogers, following her wishes, freed adult slaves Pompey and Phebe outright and agreed to manumit children Lucy and Robert at age 21 years. Dorcas Montgomery and Mary Sanderson both liberated their 40-year-old women Violet and Flora immediately. Women figured prominently among Episcopalians who emancipated slaves soon after passage of the abolition act. They were six of sixteen Episcopalians who freed slaves during 1780, 1781, and 1782.[30]

Fewer Philadelphia Presbyterians owned slaves in 1780 than Episcopalians and they withdrew from slaveholding to a much greater extent during the 1780s, but they also freed blacks in a smaller proportion. While slaveownership among Presbyterians declined by three-fourths between 1780 and 1790, only 28 percent of Presbyterians who owned slaves in 1780 signed manumissions compared with 40 percent of Episcopalians (Table 5–6). The remainder who withdrew from ownership of human beings apparently released their slaves informally or sold them, or their blacks died or executed successful escapes. Though George Bryan and the Presbyterian party had sponsored the act for gradual abolition they failed to inspire any immediate movement for emancipation among co-religionists who owned slaves. From 1780 to 1783 an average of only one Philadelphia Presbyterian freed slaves each year; their average rose to three per annum from 1784 to 1786, shortly before the Synod of New-York and Philadelphia took a stand on slavery. The Presbyterian church in 1787 issued a statement favoring the gradual abolition of slavery but made no demands on its slaveholding members. Thus by adopting a corporate position on the issue it went further than the Episcopalians, but still Presbyterian slaveholders decided on their own authority whether to release their blacks.

The Synod of New-York and Philadelphia considered the issue in 1787 when its Committee of Overtures submitted a vigorous statement regarding the rights of all human beings to freedom and urged that the churches under the synod's jurisdiction be instructed to "do everything in their power consistent with the rights of civil society, to promote the abolition of slavery, and the instruction of negroes, whether bond or free." The synod adopted a weaker stance, however, one that urged slaveowners to prepare their slaves for liberty through education and allow them to work for their freedom. The synod believed "the final abolition of slavery in America" was a worthy aim but wanted no radical emancipation. A decade later the Presbyterian General Assembly condemned slavery in principle, but even then it allowed local jurisdictions to work out their own policy.[31]

Francis Alison, Philadelphia's eminent Presbyterian clergyman, epitomized Presbyterian ambivalence toward black bondage. He had spoken as early as 1768 of the "wickedness" of slavekeeping and the divine wrath that it would incur, though he did not provide for the freedom of his five slaves until he wrote and amended his will in the late 1770s, and even then he directed that they should serve until age 30 or 31. Any children born to his woman Rose before she achieved freedom should serve to age 30 and then be released, "the service of any child, till it be so old, being judged sufficient to compensate for its education & nourishing, and all the hazards of its dying before it be able to pay these expences." In his will Alison wrote, "With respect to my black servants, I cannot find that the Scriptures have any where condemned Slavery, as what is in all cases unjust & wrongful, but rather seem to [?] & give it countenance;" but he ordered his slaves freed because he believed that slavery "leads bad men to inhumanity, injustice, & oppression, & is beneath the benevolence of the Christian Religion, & that freedom & liberty in Civil Government, which men greatly desire."[32]

Alison's successor at First Presbyterian, the Rev. John Ewing, owned no slaves and so provided a less ambiguous example to his congregation. City Presbyterians were slower than Episcopalians to manumit, but when they chose to do so they were much less likely to require additional service or payment from adult blacks. Robert Knox of Southwark in his 1784 will directed his man Harry to serve the widow for six months after his death, a comparatively short term in the 1780s and 1790s, and gave Harry £50 for past services. Presbyterian leader Charles Pettit in 1781 freed Daniel Gilmore whom he had only recently purchased at a public sale in Trenton, and in fact may have bought him in order to bring about his release. Gilmore had been on

3-254

I do hereby certify that the bearer William Grubber formerly my servant, has been duly emancipated according to law in Pennsylvania. — whilest he lived with me, he was sober, honest, and faithful. He leaves me with the affections, and best wishes of every member of my family; and I do hereby recommend him to the protection, and friendship of all persons who love integrity; and goodness of heart in their humble, as well as in their more distinguished forms. ——

Benj'n Rush. M.D.
Professor of Medicine
in the University
of Pennsylvania.

Philadelphia
18th May 1793.

Certificate of freedom provided by Benjamin Rush for his slave William Grubber. In 1788, Rush had signed a manumission pledging Grubber his liberty after six years additional service. Courtesy of The Pennsylvania Abolition Society Papers, Historical Society of Pennsylvania.

board a British vessel taken as a prize and condemned by the New Jersey
Court of Admiralty.[33] Attorney Jared Ingersoll freed Hamlet without condition
in 1784, and two years later, Ingersoll, William Bradford, Jr., and Charles
Pettit, as executors for Joseph Reed, freed his slave Thomas Henderson in
accordance with Reed's wishes. Penelope Hailey, who in 1786 freed her
woman Amy unconditionally, was the only Philadelphia woman identified as
a Presbyterian to free a slave in the 1780s and 1790s.[34]

The Methodists took a stronger stand against slavery than the Presbyterians.
Francis Asbury, who became the first bishop of the American Methodists,
made a commitment to antislavery as early as 1778. At the Christmas conference in 1784 for organizing the American Methodist church the denomina-
tion laid down policy for requiring all members to free their slaves and for
denying admission to anyone who owned slaves. Fierce opposition in the
South brought a rescinding of the ban a year later, but denominational leaders
continued to speak against the institution. For example, Freeborn Garretson,
who had convinced Richard Allen's master of the sin of slaveholding in 1779,
preached in the city in the same year and in 1793 became the presiding elder
of the Philadelphia Methodist Conference.[35] Mostly composed of families of
lesser wealth, the city's Methodists were never involved heavily in slaveholding, but the few who did hold slaves had released them or otherwise withdrawn from slaveholding by 1790.

Slaveownership among other religious groups in Philadelphia also declined
in the 1780s, with the number of slaveholders among German Reformed,
German Lutherans, Baptists, and Jews falling by over half (Table 5–6). In
1790, as in 1775, all of these groups, with the exception of Jews, comprised a
smaller percentage of slaveholders than their proportion in the city's population warranted. Jewish slaveowners numbered only six in 1790 but they
formed a relatively large segment of the tiny Philadelphia Jewish community.
Though ten Catholics and four German Reformed freed slaves, the surviving
records reveal few actual manumissions for the other groups, so the decline in
slaveholding from 1780 to 1790 appears to have occurred mostly because their
slaves fled or because masters sold their slaves or acquired no new slaves to
replace those who died.

In the 1790s slaveholding dropped precipitiously among all religious
groups still involved in the practice. Eighty-four percent of the city's owners
in 1790 had divested themselves of slaves by 1800. At the turn of the century
Episcopalians were still the largest group of owners identified by religion, but
they numbered only eight.

In Chester County and elsewhere in rural Pennsylvania, as in Philadelphia,
Quakers eradicated slaveholding among their membership by the early 1780s,

well before other churches. Fifty-two Chester County Friends signed manumissions during the years from 1766 to 1779 and seven more took that step
by 1784. At least one but probably few others still held slaves for life after that
year (Table 5–8). Episcopalians (including Swedish Lutherans) and Presbyterians were the other major slaveholding groups in the county. Both trailed
the Quakers in freeing slaves, with the majority of Episcopalians divesting
from slavery in the 1780s and most Presbyterians holding out until the 1790s.

Generally resisting the antislavery impulse through the war years, Chester
County Episcopalians underwent a marked change in the 1780s. In 1780, over
one-third of slaveowners whose religion is known were Episcopalian, but ten
years later all but seven of these forty-one masters and mistresses had given up
their slaves (Table 5–8). Few Chester County Episcopalians left formal manumissions, however; most gave up slaveholding during the 1780s by sale, by
not replacing slaves who died or fled, and perhaps by informal release. We
have found manumissions for only eleven of the Episcopalians who withdrew
from slaveholding during the 1780s, and four of them freed blacks in 1780 in a
decidedly lukewarm manner: they were among nine Chester County owners
who registered twelve blacks for terms of service shorter than slavery for
life.[36] Whether these cases can be considered manumissions, effectuated ironically by means of an instrument designed to perpetuate slavery, or whether
the blacks involved had been freed previously (or even born free) and their

TABLE 5–8. Religion, Slaveholding, and Manumission in Chester County,*
1780–1800

	Slaveowners 1780	*Manumitters** 1780–90*	*Slaveowners 1790*	*Manumitters 1791–1800*	*Slaveowners 1800 (Census)*
Quaker	3	7	0	1	0
Ex-Quaker	19	5	9	3	4
Episcopalian	41	11	7	1	3
Presbyterian	43	2	36	6	12
Baptist	7	0	5	0	0
Rom. Catholic	2	0	1	0	0
Unknown***	86	6	55	7	21
TOTAL	201	31	113	18	40
NON-QUAKERS	198	24	113	17	40

*Includes Delaware County after 1789.

**Manumitters are counted only the first time they freed a slave.

***In many cases, these slaveholders were affiliated with no church.

Sources: Chester Co. Slave Register, 1780; U.S. Bureau of the Census, *Heads of Families*, 59–75,
98–104; manumissions; church records; U.S., manuscript census, 1800.

masters were attempting to ensure that they would serve out their terms of indentured servitude, is unclear. At best they were half-hearted manumissions, for though they set a date for freedom, they all entailed additional service.

All but one of the Chester County Episcopalians who manumitted slaves in the 1780s and 1790s entailed freedom with additional service or payments. The Rev. George Craig, longtime minister of St. Paul's Church in Chester and St. Martin's Church in Marcus Hook, freed his woman Phoebe and her daughter Amy in his 1782 will but required Phoebe to pay his executors £75. He freed his man Tom immediately upon his death, but his black boy Phil and mulatto boy Jack would be bound out to learn trades if it could be done without a fee, otherwise to learn husbandry until age 21 and then be hired out for the benefit of Craig's estate for seven years. Lewis Gronow, a Tredyffrin farmer, in 1782 freed his man York six months after his death and provided for his support in case of sickness or misfortune. He freed two mulatto boys, Aaron and Moses, at age 25, and directed that their brother Simon, the property of Gronow's stepmother Isabel Gronow until her death, should also be freed when she died. Apparently the three boys were sons of Phillis, a "mulatto wench" who had been freed by Lewis's father John in 1776 and was now living with the son. Isabel Gronow confirmed Simon's liberty in her 1788 will and gave him a colt, two sheep, and all wages due for his labor then in the hands of John Brown and Peter Bones. Williamina Moore of Moore Hall in Charlestown was the widow of William Moore, esquire, who in registering ten slaves in 1780 had been one of the county's largest slaveowners. Mrs. Moore freed three mulatto slaves in her 1784 will and mandated that Harry, a boy, should be educated and freed at age 28 or earlier at the discretion of Moore's executrix, her daughter Williamina Bond.[37]

Most Chester County Presbyterian slaveholders remained adamant in their resistance to abolition through the 1780s. Despite the leadership of Philadelphia Presbyterians in securing the gradual abolition act in 1780 and the withdrawal from slaveholding by many of their co-religionists in the city, few of the county's Presbyterians would budge. Between 1780 and 1790, slaveholding declined among Chester County Presbyterians by only one-sixth, as opposed to 83 percent among Episcopalians and 53 percent among ex-Quakers (Table 5–8). Of slaveholders on both the 1790 and 1800 federal censuses for whom religion is known, about 62 percent were Presbyterian.

While it is difficult to pin down the reasons why Chester County Presbyterians responded to abolitionism later than co-religionists in the city, it is significant that these two groups belonged to different presbyteries within the Synod of New-York and Philadelphia. The elders and ministers of most

Chester County Presbyterian churches belonged to the New Castle Presbytery, which gathered church leaders from Delaware, northern Maryland, and Chester and Lancaster counties in Pennsylvania. Therefore, influential Chester County Presbyterians lacked frequent contact with fellow divines in the city like Francis Alison, who pondered deeply the righteousness of slavery, and John Ewing, his successor, who apparently never owned slaves. Instead, the Chester County Presbyterians met with their neighbors to the south and west and developed little concern about the morality of holding slaves. In 1790, ministers James Anderson of Middletown church, John E. Finley of Fagg's Manor, and Alexander Mitchell of Upper Octorara still owned slaves. The Rev. John Carmichael of Brandywine Manor, who died in 1785, had owned a black female in 1774 and his widow was listed in 1790 as a slaveowner. All were pastors of congregations belonging to the New Castle Presbytery. In fact, only two of the Chester County ministers of this presbytery did not own slaves at this late date. Thus, congregations had little encouragement to manumit their slaves. Before 1790 it is unlikely that spiritual guidance included exposition of biblical passages to suggest that slavery was wrong or visits to families to nudge slaveholders toward manumission: the clerics, like many of their congregants, held on to their slaves. In contrast, a minister of the one Presbyterian church in Chester County that belonged to the Philadelphia Presbytery distanced himself from slavery much earlier. The Rev. John Simonton of Great Valley Presbyterian Church had owned two taxable slaves in 1774—a man and a woman—but he had none to register in 1780.[38]

The synod's 1787 resolution, which supported gradual abolition of slavery, apparently made Chester County Presbyterians uncomfortable, encouraging them to move away from slavery during the 1790s. Presbyterian slaveholders declined from thirty-six in 1790 to twelve in 1800, and we know of no ministers who still owned slaves at the turn of the century (Table 5–8). As we have identified only six Presbyterians who manumitted blacks by will or by deed in the 1790s, including James Boyd, who had consistently resisted abolition in the Assembly, it is clear that divestment from slavery among Chester County Presbyterians hardly entailed ardent abolitionism. The decade did, however, bring considerable change within this group.

In the 1780s, abolitionism penetrated the armor of urban slaveowners much more successfully than that of Chester County masters. Thirty-eight percent of non-Quaker Philadelphians who held slaves in 1780 freed them during the 1780s; only 12 percent of the equivalent group in Chester County did so. City residents experienced more pressure to manumit and had greater access to the means. Anthony Benezet, John Pemberton, Thomas Harrison, and other PAS members approached owners to free their slaves and helped blacks raise funds to purchase themselves. In the 1780s, 86 percent of non-Quaker Philadelphia manumissions were issued through the PAS or Friends meetings and only 16 percent by will. In contrast, only 22 percent of Chester County slaves released by non-Friends were emancipated under auspices of the Friends meetings and 57 percent were freed by will.

Philadelphia manumitters, in the decade following 1780, were also more likely to free blacks without conditions than Chester County emancipators. Only one-fifth of adult slaves freed by city slaveowners during the years from 1780 to 1790 had to serve additional terms or make payments, but one-half of Chester County freed men and women faced such conditions during that decade. Of the sixteen Philadelphia manumitters who placed restrictions on the freedom of adult blacks, ten were Episcopalian, one was German Reformed, one was Catholic, and four had no identifiable religion. In the country, over three-fourths of Episcopalian, Presbyterian, ex-Quaker, and manumitters unidentified by religion placed restraints on the freedom of one or more of their adult slaves. Furthermore, non-Quaker manumitters in Chester County in the 1780s expected their slaves to serve longer terms of service than Philadelphia emancipators. While only 27 percent of males and 40 percent of females released by these rural masters were under age 26 at the time they received actual freedom, 60 percent of blacks freed in the city were age 25 and below (Table 5–9). On all counts, then, Chester County non-Quaker slaveholders lagged behind their urban counterparts in the 1780s. They were less likely to free slaves, and when they did free them, they more often waited until their deaths and entailed the blacks with additional service or payments.

In the 1790s, comparison of the numbers of Philadelphia and Chester County slaveholders becomes more difficult because many of the urban manumitters, like John Beale Bordley, were new arrivals who declared their intentions to reside in the city and then were forced within six months to release their slaves outright or manumit and immediately indenture them.[39] In the final decade of the century, 146 city masters and 18 Chester County owners freed slaves (Tables 5–6, 5–8). Rural manumitters continued to release by will more frequently than emancipators in Philadelphia, but the proportion in both places dropped significantly from the 1780s. During 1791–1800 the PAS handled almost all city manumissions; in Chester County two-fifths of manumissions were testamentary, another two-fifths were by deed, and the rest were through Quaker meetings. The Philadelphia manumitters of the 1790s, mostly new arrivals to the city, were a different breed from those of the 1780s. They made sure that they would obtain years of additional service from their blacks. In the 1790s, 67 percent of male slaves and 76 percent of females

TABLE 5–9. Age at Freedom of Blacks Manumitted
by Non-Quakers, 1780–1800

Age (Yrs.)	PHILADELPHIA			
	1780–90		1791–1800	
	Males	Females	Males	Females
1–17	17 (33%)	17 (35%)	5 (8%)	2 (4%)
18–19	2 (4)	8 (17)	1 (2)	1 (2)
20–22	9 (17)	2 (4)	7 (12)	4 (8)
23–25	3 (6)	2 (4)	6 (11)	5 (10)
26–29	7 (14)	6 (13)	28 (49)	20 (40)
30–34	8 (16)	2 (4)	6 (11)	7 (14)
35–39	2 (4)	5 (11)	1 (2)	6 (12)
40–49	3 (6)	2 (4)	2 (3)	3 (6)
50+	0	4 (8)	1 (2)	2 (4)
TOTAL	51 (100)	48 (100)	57 (100)	50 (100)
	CHESTER COUNTY			
1–17	0	0	0	0
18–19	0	1 (10%)	0	0
20–22	3 (20%)	2 (20)	1 (20%)	1 (20%)
23–25	1 (7)	1 (10)	1 (20)	1 (20)
26–29	3 (20)	2 (20)	3 (60)	2 (40)
30–34	5 (33)	3 (30)	0	0
35–39	2 (13)	1 (10)	0	1 (10)
40–49	0	0	0	0
50+	1 (7)	0	0	0
TOTAL	15 (100)	10 (100)	5 (100)	5 (100)

Note: Includes only blacks whose ages are known.

Source: Manumissions.

received freedom only at age 26 or above. Whereas only one-fifth of adult
blacks freed in the city in the 1780s had conditions placed on their freedom,
65 percent of men and women manumitted in the 1790s had to continue to
serve their masters for a certain number of years or pay for their freedom. As
we shall see in the next chapter, slaveowners forced to free their blacks used
the system of indenture to wrest labor from the African-Americans for the
greater part of their productive lives. As slavery disintegrated in both city and
country, the distinction the Assembly had made between slaves born before

1780 and their children born after that date disappeared. Some masters touched by antislavery sentiment nevertheless burdened their bondsmen and women with years of servitude, and new residents required by law to emancipate their slaves took advantage of a legal code that allowed them to exploit the labor of the blacks for long terms. City manumitters in the 1790s also tended to delay freedom for black women longer than for men, as 22 percent of females, but only 7 percent of males, were freed at age 35 or above (Table 5–9). These owners either valued the women's labor or planned to obtain the service to age 28 of any children they might bear. Chester County slaveowners also tended to hold on to women of childbearing age and to release slaves only after they had served past their mid-20s. In the 1780s and 1790s they freed nineteen men but only twelve women, when according to the 1800 county septennial census, 25 men and 32 women were still in bonds.[40]

As we evaluate the contributions of various groups of people to the dismantling of slavery in Pennsylvania it becomes clear that the situation was much more complicated than the simple outpouring of abolitionist sentiment. In the aftermath of the passage of the gradual abolition act, slaveholding declined in both Philadelphia and the hinterland, but in both places only a minority of owners recognized that perpetual bondage was wrong. Indeed in Philadelphia in the 1780s the number of escapes by slaves nearly matched manumissions; city slaves, deeply disappointed by the 1780 legislation that kept them in bondage, demonstrated their outrage and "stole themselves."[41] Owners certainly heard the pleas of their slaves but weighed a number of considerations in deciding whether to manumit. In Philadelphia, artisans and mariners, with limited resources, more often sold slaves (or lost them by flight) than freed them. Wealthier city dwellers—merchants, officials, gentlemen, and affluent widows—often wanted to keep retinues of slaves but could also afford the loss of assets that accompanied emancipation. In Chester County, where residents had invested recently in slaves, manumissions came more sporadically and slowly. Scots-Irish Presbyterians from the western part of the county were especially reluctant to release their slaves.

The misfortune of the transition from slavery to freedom in Pennsylvania was that the decision to manumit, made so grudgingly by many owners, had such limited practical benefits for slaves. The law requiring black Pennsylvanians born after March 1780 to serve until age 28 set the standard by which owners retained the labor of freed blacks through the prime of their lives.

6

After Freedom

The manumitting sentiment that overtook many, albeit a minority, of Pennsylvania's slaveholders in the 1780s and 1790s led to the release from bondage of hundreds of slaves. The desire of slaveholders to be quit of the system of bondage, however, did not mean that their need for cheap labor and a flexible system for obtaining it had diminished. In an expanding late eighteenth-century economy, both rural and urban Pennsylvanians sought a dependable, convenient, and inexpensive labor force—always the goal of employers.

This compelling desire for cheap labor reshaped the lives of former slaves in much less satisfying ways than they might have anticipated. Both masters and slaves regarded emancipation as a significant event. Masters could imagine themselves as contributing to the elimination of the new nation's most noxious cancer. Blacks could enjoy immediate freedom or look forward to a specific date when they would be free, and they knew that their children would not be born into slavery. But no matter how emotionally fulfilling, on the practical level liberty held less for Pennsylvania's African-Americans than they might have wished. Ex-slaves who remained in the state after manumission and those who migrated into the region during the early decades of the Republic almost always took places on the bottom rung of society, with no land and little personal property or security. Most of them, especially in rural areas, remained there throughout their lifetimes. Indeed, as Pennsylvanians learned that they could retain access to the labor of their former chattel, masters quickly reaped the psychic benefits of manumission with little financial penalty. Many blacks remained in a state of semi-freedom well into the nineteenth century as white employers learned how to manipulate the labor market in the era of manumission and work the laws governing servitude to their advantage.

In understanding how freedom came only by degrees, it is important to keep in mind the long-range changes occurring in the labor system over the course of the eighteenth century. Before 1750, both rural and urban producers with capital to spare and need for full-time laborers invested in European indentured servants and African slaves. Philadelphians, with greater wealth, better access to the auction block and West Indian suppliers, and perhaps fewer scruples against slavery, purchased blacks more frequently than their rural counterparts, who relied more heavily on white indentured servants. After the Seven Years' War, and after passage of the stiff import duty on slaves in 1761, slavery declined quickly in Philadelphia; but it persisted among wealthy farmers and entrepreneurs in Chester County and other parts of rural Pennsylvania even after enactment of the gradual abolition act of 1780 mandated its eventual demise.

In the second half of the eighteenth century, employers began to appreciate the advantages of wage laborers or other laborers who did not need to be provided for after their physical resources dwindled. The severe recession following the Seven Years' War and the economic chaos of the Revolutionary period taught the lesson that labor procurable in smaller packages was often preferable to extended or lifetime bound labor.[1] Increasing the appreciation of employers for the more flexible wage labor system was the presence of a growing pool of free laborers. This growing supply had much to do with the escalation of real estate prices, both in rural and urban areas, which made it more difficult than earlier for native sons and daughters, new immigrants, and servants who had finished their terms to set up their own shops or farms. After mid-century, merchants, craftspeople, innkeepers, ironmasters, millowners, and large farmers could draw on increasing numbers of free workers to hire by the year, month, week, day, or task. Or, they came to realize that they could depend on young black laborers who had been signed to indentures binding them into their late twenties. Many black Pennsylvanians released during the late eighteenth century entered this labor pool, as did thousands of black migrants who arrived around the turn of the century from Maryland, Delaware, and states further south. But they often entered under harsh conditions that must have made freedom seem like a mirage. We now look at how slaves, once freed, were fitted back into the labor force in the early Republic first in Philadelphia and then in rural Chester County.

this may Certifie To all parsons To whom it may Concern that Negro James Griffen is a Free man and has Liberty To pass or To Repass as a Free man through any County or State and has this Day made application for a pass To Travel unto Philadelphia on horse back and this may Certifie that the Baiver James — Griffen has Liberty as a Free man with his Creature Bridle and Saddle To pass from Sussex County through any other County or State and has Liberty To act and perseed in Every manner of Busyness as Fare as is Lawful as he may Chuse or think proper To undirtake To Doe this To any Gentilman To whom it may Concern from ——— Isaac Moore

Tifts Ellenor Moore ——— May 21 Day 1793

Certificate of freedom provided by a Delaware master for James Griffen, who was headed for Philadelphia. Unlike many ostensibly free individuals who arrived in the city with long indentures, Griffen had received an outright release. Courtesy of The Pennsylvania Abolition Society Papers, Historical Society of Pennsylvania.

African-Americans who entered the Philadelphia labor market between 1790 and 1820 faced many barriers to success. Some were beset by physical problems resulting from harsh treatment under slavery. More were accustomed primarily to rural work routines and lacked urban skills. And all had to cope with increasing immigration (though interrupted from 1807 to 1815 by the Jeffersonian embargo and the War of 1812) that pitted them against Irish, English, and German immigrants, especially the Irish, in the competition for jobs at the lower levels of the occupational hierarchy.

Thousands of free African-Americans had to fit themselves into niches in the urban economy in the early national period. In 1790, when federal census takers first enumerated the nation's population, 1,849 free blacks—4 percent of the population—lived in the city (Table 1–4). The rapid influx of newcomers more than tripled that number in the next ten years—to 6,028. In the early nineteenth century the influx of newcomers tailed off; but census takers counted 8,942 free blacks in Philadelphia in 1810 and 12,110 a decade later—about 10 percent of the population.

Most of these African-American urban dwellers took their places at the bottom of the job hierarchy as common laborers—stevedoring on the city's busy docks; digging graves, wells, and house foundations; and toiling as chimneysweeps, ashmen, porters, waiters, bootblacks, and, in the case of women, clothes washers. Many young men, perhaps as many as one of every four, made their living at sea for at least a few years.[2]

Despite the obstacles to advancement, a sizable number of free blacks, probably one of every ten, found a way to climb the ladder of material success at least a rung or two.[3] A few ascended the ladder so impressively that even ambitious white Philadelphians might have envied them—and in fact resentment of successful blacks became an ingredient of rising white hostility by the 1820s.[4] For several reasons, the city offered many more opportunities than the country for aspiring former slaves. First, the range of occupations was much wider, and many free blacks who had acquired artisan skills as slaves found master craftsmen who valued their industry and would give them employment. Such a man was Moses Williams, whom Charles Willson Peale hired as his first silhouette cutter and general assistant when the latter opened his museum in 1786. Second, as the black community grew, its residents willingly supported black carpenters, tailors, shoemakers, bakers, teachers, and many others who provided services and crafted articles. This allowed people like Eleanor Harris, an African-born former slave, to become a "well-qualified tutoress of children" in Philadelphia in the 1790s. By 1810, at least a dozen black teachers and clergymen served Philadelphia's African-Ameri-

Portrait of the Rev. Richard Allen (1813), founder of the African Methodist Episcopal Church. Freed in 1780 by his Delaware master, Allen was a prominent abolitionist and advocate for black Philadelphians. Courtesy of The Library Company of Philadelphia.

cans, and by 1816 the community even had need of a black fencing master.[5]
Third, by dint of its concentrated population, the urban milieu provided
opportunities for black entrepreneurship, usually on a small scale.

Only the most talented and persistent could take advantage of these opportunities; but men like James Forten, who took over the thriving sailmaking
business of Robert Bridges, for whom he had worked for twelve years,
achieved a degree of success almost unthinkable in rural areas. By 1807,
Forten had a racially mixed crew of thirty men at work in his sail lofts that
turned out precisely cut sails for many of Philadelphia's largest sailing ships.
Only a few entrepreneurs matched Forten's scale of operations—the food
caterer Robert Bogle and his competitors, the former Santo Dominguan slaves
John Baptiste and Peter Augustine, the beer bottler Robert Montier, and the
fabulous musician Francis (Frank) Johnson, described in 1819 as "leader of
the band at all balls, public and private; sole director of all serenades . . .
inventor-general of cotillions.[6] Further down the entrepreneurial scale were
people such as the fruitseller Robert Gray; carters such as John Volair and John
Hageman; the many oystermen whose vending carts and charcoal heaters were
familiar sights on Philadelphia's street-corners; and the master chimneysweeps
whose young apprentices called out their trade throughout the city. Ranged as
they were along a spectrum of wealth and occupations, the self-employed free
black artisans, shopkeepers, proprietors, and professionals had one thing in
common: a largely autonomous existence that allowed them the maneuvering
room to make decisions about their work schedule and the way they conducted
their businesses, large and small.[7]

It is difficult to say how many former slaves in Philadelphia achieved at
least modest material success in the early nineteenth century. A sense of
proportion can be gained, however, from the fact that by 1820 about one
of every nine black heads of household owned real property. If this rate of
property ownership compared poorly with the white population in general, it
was probably only slightly lower than among what is a more realistic comparison group—recently arrived immigrants from impoverished backgrounds.[8]

For many more black Philadelphians, the reality of urban life was anything
but bright. The almshouse records, which have survived almost intact for the
half-century after 1790, spell out the details on hundreds of sick, disabled,
hungry, and homeless sojourners who made their way to the city's largest
building to seek medical aid, find shelter from bitter weather, give birth, find
refuge for a child they could not support, or simply to die with the prospect of a
decent burial. Their numbers were very small, however, in two almshouse
censuses in the early nineteenth century—54 in 1806 and 55 in 1810 among a

black population of about 8000–9500 in the city. In fact, in proportion to their population, black Philadelphians passed through the almshouse doors less frequently than German and Irish immigrants.[9] The number of black inmates at the almshouse would grow in the second quarter of the nineteenth century, although the extensive system of mutual aid societies established by black men and women provided an alternative means of dealing with the unfortunate.[10]

Part of the relative success of urban African-Americans in avoiding the almshouse and the extremities of poverty may relate to the extensive number who remained indentured into their late twenties and the large number of others who, while free of indentures, remained within white households where their opportunities were severely restricted but shelter, food, and clothing were assured. In 1790, half of the city's free blacks lived in white households and ten years later census takers counted 56 percent of the black population working and residing with white families.[11] What proportion of these was indentured and what proportion free domestic servants is impossible to ascertain; but the indenturing books of the PAS show a sharp decline of indentures in the early nineteenth century (Table 6–1). By 1820, almost all slaves had been manumitted and most of the children born to slaves after 1780 had completed their long indentures.

This decline of indenturing and the completion of most indentures also account for the sharp decrease in the early nineteenth century of the percentage of Philadelphia's African-Americans who lived in white households—from 56 percent in 1800 to 30 percent in 1810 and 27 percent in 1820. By the last year, two-thirds of the African-Americans living in white households were female, undoubtedly doing domestic labor for the most part. Many blacks in the city had signed indentures as a condition of their emancipation, and many more found that living in a white household was the best waystation to an autonomous existence. But gradually, most of them worked their way clear of this dependency, establishing households of their own.

The situation of black Philadelphians who moved from perpetual servitude to limited servitude under indentures is worthy of careful consideration. Such a system had a triple utility. First, it provided compensation to slaveowners for whom slaveholding had become either morally repugnant or economically disadvantageous. Second, it was the labor system by which white slavemasters quitting the business of compelled labor recaptured the labor power of the region's slaves. Third, it was the intermediate station that thousands of blacks on the road to freedom occupied, some willingly and some reluctantly, for many of their most productive years.

In creating a twilight zone between slavery and freedom, Pennsylvanians gave new life to the old but decaying institution of white indentured servitude

TABLE 6–1. Indentures of Free Blacks in Philadelphia, 1778–1820

| | INDENTURES | | | | INDENTURES | | |
YEAR	Male	Female	Total	YEAR	Male	Female	Total
1778	2	0	2	1800	191	67	258
1779	1	2	3	1801	71	59	130
1780	2	3	5	1802	23	28	51
1781	0	2	2	1803	25	32	57
1782	10	8	18	1804	44	40	84
1783	9	16	25	1805	25	15	40
1784	14	18	32	1806	26	20	46
1785	24	16	40	1807	34	16	50
1786	17	9	26	1808	32	26	58
1787	14	7	21	1809	23	12	35
1788	14	6	20	1810	27	27	54
1789	10	9	19	1811	37	20	57
1790	13	11	24	1812	25	18	43
1791	15	12	27	1813	21	24	45
1792	59	48	107	1814	24	26	50
1793	67	65	132	1815	23	26	49
1794	161	144	305	1816	26	29	55
1795	149	131	280	1817	21	15	36
1796	128	104	232	1818	11	5	16
1797	77	93	170	1819	5	10	15
1798	67	58	125	1820	4	2	6
1799	56	47	103	Total	1627	1326	2953

Source: PAS Papers Indenture Books, Reels 22–23, HSP.

and, in the process, arrived at a new understanding of what constituted free labor. As recently as the mid-eighteenth century, bound servants had constituted as much as a quarter of Philadelphia's labor force, but by the eve of the Revolution they made up no more than 8 percent of those who worked with their hands. By the end of the Revolution, the contribution of indentured labor to the city's economy amounted to less than 7 percent of all workers, and the total number of indentured servants, which had exceeded 2000 in the early 1750s, had fallen to fewer than 400.[12] Then, in the late 1780s, the number of indentured servants, a majority of them black, began to rise sharply, probably reaching about 2000 by the end of the century. Thus the early stages of the manumission movement also spurred a revival, at least for a few decades, of the indenturing system that had been declining rapidly in the late colonial era and had virtually ceased to function during the Revolution. The first historian of Pennsylvania's black population, writing nearly eighty years ago, took note of this condition of half-freedom under which thousands of blacks released from slavery after the Revolution spent much or all of their lives. "There was no instantaneous creation of a great body of freedmen," wrote Edward Turner. Rather there was a "slow rise" from "complete servitude to complete freedom" and during this transition blacks were "compelled to halt for long periods on [the] way up."[13]

In reviving the indentured labor system with much longer terms of service, Pennsylvanians retained some of the odious characteristics of slavery. Just as a slaveowner's property rights in slaves allowed him or her to sell a bondsman or bondswoman at will, the masters and mistresses of indentured laborers could dispose of their servants at their whim. The Philadelphia newspapers give evidence of the lively market in what became units of labor, regularly carrying advertisements for servants—black, mulatto, white, Indian, East Indian, German, Irish, Dutch, Welsh, Scots, Portuguese, and English. A large number of the advertisements offered children, sometimes as young as four years— testimony to the fact that hundreds of black children grew up without their parents in the households of one, two, three, or more white masters or mistresses.

An 1813 advertisement, placed by a Philadelphia firm in a Chester County newspaper, reveals how the tentacles of the market in bound labor extended from city to country. Baker's General Intelligence Office, on Fourth Street between Chestnut and Walnut, offered for sale thirteen black servants, of whom seven would serve to age 28 or longer. One was "an excellent house girl, a mullatto, 20 years old and 8 [years] to serve, from Wilmington, [Delaware], a washer, ironer, seamstress, and child's maid, good tempered, &c." Baker's also offered to bind "White Girls, 14, 11, 10, 8, 6, 5 and 4; White Boys, 16, 14, 13, 12, 11, 10, 8, 7, 5 and 4; Black Girls, 9, 7 and 4; Black Boys, 12, 11, 10 and 6."[14]

Masters were anything but sentimental in disposing of unsatisfactory servants, but servants could sometimes make this work to their advantage. Understanding the brisk market for unexpired indentures, servants who detested their masters could malinger or work poorly in order to encourage their own sale. William Cobbett, the English journalist whose venomous pen brought almost daily drama to his brief career as a Federalist writer in Philadelphia, withheld none of his contempt for his 16-year-old servant, whom he described in a runaway advertisement as having a face "constantly well besmeared; his eyes are gray, and have a Jewish leer; his mouth is a good deal sunk, the corners beautified with tobacco juice, and the inside with a set of teeth bearing, in colour, an infinite resemblance to corruption issuing from a stale wound."[15]

This commoditized character of indentured labor had always existed in the American colonies and had always been resisted by large numbers of servants who fled severe masters. But the extension of the bound labor contract to age 28 and the consequent susceptibility of black men and women to sale, exchange, or lease for a decade of their adult lives blurred the line between slave and indentured labor, a line that had been more distinct when servitude was usually limited to seven years and usually did not last beyond age 21.

While the contrast between indentured and slave labor diminished, the distinction between indentured and free wage-labor grew sharper because of the broad redefinition of the labor relation in the first third of the nineteenth century. At the heart of this redefinition was the growing idea that an employer could control the property in a hired laborer only so long as the employee chose to remain in the contractual relationship. A part of the new more egalitarian paradigm of the post-Revolutionary period, this concept stripped employers of coercive rights, including that of forcing a laborer to complete a contract if the hired person, for whatever reason, found the bargain no longer to his or her liking. Thus labor came to be thought of as involuntary, or unfree, in any situation where a laborer could not repossess the property in his or her labor. In essence, the situation of free labor was becoming freer in the very era when indentured servitude, the lot of thousands of blacks emerging from slavery, had been extended so as to become more like a limited form of slavery.[16] The increasing association of indentured labor with black Americans made the very idea of an indenture offensive to whites. "No person," averred the Pennsylvania Supreme Court in 1812, "to whom wages could be due for his services, would endure the name [of indentured servant], as it would be considered offensive and a term of reproach."[17]

In the late eighteenth century, Philadelphia became not only a virtually slave-free city but also a city whose thriving commerce included a lively traffic in men, women, and especially children who were released from slavery but were not yet free. Hundreds of slaveowners in the broad region for which Philadelphia served as the commercial center, encompassing southern New Jersey, Delaware, the northern Chesapeake, and the eastern counties of Pennsylvania, liberated their slaves and sent them to the Delaware port under indenture.[18] From one point of view, this confirms the image of Philadelphia as a center of humanitarianism. But the role of the city in attracting newly freed blacks, as the indenture books maintained by the PAS indicate, had much to do with a mutually advantageous contract between urban producers who needed cheap and closely supervised labor and slavemasters in Philadelphia's trading orbit who wished to receive compensation for their slaves in an era when slaveholding was for many becoming both economically disadvantageous and unconscionable. A report to the state Senate stated that Pennsylvania residents would pay "about half the usual price of a slave" in the South "for this limited assignment."[19] A country slaveowner would agree to free a slave while simultaneously indenturing him or her to an urban employer, who would pay a considerable sum for a ten- or twelve-year-old indentured servant whose term of service ran until his or her twenty-eighth birthday.

The indenturing of manumitted slaves began slowly in the last years of the Revolution in Philadelphia. Fifty-five blacks were indentured by the almshouse managers or under the auspices of the Abolition Society from 1778 to 1783. The almshouse managers directed a steady stream of black children into white homes, including some as young as the two-year-old Eleanor, assigned to grocer John Dorsey to serve for twenty-two years.[20] For the remainder of the 1780s, another 158 blacks were bound to long-term labor contracts (Table 6–1).

In indenturing manumitted slave children, slaveowners were following a well-established precedent. Binding out the children of indigent parents was a common expedient on both sides of the Atlantic for holding down the cost of poor relief and teaching the offspring of the laboring poor the habits of industry and morality. To be reared in a respectable home of a merchant, master artisan, or doctor, where the child would be taught to read and write and trained up to a skill (housewifery in the case of almost all girls), was in theory a benefit to a child born into an impoverished family. Those who accepted such children into their families provided room, board, and moral guardianship in exchange for extended labor by a young person in the adolescent and early adulthood years.

While following an ancient precedent, the process of indenturing freed slaves contained one new and vitally important feature. Whereas imported indentured servants served a term that rarely exceeded seven years and averaged four years, manumitted slaves were usually indentured as a condition of their release to age 28.[21] Aside from the obvious economic advantage of this innovation, its rationale seems to have come from the 1780 gradual abolition law that specified that children born to slaves after March 1, 1780, should serve their mother's owner for 28 years. For those inclined to liberate children born into slavery *before* the law was passed, or to give freedom to young adults, no less a term of service must have seemed justifiable. Moreover, the Philadelphia overseers of the poor, shortly after the 1780 law was passed, began binding out the children of black paupers to age 28, further establishing this as the norm. The law had always allowed the overseers and the almshouse managers in Philadelphia to bind out the children of poor white parents until they reached their majority—18 years of age for girls and 21 for boys. But the 1780 law seems to have given them the precedent for extending the service of black children far beyond that of their white counterparts.[22]

Not everyone who manumitted slaves took advantage of the new extended labor contracts that were possible. When releasing their slaves, almost all Quakers followed the practice prescribed by Philadelphia Yearly Meeting of indenturing the children of these bondspersons only to age 18 if female and age 21 if male, thus making no distinction between black and white indentures. But most others wanted to maximize their profit in the labor of those whom they indentured after releasing from slavery. For example, in making a decision to free a young girl of fifteen while binding her as a house servant to age 28 rather than age 18, a master could increase the productive labor that could be extracted under such an indenture from three to thirteen years. Moreover, if he wished to sell her services to a neighbor, this extension of her obligation could greatly increase the price her indenture could command. If it were a 14-year-old boy, who if white would have been released at age 21, the manumitting master would be able to double the years of the indenture—from seven to fourteen. The PAS recorded 208 indentures of blacks in the 1780s, 55 percent of them males. Two-thirds of these indentures bound the African-Americans involved to age 28 and another sixth until age 24 to 26. Although some members of the Abolition Society may not have approved of this practice, they acceded to it in many of the indentures that they arranged.[23]

As slavery broke up in Pennsylvania, the practice of indenturing blacks to long terms of service created a substitute form of labor that in some ways was more efficient than perpetual servitude. Black children could be indentured at eight or ten, or even earlier, and their labor put at the disposal of the master for several decades. The master received the services of young black men and women during much of their most physically productive years and was relieved of supporting such persons, as under slavery, after their physical resources dwindled. Many laboring people did not live to see their thirtieth birthday and physical depletion among laboring people often began in their thirties.[24] Therefore, much of the labor value of a young black could be extracted at a reasonable cost under an indenture system that did not release men and women until age 28.[25]

From one perspective, slaveowners could rationalize the long-term indenture as a form of apprenticeship that trained black youths for employment and citizenship; yet it differed enormously from that ancient institution, which usually extended to the eighteenth year for females and the twenty-first year for males, in taking labor without pay for a full ten years beyond the usual end of an apprentice's term for women and seven years for males.[26] For some black parents just emerging from slavery indenturing their children was an option, though not a very desirable one, for making ends meet in the city. By agreeing to bind out their children to white families on long-term indentures, they reduced the demands on their own slender incomes and, in the best cases, obtained at least rudimentary education for their children. The PAS indenture books contain 39 cases from 1778 to 1790 of black parents binding out their children, but in almost every case these parents would only bind their daughters to age 18 and sons to age 21. Some black adults indentured themselves as well, usually for seven years or less. But from another perspective the system was primarily a means of providing cheap labor for white masters. It is difficult to determine the exact cost of indentured labor or to compare it with that of slavery, but one Irish immigrant in the city in 1791 believed that the time of a servant could be purchased for "about the eighth part of the wages they [masters] would have to pay" a native Pennsylvanian.[27]

By the early 1790s, with the number of slaves in the city reduced to a few hundred and in eastern Pennsylvania to about one thousand, labor-hungry Philadelphia masters had soaked up much of the supply of indentured black labor. But then the availability of indentured African-Americans began to grow, if the PAS indenture books are an accurate reflection of these trends.[28] This occurred in part because of a new regional supply of manumitted slaves and in part through an unusual new influx of indenturable blacks from outside the country. From 1792 to 1800 the average number of indentures recorded annually by the PAS increased nearly eightfold from the previous decade— from about 20 to about 190 per year (Table 6–1). Of the 1,712 indentures from 1792 to 1800 recorded by the Abolition Society, 55 percent were male. Only about one-fifth of these 1,712 persons had been slaves in the city. The others were part of a stream of slaves brought or sent to the capital city by arrangement to be released and indented.

A steady traffic in black youths from neighboring New Jersey, Delaware, and Maryland, and a few from more distant points, can be traced in the PAS indenture books. No doubt some masters who were deeply troubled by the morality of slaveholding released their slaves outright or allowed their slaves to buy their freedom if they had the resources to do so, and some of these fortunate persons found their way to Philadelphia. But many more African-Americans who arrived in the Delaware River capital had been released from their bonds as the result of a master's desire to rid himself of slaves but to recapture most or all of his investment.[29] A slaveowner could obtain the fullest compensation by selling slaves to Virginia, Maryland, or further south.

But for slaveowners tinctured with moral doubts about slavery an alternative course of action was to take or send young slaves to Pennsylvania under articles of manumission that specified that the black would be indentured to a merchant, artisan, mariner, or farmer who would pay a price for six, ten, or even as many as twenty-five years of indented labor. Adam King, of Georgetown, Delaware, for example, gave power of attorney to ship captain John Hand, on his way to Philadelphia, to "dispose" of two slaves he was freeing but who were to be sold as indentured servants, a boy until he was 28 and a girl until she was 21 or longer "if the Laws of the State will Admit of it."[30] Thus, eastern Pennsylvania employers filled their labor needs while slaveowners in neighboring states salved their consciences but protected their pocketbooks.

A large part of the sudden rise in indentures in the 1790s was triggered by a completely unexpected expansion of the labor pool caused by black rebellion in St. Dominique. A few French slaveowners had drifted into Pennsylvania before the rebellion erupted in 1791, and they had been obliged to free their slaves by the six-months clause of the 1780 act. But beginning in 1792 shiploads of French Catholic slaveowners poured ashore in the Delaware port. When their pleas for exemption from the 1780 law failed, they had two options. Either they quickly left the state or, to minimize their loss, they freed their slaves just before the six-month limit expired while simultaneously signing them to indentures. From 1791 to 1795, 284 French slaveowning immigrants in Philadelphia freed 442 slaves, and with few exceptions they signed them to extended indentures or sold their indenture to another Philadelphian. The number tapered off rapidly after 1795; 24 French masters freed 30 slaves from 1796 to 1800 and another 26 slaveowners freed 35 slaves from 1801 to 1810.[31]

Most of the black Santo Domingans were apparently willing to sign such indentures because, without resources and language skills, they believed a period of indentured labor was necessary for them to make the transition to the land in which they found themselves. In many cases, the refugees had arrived with only slave children, and they were ordinarily indentured until they reached age 28. For example, Jacques Chauvet freed three slaves—Filette, Simon, and Jaime—in 1795 but the indentures of the three ran, respectively, to 1807, 1808, and 1815. Annette LaChicolle freed five slaves in the same year, but the indentures began on the day after manumission for Marguerite, who was to serve for 10 years, Taine for 12 years, Egle for 14 years, Diguene for 18 years, and Marie for 10 years. John Barbarin, arriving in 1794 with twenty-five slaves, lost all the progeny of his female slaves, who were born free in Pennsylvania, but he retained the services of his slaves, released after six months and immediately signed to long-term indentures that extended in the most extreme case until 1822. According to the PAS records, of the 508 French slaves manumitted in the city between 1787 and 1810, only 45 were given outright releases; two others were allowed to purchase their freedom. All the others were signed to indentures, usually for the maximum time allowed by Pennsylvania law.[32]

When the federal census takers made their rounds in 1820, forty years after the gradual abolition act was passed by a radical legislature in the midst of revolution, most of Philadelphia's black citizens had worked their way free of bound labor. One of four blacks (27 percent) still lived in white households, but most of these were single men or women or children, not black families. A single black, usually a woman, lived in more than 60 percent of the white households where the census takers found black Philadelphians.[33] Overwhelmingly, they were domestic servants, as indicated in Table 6–2 which shows that by this time widows and single women, merchants, proprietors, officials, and professionals—the vast majority of them desirous of black labor primarily for domestic service—far outnumbered artisans, mariners, and laborers, who in many cases might have employed black labor for other than domestic skills.

By 1820 the transition to a free-labor force was well advanced after a two-generation pause that had allowed for the recapture of black labor released from perpetual bondage. In Philadelphia, industrialization was well under way, and, after the depression of 1818–22 that momentarily slowed its pace,

TABLE 6–2. Occupation of White Philadelphians
with Black Household Residents

	1783–90	1800	1820
Merchants	24 (25%)	283 (26.5%)	245 (21.1%)
Proprietors	24 (25%)	147 (13.8%)	161 (13.9%)
Professionals	14 (14.6%)	152 (14.2%)	189 (16.3%)
Gentlemen	—	56 (5.2%)	54 (4.7%)
Women	7 (7.3%)	73 (6.8%)	278 (24.0%)
Artisans	17 (17.7%)	241 (22.5%)	159 (13.7%)
Officials	4 (4.2%)	38 (3.6%)	30 (2.6%)
Laborers	2 (2.1%)	20 (1.9%)	9 (0.8%)
Unknown	4 (4.2%)	59 (5.5%)	35 (3.0%)
TOTAL	96	1,069	1,160

Sources: 1783–90—PAS Indenture Books; 1800 and 1820—manuscript federal censuses.

would surge forward rapidly. Black Philadelphians, whose complete emergence from bondage had been retarded by the revived indenture system for two generations after the Revolution, were not welcomed by employers as part of the new factory labor system. Their places as domestic workers and unskilled laborers, except as they were able to operate in carts and entrepreneurial roles within their own emerging black community, had already been worked out.

Over the four decades after 1780, the African-American population grew in the countryside as white farmers quickly appreciated the benefits of exploiting the labor of newly freed slaves. Immediately after the Revolution, at the same time Philadelphia's black population rose phenomenally, the number of blacks in Chester and Delaware counties tripled, increasing from 600 in 1783 to 1,843 in 1800. Their percentage of the population rose from 2.7 percent in 1790 to 4.8 percent in 1810 and to 6.5 percent in 1820 (see Table 1–8). Rural producers, like their city counterparts, eagerly bought up the indentures of blacks freed by masters from outside the state who recognized in the Pennsylvania servant market a way to unburden themselves of the onus of slavekeeping while absorbing little financial loss.

Rural black Pennsylvanians, to an even greater extent than liberated men and women in Philadelphia, found that freedom came only in stages and opportunity was curtailed. Throughout the period to 1820, a higher percentage of rural blacks remained in white households, and in general, life offered fewer rewards to liberated slaves in the countryside than in the city. Chester and Delaware counties had no James Forten, Richard Allen, or Robert Bogle. A few black families acquired farms of as much as 100 acres, but rural society lacked the fissures that allowed ambitious city folk, in the decades immediately following emancipation, to rise toward the top. African-Americans emerged from slavery long past the time when land was easily acquired in eastern Pennsylvania. Like newly arrived European immigrants, blacks with little capital would have to seek their fortunes on the frontier if they aspired to the yeoman ideal of a family-sized farm. But for newly freed blacks, the frontier offered more risk than opportunity. If one left the neighborhood of his or her former owner, or the purview and protection of Friends meetings and the PAS who kept records of manumissions, only a piece of paper, a certificate of freedom that could easily be destroyed or lost, prevented reenslavement.

After freedom the lives of blacks in Chester and Delaware counties remained intertwined with those of whites. In 1790 the proportion of African-Americans living with a white head of household was 58 percent; the percentage rose to two-thirds ten years later, and then dropped to 55 percent in 1810 and to 44 percent in 1820, but remained higher than in Philadelphia, where in 1820, 27 percent of blacks lived in white households.[34] The majority of free blacks listed in rural white households lived with at most one other ex-slave; they were generally live-in domestic servants or farm workers. Some were slaves born before 1780 who were promised freedom at maturity or older. Others were the freeborn children of slaves who owed service until they reached age 28. Joining these country-born servants in large numbers during the late 1780s and 1790s, and in smaller proportions thereafter, were blacks brought in from other states and indentured to Pennsylvania farmers. The PAS coordinated part of this effort, but residents along the southern tier could readily make contacts themselves with slaveowning neighbors in Maryland and Virginia. The trade in black indentured servants continued in rural Pennsylvania through the early nineteenth century, even after the PAS had greatly reduced its participation.

Children and young adults comprised the largest proportion of free blacks in white households, as masters retained the services of nominally freed slaves and their children through their most productive years. As late as 1820, three-quarters of young black men and 58 percent of young women aged 14 to 25 were working in the households of whites. For example, Quakers Cadwalader and Ann Evans of Edgmont freed slave Tobias sometime before 1768, allowed him a house and garden, and permitted his wife Sarah to go to live with him around 1773, several years before she officially received freedom. Their children were also manumitted but several were required to serve the white family until maturity, to age 18 or 20 for the girls and to age 21 for the boy.[35] Walter Hood, a white Oxford Township farmer, in 1790 had four free blacks in his household. They were children born in the 1780s to two young slave women, Sall and Jean, and obligated to serve Hood and his family to age 28. After Hood died in 1792, two of the bound black children remained with their mothers in the service of Hood's heirs, but the others were sold in the vendue of Hood's estate. Mint, the oldest of the children born in "freedom," would not begin to work for herself until 1812.[36]

Rural white households also included blacks who had been slaves elsewhere but had been brought to Pennsylvania, freed, and bound as servants or apprentices with specified terms. The PAS served as the agency for much of this activity. In 1800, for example, the PAS Committee of Guardians drew up indentures for 134 Africans saved from two illegal slave ships by the sloop of war *Ganges*. Appalled by the condition of the victims, in chains, starving, and naked, the PAS and black leaders provided clothing, food, and tents for shelter. Apparently nobody offered to take the Africans back to their home-

THIS INDENTURE witnesseth

THAT *Darrah* Ganges, by and with the consent of ROBERT PATTERSON and THOMAS HARRISON, members of the Pennsylvania Incorporated Society for Promoting the Abolition of Slavery, he being one of those persons captured on board the Phebe, by the sloop of war the Ganges, commanded by John Maloney, Esq. hath put h *er* self and by these Presents, the said *Barrah* Ganges doth voluntary and of h *er* own free will and accord, put h *er* self Apprentice to *Mark Wilcox of Delaware county Paper maker & farmer* to learn the *of housekeeping* Art, Trade and Mystery, and after the manner of an Apprentice to serve him the said *Mark Wilcox* his Heirs and Assigns from the day of the date hereof, for and during, and to the full end and term of *Four* years next ensuing. During all which term the said Apprentice h *er* said Master faithfully shall serve, his secrets keep, his lawful commands every where readily obey. *s* he shall do no damage to h *er* said Master's goods, nor see it to be done by others, without letting or giving notice thereof to h *er* said Master. he shall not waste h *er* said Master's goods, nor lend them unlawfully to any. he shall not commit fornication, nor contract matrimony within the said term. *s* he shall not play at cards, dice, or any other unlawful game, whereby h *er* said Master may have damage. With h *er* own goods nor the goods of others, without licence from h *er* said Master, he shall neither buy nor sell. *s* he shall not absent h *er* self day nor night from h *er* said Master's service without h *is* leave, nor haunt ale-houses, taverns or play-houses ; but in all things behave h *er* self as a faithful apprentice ought to do, during the said term. And the said Master shall us the utmost of h *is* endeavours to teach, or cause to be taught or instructed, the said Apprentice in the trade or Mystery of *Housekeeping* and procure and provide for h *er* sufficient Meat, Drink, Wearing apparel, Lodging and Washing, fitting for an Apprentice, during the said term of *four* years *to Endeavour to Teach her to Read & Write*

and when free, to have two suits of apparel, one whereof to be new.

This Indenture not to be assigned, without the consent of the Committee of Guardians of the Pennsylvania Incorporated Society for the Abolition of Slavery.

And whereas a Bond is this day given by *Mark Wilcox and*

to John Hall Esq. Marshal of the United States for the District of Pennsylvania, in the sum of Four Hundred Dollars, conditioned, that if the suits brought or to be brought by the claimants of the Phebe or her cargo : and the Court should determine that *Darrah* Ganges is a Slave, then, and in that case, he is (if alive) to be surrendered to the said Marshal or to his assigns on demand.

[L. S.]

AND for the true performance of all and singular the covenants and agreements aforesaid, the said parties bind themselves each unto the other firmly by these presents. IN WITNESS whereof, the said parties have interchangeably set their Hands and Seals hereunto. Dated the *fifth* day of *March* in the year of our LORD one thousand eight hundred *one &c.*

Sealed and delivered in the presence of } *Darrah* *Ganges mark*

John B. Foster
Thos. Newlin

lands, so the PAS set to work arranging indentures with employers in Philadelphia and surrounding counties. The PAS arranged terms of four or five
years for adults and to age 18 for girls and to 21 for boys, briefer than those
expected by most masters. Twenty-seven men and boys apprenticed in Chester
and Delaware counties were to learn farming and a few would also be trained
as millers or tanners. Nine women and girls were to learn housewifery.[37]

Pennsylvania farmers procured bound black laborers from the South on
their own. George Brinton, a substantial farmer of Chester County, purchased
several slaves from Delaware and Maryland farmers. He then freed them, as
required by law, but required them to work off the purchase price. His strategy
was not wholly successful, for several of the servants fled and another requested leave to find a new master after only a year. John Clark of Lancaster
County in 1814 bought for $360 two young blacks from Levi Boulden of
Delaware. Boulden first petitioned the Pennsylvania courts for permission to
transfer the children on condition they would be free at age 28. The justices
agreed and the boys, Thomas and James Staats, were manumitted and bound
to Clark for seventeen and nineteen years respectively.[38]

As the growing percentage of blacks in the population of Chester and
Delaware counties clearly shows, prosperous farmers and rural craftsmen
craved the labor of ex-slaves. Families with incomes that could not have
financed the purchase of a slave, or fed, clothed, and occupied a black family
year-round, could now afford to house and employ a young apprentice or
servant. White employers included men and women from a wide range of
wealth groups—landless white cottagers like Moses Martin of Birmingham as
well as iron magnates like David Potts, who owned a furnace, stamping mill,
and over 4000 acres of land. The average acreage of all farmers who had black
servants in their households was 135 acres in 1820, down from 166 acres in
1800.[39] Over the first two decades of the nineteenth century, increasingly
more ordinary farmers and rural artisans exploited the labor of blacks. Sixteen
percent of white households in 1800, and 21 percent in 1820, had direct
access to the labor of black servants, apprentices, or cottagers, and their
neighbors also profited from the labor of blacks.[40] In 1820, over one-fifth of
white families with free African-Americans had only one boy or girl under
age 14; only 6 percent of these households had four or more blacks. Middling
and more prosperous farmers and craftsmen, many of whom could never have

---

Indenture for Darrah Ganges, rescued from the slave ship *Phebe* by the sloop of
war *Ganges*. She was apprenticed for four years to learn housewifery in the
household of Mark Wilcox of Delaware County (1801). Courtesy of The Pennsylvania Abolition Society Papers, Historical Society of Pennsylvania.

afforded a slave, eagerly sought black apprentices and servants, especially boys but also girls.

Contrary to the case in Philadelphia, where black women and girls outnumbered males on the census, rural employers favored men and boys.[41] The sex ratio (males to females) for free blacks under age 14 was 1.13; for ages 14 to 25, 1.20; and for ages 26 and over, 1.30. Black men were migrating into the counties looking for work or freed by Maryland and Delaware masters and indentured to labor-hungry farmers. They clustered in fertile areas near the Delaware border, up the Brandywine Valley, and along the Delaware River. Sixty percent of blacks in white households were male; fully 43 percent were boys and young men under age 26. Farm families, who comprised the great majority of white rural households that contained African-Americans, favored young men, but as was true earlier of slaveowners, they also employed black women and girls. Craftsmen, millowners, and operators of forges, rolling mills, and other ironworks, many of whom also ran farms, preferred males. Differences in preferences, and thus of sex-typing in employment, are especially visible in the case of female household heads. White widows and other women who operated farms employed an equal number of African-American males and females in their households. Widows who did not farm, but ran a shop or household, greatly preferred women and girls.

Thus, white farmers and artisans of rural Pennsylvania benefited greatly from the breakdown of slavery. Emancipation here was truly "philanthropy at bargain prices." And as in Philadelphia, indentured servitude retained its commoditized character, which increasingly after the turn of the century affiliated it more closely with slavery than with free labor. Several cases illustrate both how seriously rural white masters took the obligations of their black servants and how strenuously servants resisted their continuing bondage in a changing labor environment. Owners viewed their bound servants, whether slaves to whom they had promised freedom or the freeborn children of slaves, in much the same way as had masters of servants and slaves before the Revolution—as laborers owing years of service in return for the price of purchase. Servants, on the other hand, grew impatient when freedom proved elusive. Elisha Price of Chester, for example, had promised to free 39- or 40-year-old Peter within four years, "on condition of his serving him faithfully," but Peter, who had "been a run away almost ever since he was 20 years of age" decided that life was too short to spend four more years in bondage.[42] In another case, Lewis, the 18-year-old son of a slave woman, fled at his master's death when he learned that he was to be bound to another man. The new master, Thomas Henderson, petitioned the Chester County court to extend Lewis's service beyond age 28. The court ordered the absent Lewis, an ostensibly freeborn individual who already was bound to spend his prime years in bondage, to serve an additional seven months as recompense for his absence.[43]

When blacks finally gained freedom, either directly from slavery or, more frequently, from servitude, they confronted a social structure that ranged from wealthy farmer-entrepreneurs like ironmaster Thomas Bull; to more ordinary farmers with landholdings of 100 to 200 acres; to tenant farmers who rented sizable acreages and artisans who leased their houses or shops; to cottagers who by contract agreed to work for landlords for a specified number of days in exchange for housing and certain privileges; to day laborers without contracts who obtained shelter and employment where they could. Few black families rose above cottager status. In the forty years after passage of the gradual abolition act, prospects for upward mobility remained dim.

Few of the 104 black heads of household listed on the 1790 census possessed sufficient property to be taxed. Our attempt to locate manumitted blacks on tax assessment lists yielded meager results. Only one black person in Chester and Delaware counties owned land outright before 1790—William Boulton of Marple. On the 1783 census and tax list, he was taxed for 100 acres of land (part of which he probably leased), two horses, three cows, six sheep, two dwelling houses, and two other buildings. By 1802 his property was diminished, as he was rated for only thirty acres, a cabin, a barn, two horses, and a cow. We have no firm information about his background or how he amassed his property, but it is possible that a white woman in his household was his wife and that she had brought property to their marriage. Besides Boulton few blacks appeared on the tax rolls.[44] Even a man like Oran Hazard, who was freed in 1766 and settled on part of his ex-master's farm where he is reputed to have raised good tobacco, was not taxed directly. Though registered in Middletown Township on the 1790 census with his wife and children, he was not considered taxable. His will, probated in 1796, suggests that he had very little wealth.[45]

By 1800, additional black heads of household had small farms, but opportunities to obtain land, even as tenant farmers, remained bleak. At the turn of the century, 12 of 129 (9 percent) African-American families held plots of land ranging in size from a "lot" to 40 acres, with a mean of fourteen acres. This rate of property ownership was similar to that in Philadelphia, where one of every nine black households owned real estate. Clearly, even the most successful former slaves were still living on the margin twenty years after passage of the gradual abolition act.[46] And two decades later, in 1820, conditions had hardly improved. Thirty-seven of 462 (8 percent) black households owned pieces of land from lot size to 100 acres, with a mean of twelve acres. Eight additional families rented farms ranging in size from five to 100 acres. By renting, blacks gained access to larger acreages, for on average these tenants farmed 36 acres.[47]

One step below blacks who scraped together the resources to buy or lease farms were cottagers, families who worked for the landlord and neighbors, lived in small houses, gardened small plots, and perhaps ran a pig in the lane. Since the mid-eighteenth century, Chester County farmers had been building cottages on their farms to house increasing numbers of free laborers. Called "inmates" on the tax lists, they were mostly men with families who earlier in the century had boarded in the houses of their landlords but after 1750 more often had cottages of their own.[48]

As early as the 1720s, most blacks released from slavery and servitude in Chester County became inmates or cottagers. Even ex-slaves who received at emancipation small acreages for use during their lifetimes held no title to the land and could not devise it to their heirs. Mingo, emancipated in 1723 and thus one of the first free blacks in Pennsylvania, went to work for Joshua Johnston, a Quaker farmer of London Grove who lived about five miles from Mingo's former owner. Mingo purchased a grubbing ax, a pitching ax, and a gun with his wages and stayed with Johnston for nearly twenty years. He apparently supported himself until 1771, at age 78, when he requested assistance from the overseers of the poor.[49] Liberated a generation after Mingo, in 1751, Negro Bilha was able to establish a household with the £25, household items and furniture, books, clothes, provisions, and a mare bequeathed to her by owner Deborah Nayle. At her own death, Bilha possessed an estate valued at £108, but owned no land. She supported herself with investments and probably by working for her landlord and neighbors.[50]

Two sisters and a brother, manumitted around 1770 by Peter and Thomas Worrall of Middletown, also established themselves as cottagers. Prudence Ford, Jane Salmon, and Cuff King apparently shared a household on Thomas Worrall's land. When he wrote his will in 1778, King claimed that he had "been working for myself about Nine years, in which time I have acquired Some Small Personal Estate," which included cash, book debts amounting to almost £11, clothing worth about £20, a set of bells for a team, an ax, sickle, gun, and knife.[51] Salmon and Ford had possessions worth £17 10s and £11 4s respectively when they died, including clothing, a small amount of furniture, and spinning wheels, flax, tow, wool, axes, and a hoe. Salmon stated in her will that she, like her brother, had been "working now some Considerable time" for herself.[52]

John Beale Bordley, who had plantations in both Maryland and Chester

County, and had manumitted eight slaves in 1762, 1792, and 1800 and three more in his will, but still kept many blacks in slavery when he died in 1804, recognized that the cottager system provided labor when needed while relieving the landlord of responsibility for feeding and clothing indentured servants and slaves—as well as finding work for them to do year-round. The cottager system, he argued, was well-suited to mixed agriculture and might be advantageous in raising tobacco as well. In 1801 he wrote, "When *slavery* shall cease or be inhibited, in our country, where or how are means of cultivating the lands of the southern and middle states to be found?" Thinking, perhaps, that slavery might soon end in Maryland just as it was dying in Pennsylvania, Bordley encouraged farmers to turn to free laborers, particularly cottagers. These workers, modeled on English cottagers, already could be found in Chester County, as well as in other northern states. They should be rented "a small very confined house called a *cottage*," measuring—for a husband, wife, and children—12 by 16 feet with two floors. "A small garden is allowed to the cottage; which gives employment and comfort to the wife and children; but not an inch of ground is otherwise allowed for *cultivation* of any sort, which might tend to draw the cottager from the farmer's business, to attend to an enlarged employment of his own."[53]

The legal foundation for the cottager system was an annual labor contract, signed each spring, which provided flexibility for both employer and cottager but permitted the latter little hope for upward mobility. In return for agreeing to work for the landlord for a stipulated number of days during the year, cottagers rented or received at low cost lodging and certain privileges, such as use of a half-acre to grow flax and permission to graze a cow, run a pig, take apples for cider, and cut firewood. Their agreement stated that the cottager must be available to work for the landlord during harvest and other specified times. Cottagers made a variety of agreements with their employers, with established wages for various jobs. Harvest wages were highest because that was when the need for labor was most critical. All available hands went into the fields to reap. At lower rates men plowed, dug ditches, split rails, hoed corn, and performed the myriad jobs farming entailed. Those will skills made and sold shoes, cloth, wooden casks, and such to their employers and neighbors. Those without craft skills did general labor for other farmers in the locality as the requirements of their own landlord permitted. Women assisted in the landlord's house and spun, but they also worked in the fields and garden, making hay, reaping wheat, and digging potatoes. The cottagers, assuming they fulfilled their labor obligations, were thus assured a certain income from which to pay the rent and charges for other goods and services the farm owners provided. They were free to work for others during "off" days, just as the employers were free from paying for more labor than they needed.[54]

The cottager system, like wage labor in the city, ideally suited the needs of many employers. Rural landlords could guarantee help for themselves during crucial times in the growing season but did not need to keep workers busy year-round or provide sustenance, as was necessary under slavery. The number of cottagers, white and black, appearing on the tax lists increased from 183 in 1750 (6 per 100 landlords and other potential landlords) to 1,557 in 1799 (31 per 100 potential landlords) to 3,030 in 1820 (41 per 100 potential landlords). In addition, there were many more cottagers living in the country who did not appear on the tax lists because they were too poor to be taxed or too mobile to be caught by the tax assessor.[55] Among these untaxed cottagers were most free black families. Of 129 black heads of household in Chester and Delaware counties on the 1800 census, only two were described as inmates, or cottagers, on contemporaneous tax lists. By 1820, 25 of 462 (5 percent) black heads of household were listed as cottagers on the tax rolls. A few had horses or cattle, but most were taxed only for a dog.

Under the cottage arrangement, blacks had more freedom than they had as servants or slaves because they could move around from year to year seeking better situations and could do what they desired on off-days. Still, they lived on someone else's land and daily confronted the generally accepted belief among whites that African-Americans were an inferior race who needed assistance and direction for survival. If blacks had been owned by Quakers, as was the case for many ex-slaves in Chester and Delaware counties, committees from local meetings visited to investigate their behavior and give advice on finances, including labor agreements. For example, when in 1779 the members of Concord Monthly Meeting knocked on the doors of most of the free blacks in their area, in addition to inspecting and settling accounts according to contracts with employers, they advised couples with large families to put out their children as apprentices both to ease the burden on the parents and provide training for the children. The Friends also arranged for schooling of black children and encouraged spiritual growth, but they did not permit blacks to join the Society until the 1790s, when very few did in fact seek membership.[56]

In their households, blacks carved out some space independent of whites, but too often they found that former status as slaves and limited resources undermined their autonomy. By 1820, only slightly over half of blacks in Chester and Delaware counties were counted as living in black households; average household size for African-Americans had increased only from 3.3 persons in 1790 to 4.7 in 1820, an indication that children were leaving families at early ages. Cottagers experienced conditions much like sharecroppers in the southern United States after the Civil War. Some became indebted to their landlords if they purchased supplies in excess of their wages. A 1771 petition to the Chester County court illustrates the nightmarish situation a free black could get into if he failed to earn enough to cover his expenses. John Starrett of East Nantmeal told the court that Thomas Butcher, a free black man living in the same township, was indebted to him for various sums amounting to over £40. To make satisfaction, Butcher agreed to bind his two young children to Starrett, who took the children and maintained them with that promise in mind. Butcher was "Importuned and Overpersuaded," however, by one Samuel Patrick, to whom he bound the children instead of to Starrett. Butcher then fled. Starrett claimed that the local overseers of the poor knew the case well and had been prepared to bind the children to him according to the 1726 law, but Butcher absconded before they had a chance to do so.[57] While the petition presents only one side of the case, we can see how economic hardship could lead to dependency and the breaking up of families. When parents got into debt, children became pawns. The 1726 law enabled justices to bind out children even without parents' consent, and the Butcher case suggests how creditors could make the law work for them. While the 1726 law was repealed in 1780 with passage of the gradual abolition act, binding out children remained a necessity for hard-pressed parents.

Below cottagers on the social scale were blacks who lived in grinding poverty and sometimes landed in the almshouse or jail. Thomas Butcher, through ill fortune or misdeed, fell into this status, as did perhaps 10 to 15 percent of the black population of rural southeastern Pennsylvania during the first two decades of the nineteenth century. Stories from the almshouse records detail the misery experienced by former slaves abandoned without resources by local masters, and fugitives or manumitted blacks from the South who arrived destitute and ill. They roamed from township to township seeking work and sustenence. When winter weather descended, they sought shelter in the poorhouse; when hunger forced them to steal, they often went to jail. Dabbo Ganges, probably one of the Africans rescued by the *Ganges* in 1800, drifted from one farm and ironworks to another, working the fields, cutting wood, and bleaching linen. To survive in the winter, he "would enter a white's house at random, seat himself by the fire or stove, and announce his intentions to break bread and lodge there." Later, in his old age and after economic depression struck in 1837, he turned more often to the Chester County almshouse.[58]

Jacob Stephens also had pluck, but his strategy for survival on at least one occasion was less savory. A deposition given by a black man, George Brown, probably a cottager, details the efforts made by the two men, one a drifter and the other more settled, to earn their living during a week in March 1792. Soon after Brown met Stephens they went "to hear whether the *Queen of Morocco* had come in and on inquiry were told she had not come in on Sunday night." They stayed over at a black man's house in the port town, probably Wilmington, and the "next morning we set off and got to my house abt half after 12 oClock then we went to John Baldwins & told him we came about the flax he told me that we should go to work at it[.] I then went to scutching & Jacob Stephens to breaking[. W]e continued at work till fourth day [Wednesday] evening following & I continued at work till next day morning when it began to rain & I left off work on fifth day morning." Stephens left Brown, saying he would go elsewhere to get work, but apparently finding none, resorted to theft instead. He returned to Brown's home Saturday morning with a ham and a piece of beef and persuaded Brown to take the meat in exchange for his violin, which could be transported more easily. When Brown learned that the meat had been stolen he reported the incident and cooperated in Stephens's arrest.[59] Jacob Stephens was part of a rural underclass of whites and blacks who escaped a quotidian existence of working for paternalistic white landlords but who, given the uncertainties of weather, crops, and ship arrivals, risked utter destitution.

After freedom, then, blacks in Chester and Delaware counties found their opportunities limited. In 1820 a large percentage still lived in white households and few black householders had land. And of African-American landholders, just a handful held sufficient acreage to support their families without supplementing their incomes by working for others. Only four black families (of 462) had more than fifty acres and at least two of these were tenants. In rural Pennsylvania, land was the financial measure of a man and his family though it was increasingly difficult for whites as well as blacks to obtain. African-Americans entered the real estate market well after land prices had started to soar. Like more and more white folks coming of age, the most that blacks could hope for was a cottage, a half-acre garden, and a labor contract to work a specified number of days. Even blacks whose manumitting owners provided a small farm with which to earn their livelihoods had no right to pass the land along to their heirs. Any dreams of a farmstead in early nineteenth-century Pennsylvania proved to be as empty as later promises of "forty acres and a mule."

In Philadelphia, African-Americans found the way to wealth more open, and the large, concentrated black community offered opportunities for entrepreneurship unknown to men and women in the country. Still, the great majority of urban blacks had difficulty overcoming the obstacles of limited capital and low estimations of their abilities held by whites. Most black men in the city worked as day laborers and women washed clothes and served as domestics even in the years around the turn of the century when the success of James Forten, Richard Allen, and Eleanor Harris seemed to promise opportunity for all.

Thus in freedom even more than in slavery, blacks were a versatile, efficient labor force suited to the requirements of the urban market and rural economy based on grain and livestock agriculture. As slaves, African-Americans had worked side-by-side with masters and their families, white indentured servants, and wage laborers on farms, in shops and houses, and on ships and wharves. They moved from job to job by the hour, day, week, or year providing services as needed. In freedom, black men and women continued to work for others, living in white households as servants and apprentices, or renting houses or cottages and working for wages. As laborers, cottagers, and servants, blacks filled the needs of labor-hungry producers in both city and country. Philadelphia artisans, merchants, and ship captains quickly claimed the labor of the thousands of blacks who entered the city during the early years of the Republic. In Chester and Delaware counties, where in 1820 the percentage of free blacks in the population was over three times what it had been under slavery, less affluent yeomen and artisans could afford to build a cottage on their land or acquire an apprentice or servant to live in their homes, whereas only wealthy farmers and rural entrepreneurs had been able to invest in slaves and keep them occupied year-round. In making contracts with cottagers and wage laborers, employers paid only for the labor they needed. The masters of bound servants obtained their service during the prime of their lives and then left them to shift for themselves, or turn to the almshouse, when less physically able. Emancipation proceeded apace in late eighteenth-century Pennsylvania, in both Philadelphia and its hinterland, as artisans, merchants, farmers, and entrepreneurs learned that they could release their slaves with little financial loss, take advantage of a burgeoning servant trade in recently released slaves, and turn to a sizable pool of free black workers for cheap, menial labor. In deciding to release their blacks such manumitters experienced only the slightest tinge of antislavery sentiment. The prospect of a more efficient work force, exploiting black men and women during their most productive years, or obtaining labor only for the hours or days needed, loomed much larger than altruism in these emancipators' minds.

7

The Legacy of Antislavery Reform

If the freedom road for black Pennsylvanians was twisted, narrow, and obstacle-filled, it would have been even more so without the work of the Pennsylvania Abolition Society. Few African-Americans emerging from bondage had the wherewithal or the legal knowledge to fight for the small gains the PAS laboriously extracted from a generally unsympathetic society and legal system. Yet the stance of the Society was ambiguous and paradoxical. Like the Society of Friends, who continued to provide most PAS members in the early nineteenth century, the PAS helped to end slavery in Pennsylvania and assisted hundreds of individual slaves by preventing their reenslavement and by wringing small advantages from a society dominated by and for whites. At the same time, however, the PAS cooperated in the creation of a new system of labor and social relations that exploited black labor and left those who had been unshackled little opportunity for upward movement in society. Their efforts went toward reforming their society by ridding it of perpetual and hereditary racial slavery; but they had little energy or imagination for restructuring their society so that former slaves could compete equally with white citizens.

One of the PAS's priorities in the twilight of the slave era was to temper the harshness of the indentured servitude middle ground occupied by so many manumitted blacks. The PAS was particularly opposed to the binding of black children brought in from other states to age 28, regarding this as exploitative and illegal. They argued that the same law governing the indenturing of white children ought to apply to blacks, that is, that boys could be bound until age 21 and girls to age 18. Spurred by the large number of French slaveowners who were binding their recently released slaves until 28 years of age, the PAS brought a suit before the Pennsylvania Supreme Court in 1794 to secure the freedom of a black indentured servant named Robert, who had fled his mistress and approached the PAS for help. Brought into the state in 1779 as a slave, Robert had been freed in 1784 at age 14 on the condition that he sign an indenture to serve until age 28. Finding that Robert had never been registered properly as a slave in 1780, the court declared that he was legally free at the time he signed the indenture in 1784 and thus could be bound only to age 21. But in affirming that free blacks could be bound only under the terms that applied to whites, the court also declared that those bound to an indenture in another state or indentured as a condition of release "from a longer servitude" could be legally obligated to serve until age 28.[1] The PAS won Robert's release from his indenture on the technicality of his improper registration but lost on the larger issue. Through the court's ruling, Pennsylvania would remain for decades a labor market in which manumitting masters, for whatever motive, could sell the labor power of the slaves they were freeing for the greater part of the slaves' productive lives.

At the end of the eighteenth century, the PAS confronted a new stratagem devised by white employers for maximizing their investment in confined black labor. When the daughters of slaves born after 1780 started reaching childbearing age in the mid-1790s, their owners saw a new possibility for extracting labor from their wombs. These female children of slaves were legally obligated to serve their mother's master, or whomever he sold them to, until age 28. Any children they bore before that age came under the master's control, although since these children were born entirely free, it might have been presumed that they could not remain indentured for more than 18 years if female and 21 if male. But many masters of such women, especially in the western part of the state, saw it otherwise and claimed their title of these grandchildren of slaves until their twenty-eighth birthdays. When the PAS brought a test case in 1811, the court upheld the master's right to 28 years of labor.[2] Not until 1824 did a lower court reverse this decision. Two years later, the state Supreme Court agreed that no person born in Pennsylvania could be compelled to 28 years of servitude unless his or her mother was born a slave.[3]

The PAS also continued to trip up unwary purchasers of indentured labor in order to procure the outright freedom of an occasional person. Timothy Matlack, the aging radical of Revolutionary days, in 1811 lost his investment in a 31-year-old mulatto woman, Hester, on the PAS's favorite technicality. Unknown to Matlack, Hester's former master had never properly registered her after her birth in August 1780 as the law required. In 1798, Hester's first master had signed a manumission for her at age 18 (thereby providing documentation of her status), bound her to a ten-year contract as an indentured servant, and then sold her to a man in Trenton, New Jersey. Hester absconded from this master. Several years later, after she was picked up as a runaway servant in Philadelphia, the court sentenced her to a five-year term of labor. When city officials auctioned this labor obligation, the highest bidder was Timothy Matlack of Philadelphia. But Matlack lost his investment when the PAS intervened and secured the court's agreement that Hester was free because her birth in 1780 had never been registered as the law required.[4]

The PAS also fought against a variety of schemes employed by masters and their agents to circumvent the abolition laws, including the pernicious business of kidnapping indentured black servants and selling them south into slavery. The longer the indenture, the longer any African-American remained at risk to be sold or taken south and, once in slave territory and without the protection of an organization such as the PAS, reenslaved. In one case in 1810 the PAS obtained freedom for Azor, an eight-year-old boy who had been indentured until age 28 without his mother's consent and was about to be taken by his French refugee master to Baltimore. The master of Azor claimed that he had been born a slave; but the court determined that the boy had been born free and agreed with the PAS's argument that he should be released. The PAS was unsentimental in such cases, in this instance not objecting when Azor's mother indentured him until age 21 to a Philadelphian.[5]

Another subterfuge used by masters moving to Pennsylvania from slave states drew the attention of the PAS. Such owners frequently brought into the state men and women whom they claimed to be slaves but who were actually free. These masters then freed their purported slaves before the six-month clause took effect and signed them to indentures that extended to their twenty-eighth birthdays. In the case of Silva, a 15-year-old girl who had been brought by her French mistress to Philadelphia from Cuba by way of Rhode Island, the PAS saw an opportunity. Mlle. Bertrand, Silva's mistress, had manumitted Silva when she reached Philadelphia, immediately indentured her for thirteen years, and then sold her as an indentured servant for $200. Silva claimed she had been tricked into signing the indenture in exchange for manumission, not understanding that she had been free from the moment she touched land in Rhode Island because Congress's abolition of the slave trade in 1807 forbid the importation of slaves into the United States. When the court ruled with Silva, she became a free Philadelphian, and her purported owner suffered the loss of the purchase price from the girl's former French owner.[6]

Kidnapping was the final area in which the PAS worked on behalf of those

KIDNAPPING.

Designed and Published by J. Torrey, Ju. Philad. 1817.

No free black was safe from the kidnappers who seized men, women, and children and spirited them to the South. Plate from Jesse Torrey, *A Portraiture of Domestic Slavery, in the United States* (Philadelphia, 1817). Courtesy of The Library Company of Philadelphia.

living in the shadowy ground between slavery and freedom. Ironically, as the number of slaves in Pennsylvania dwindled to a few hundred in the early nineteenth century, the personal freedom of blacks released from slavery grew less secure. Both the ban on importing slaves after 1807 and the disruption of the immigrant traffic from England, Germany, and Ireland, especially the latter, during the years of the Jeffersonian Embargo and the War of 1812 heightened the demand for cheap labor throughout the United States in ways that directly affected former slaves in the North. At the same time that labor demand in the North led to greater severity in the indentured labor system as it applied to blacks, the growing demand for slaves, especially in the Lower South and in the newly opened cotton lands in the Old Southwest, made the mid-Atlantic states a favorite hunting ground of kidnappers. Operating in both city and countryside, the manstealers inveigled or forced free blacks onto boats and then sailed for the South where they sold their hapless victims into slavery.

As early as 1801 the American Convention for Promoting the Abolition of Slavery, which met almost yearly in Philadelphia, reported an alarming increase in the incidence of kidnapping. In 1803, Edward Darlington, a Chester County Quaker, published an account of dozens of cases of man-stealing in the city.[7] Little deterred by the meek provisions against kidnapping in the 1788 amendment to the gradual abolition law, kidnappers roamed Philadelphia's streets and operated along Pennsylvania's border with Maryland and Virginia. Nobody with dark skin could live without fear of the body snatchers, who operated under a virtual manhunter's license provided by Congress in 1793 when it passed the Fugitive Slave Law. Under this law, slaveowners or their agents were entitled to enter free states, seize alleged fugitives, and then carry them out of the state if they could convince any local magistrate of the validity of their ownership. What made the law particularly obnoxious to free blacks and abolitionists was that local officials were obligated to assist in the enforcement of this federal statute but could not conduct a full investigation or admit the testimony of the fugitive. The law was an accommodation by free states to slave states in the early 1790s, and in making this concession the free states surrendered much of their power to protect free black citizens from kidnapping.[8]

Two incidents in 1801 demonstrated how free blacks were in danger of being enslaved so long as slavery existed to the south of Pennsylvania and the laws against kidnapping were so lax. In March of that year a man named Dana, about to sail from Philadelphia for Charleston, South Carolina, convinced a black woman to allow him to purchase a new suit of clothes for her young son. Leading the boy from his mother's home, he quickly took his prey aboard the schooner and locked him in the hold. Only because a delay in the ship's departure allowed the child's screams to be heard at the wharf was the boy rescued and the kidnapping attempt thwarted.[9]

Three months later four Delaware men in the city hired about eight black men to go with them to Kent County to chop wood and work on local farms for the summer. But the real intention was to bring the Philadelphia free blacks, once in Delaware, to the house of a Kent County man who supplied slave agents from Georgia with young black men from the North. The plan was foiled when the Philadelphia blacks overheard the plans of their supposed Delaware employers and escaped. But the slight penalties in Pennsylvania for convicted kidnappers made such incidents common at the turn of the century, and many Philadelphia free blacks were not so lucky as to escape, once they had left the city, either voluntarily or involuntarily.[10]

Even Richard Allen, one of Philadelphia's most prominent blacks, was seized in about 1806 by a southerner who had armed himself with a sheriff's arrest warrant after convincing the officer that he had his sights on a fugitive slave. Allen quickly turned the tables on the predator, who was arrested for attempted kidnapping and committed to debtors' prison when he could not make bail.[11] The incident dramatized the point that even while slavery in Pennsylvania was dying, no African-American in the North remained secure while slavery and slave hunters still existed.

The PAS, which had begun petitioning the legislature for a stronger kidnapping law in the 1790s, renewed its efforts in 1803, but the legislature did nothing. The PAS lobbied again in 1805, 1806, and 1811, but on each occasion failed.[12] In 1814 the Society grew more alarmed because of an increase in the trafficking in black children "under color of law" to satisfy a growing demand for cheap labor. Under a new stratagem, white labor contractors would tempt black parents with "small sums of money" to bind their children as apprentices; then the child's new master would sell the apprenticed black youth to the highest bidder, signing over the indenture to the buyer without the knowledge or consent of the parents. Conniving masters could make $50 to 100 in a few weeks according to the PAS, and not infrequently apprentice contracts were reassigned several times to masters far distant from the apprentice's home, which increased the risk that a youth would disappear into the abyss of slavery in the South. Taking a test case of a youth named Augustus Stephenson before the Pennsylvania Supreme Court early in 1815, the PAS received a favorable ruling that indentures of youths sold to a new master without the consent of the servant's parents were void.[13]

After the War of 1812, when the demand for slaves rose in the South, kidnappers operated more brazenly. Snatching up free blacks whom they claimed were escaped slaves, they forced them aboard small ships that slipped quietly down the Delaware River and headed south for slave territory. PAS members led a petition drive in 1816, bringing pressure on Congress for a law against kidnapping. Later that year, after the Pennsylvania Supreme Court ruled that a child of a fugitive slave woman who had been conceived after the woman reached Pennsylvania, was born free and therefore immune from the provisions of the Fugitive Slave Act of 1793, the PAS began aiding fugitive slaves, providing encouragement and legal assistance.[14] Far from lapsing into inactivity in the years following the War of 1812, as often is claimed, the Society's lawyers and committee members worked vigorously to assist free blacks and fugitive slaves. In their report to the American Convention for Promoting the Abolition of Slavery in 1817 the PAS detailed fifty-three cases in which it had intervened, thirty of them resulting in "rescuing the objects of their care from slavery."[15]

A particularly vicious case of kidnapping in the summer of 1817 seems to have further galvanized efforts to seek a stronger state law against man-stealing. William Nelson, a professional body snatcher from Maryland, only recently whipped and cropped in Delaware after being convicted for kidnapping a free black woman, arrived in Philadelphia and obtained from a Southwark magistrate a warrant against a free black woman living in the Northern Liberties and her two sons, age 22 and 16. With a companion and a deputy sheriff, Nelson burst into the house of the unsuspecting black family on a Sunday morning; when the woman's husband struggled with them as they attempted to seize her and their sons, they threatened to "blow out his brains if he made any further resistance" and then bludgeoned one of the sons into submission. The mother and two sons were dragged through the streets to the other side of town to appear before the Southwark magistrate where, as the *Philadelphia Gazette* reported, "it was uncertain that any person would know them or appear on their behalf." Luckily, some of their friends rushed to the magistrate's house, so the kidnappers were not allowed to proceed out of the city with their victims. But the black family was held in jail until the case was heard before the Supreme Court, which found in their favor. In the meantime, the same kidnappers obtained another warrant and tried to carry out a free black man working on the farm of a Philadelphia judge.[16]

While the violent case of kidnapping in 1817 was one incentive to seek a stronger state law against man-stealing, another spur came in 1819 when William Tilghman, Chief Justice of the Pennsylvania Supreme Court, ruled that certain procedures employed to protect the liberty of blacks, such as the writ of *de homine replegiando* (to redeem the body taken), were unconstitutional. Tilghman's obliteration of this protection, as the legal historian Thomas Morris has pointed out, "significantly altered, in favor of property rights, the compromise Pennsylvania had made with slavery in the 1780s."[17] Faced with this setback, and seeing attempts thwarted at the federal level to obtain greater protection of free blacks, both Philadelphia's free black leaders and the PAS increased their efforts to obtain a strengthening of the kidnapping law. Their exertions finally bore fruit in 1820 when the Pennsylvania legislature enacted a law that greatly increased the penalties for convicted kidnappers to imprisonment at hard labor for up to twenty-one years. More important from a constitutional point of view was a clause that denied lesser officials such as aldermen and justices of the peace the authority to issue writs to those who, under the federal Fugitive Slave Act of 1793, sought to reclaim purported runaway slaves. Instead, hunters of alleged fugitive slaves would have to seek their writs from higher court officials, thus making the recovery of fugitives more difficult and increasing the protection of free blacks. One of the first interventions by a northern state on a federal law, the 1820 statute was a precursor of further state limitations in the antebellum period.[18]

The 1820 law deterred some kidnappers by stiffening the penalties for this offense and limiting the power of Pennsylvania magistrates to assist them under the federal fugitive slave law. But it offended neighboring Maryland slaveowners and led within a few years to a further revision of the state law that attempted to "find a workable balance between slaveholders' claims and the protection of free blacks."[19] The PAS achieved a partial victory in 1826 by blocking some clauses that would have nullified advances made in the 1820 law. But it did not include what most abolitionists wanted—a guarantee of a trial by jury to anyone seized as a fugitive slave who claimed to be free.

The nearly total extinction of slavery in Pennsylvania by the second decade of the nineteenth century is often viewed as a triumph of humanitarianism. Alternatively, it is dismissed as the demise of a labor system that had no economic significance. In either interpretation, Pennsylvania is considered a special case, not only far ahead chronologically of its neighbors to the south in making the transition to free labor, but somehow buffered from the gut-wrenching conflict of morality, material interest, and power that characterized abolition in other slave societies.

By identifying the motivations of individuals and institutions and measuring their impact on the process of emancipation, we disentangle the forces at work in the dissolution of slavery in the Quaker commonwealth. The similarity of Pennsylvania's experience with that of other societies becomes clear. Three sets of actors helped to dismantle slavery in the state: abolitionists; slaveholders and potential slaveholders who for a variety of reasons disengaged themselves from the institution; and slaves who dared to escape or otherwise resist their bondage.

From the time of Pennsylvania's founding, a thin line of abolitionists kept arguments about the inhumanity of slavery before the public. They succeeded in convincing some slave masters to release their slaves willingly, without compensatory conditions or the threat of religious disownment, but the number was modest indeed. In the Society of Friends, a handful of conscience reformers for whom Woolman and Benezet acted as spokesmen prevailed only when they yoked their antislavery campaign to more popular tribalistic reforms. Just a few Pennsylvania legislators led by George Bryan, infected with the Revolutionary ideal that everyone had the right to be free, won passage of the abolition act in 1780 only after agreeing to uphold property rights of present owners and pledging to masters the better part of the lives of children born to slave women. The PAS, spearheaded through most of its history by a core group of Quaker artisans, small merchants, and lawyers, battled to protect the liberty of blacks and to extend their rights under the 1780 law. Their successes were sometimes exhilarating, but faced with overwhelming opposition they failed in the early decades of the Republic to achieve complete abolition of slavery in Pennsylvania or to gain adequate protection against kidnappers. The PAS, too, chose to cooperate in indenturing young men and women to long terms—even while fighting such conditions in the courts— when the alternative was continued slavery.

The motives of the PAS in its efforts to restrict the length of servitude, win freedom for blacks illegally held in slavery, and outwit kidnappers were beyond reproach. Like their eighteenth-century predecessors, Benjamin Lay, John Woolman, and Anthony Benezet, the PAS activists were bona fide altruists who wanted to stamp out the last vestiges of slavery in their state and ameliorate conditions for blacks. They were not wealthy entrepreneurs who consciously or unconsciously assisted the transition from slavery to freedom in order to provide a flexible and disciplined workforce for the new industrial order. They were a small band of reformers who used their legal skills and political savvy to win piecemeal concessions for former slaves from a largely unsympathetic society. The PAS lacked the vision of a social reconstruction that would have offered African-Americans equal footing with whites; but had they conceived of such a restructuring there is little chance that they might have prevailed. The PAS was a tiny vanguard of philanthropic reformers who lacked political clout or financial might.

Pennsylvania abolitionists from the Germantown protestors of 1688 to the PAS certainly played their part by keeping the issue alive in public discourse, but their achievements must be placed in the context of other forces—those that were more convincing to less idealistic Pennsylvanians that the heyday of slavery was past. This second and much more numerous group took into consideration the tremendously high mortality of slaves in Philadelphia, the growing restiveness of young bondsmen, the increased supply of free laborers, and the advantages of wage labor in a fluctuating economy, in making their decision to abandon the institution. They also listened to the arguments of Quaker abolitionists, radical Whigs, and the PAS activists, but their individual responses depended on the ways in which they employed slaves and their religious identification.

Philadelphia artisans and mariners, who had only recently purchased slaves during the Seven Years' War boom, were the first to abandon slaveholding when the economy soured. Many apparently sold their slaves, thus securing a return on their investment. Others failed to replace slaves who died, and a few freed their slaves. Slaveholders whose bondsmen and women were occupied in work that was not tied to a fluctuating economy—widows, gentlemen, some merchants, government officials, and wealthy farmers with additional enterprises—were much less eager to give them up. Such masters of considerable means could weather downturns in the economy without selling off slaves for capital and had the wherewithal to support a retinue of domestic servants.

Religious or moral concern and Revolutionary ideology also affected white Pennsylvanians in different ways. Most Quaker slaveholders, under threat of disownment, freed their slaves by 1780. Many Philadelphia Presbyterians, responding to the leadership of their political and religious leaders, forsook slavery in the 1780s, but their fellows in Chester County, under less pressure from leaders to free slaves and with greater economic incentive to retain them, held on for another decade. Despite the alliance of Presbyterians throughout the state on other legislative matters, they divided sharply over abolition. Anglicans with considerable wealth and no religious compunctions against slavery were the largest group of slaveholders in Philadelphia throughout much of the eighteenth century. Some freed slaves before 1780, and more after; and they gradually lessened their involvement in the institution from the 1780s on.

Manumitting owners were of course affected to some extent by antislavery sentiment—if they had wished simply to be rid of their slaves they could have sold them. But the majority allowed abolitionism to penetrate only when they recognized the benefits of exploiting the labor of blacks to age 28 and then releasing them to fend for themselves during physical decline, or of purchasing the energies of day laborers, clothes washers, and cottagers for only the time needed. Decades before emancipation in the West Indies and the southern United States, white Pennsylvanians learned that abolition need not bring a reordering of society. As servants, cottagers, and wage workers, even more than as slaves, black Pennsylvanians provided a cheap, versatile labor force in city and country.

African-Americans had a part in the extinction of Pennsylvania slavery that went beyond their fundamental interest in self-ownership. Hundreds of slaves helped to undermine the legitimacy of the institution by liberating themselves. As slaves received manumissions and the free black community grew, and when the promise of emancipation seemed to evaporate with passage of the 1780 act, the most valuable slaves—primarily young men—fled their recalcitrant owners. Other slaves resisted workloads imposed by owners, took holidays for days or weeks, committed suicide, assaults, and arson, and badgered masters for release. And when manumission for many proved to be a charade, they resisted their new bonds of indentured servitude as well. Freed black Pennsylvanians might have hoped that emancipation would bring prosperity and upward social mobility, but if so, most were disappointed. Lack of capital, fear of reenslavement, and preconceived notions held by whites of what constituted appropriate employment for blacks all constricted opportunities. In Pennsylvania, as elsewhere, African-Americans found that the freedom to achieve to the limits of one's abilities remained elusive even after perpetual bondage was destroyed.

Abbreviations Used in Notes

AHR	*American Historical Review*
CCA	Chester County Archives, West Chester, Pa.
CCHS	Chester County Historical Society, West Chester, Pa.
FHL	Friends Historical Library of Swarthmore College
HSP	Historical Society of Pennsylvania
JAH	*Journal of American History*
JNH	*Journal of Negro History*
LCP	Library Company of Philadelphia
MM mins.	Monthly Meeting minutes (men's meeting unless otherwise noted)
PA	*Pennsylvania Archives*
Pa. Gaz.	*Pennsylvania Gazette*
PAS	Pennsylvania Abolition Society
PHMC	Pennsylvania Historical and Museum Commission, Harrisburg
PMHB	*Pennsylvania Magazine of History and Biography*
PYM mins.	Philadelphia Yearly Meeting minutes (men's)
QC	Quaker Collection, Haverford College
QM mins.	Quarterly Meeting minutes (men's)
WMQ	*William and Mary Quarterly*

Notes

Introduction

1. *Pa. Gaz.*, April 19, 1730. For other examples of Franklin advertising slaves for sale, see Claude-Anne Lopez and Eugenia W. Herbert, *The Private Franklin: The Man and His Family* (New York, 1975), 291. Although many historians have written about Franklin's attitudes toward slavery and toward blacks, they have rarely mentioned his own involvement in slavery. Lopez and Herbert provide the best account to date in ibid., 291–302.

2. Franklin to Abiah Franklin, April 12, 1750, in Leonard W. Labaree et al., eds., *The Papers of Benjamin Franklin* (New Haven, 1959–), III, 474.

3. Ibid., IV, 234.

4. Ibid., IV, 229.

5. Ibid., IV, 231.

6. Ibid., VII, 273n; Lopez and Herbert, *Private Franklin*, 293.

7. Franklin's will, dated April 28, 1757, is in *Papers of Franklin*, VII, 203.

8. See ibid., IV, 229n for the telling change of wording.

9. Franklin to Deborah Franklin, June 27, 1760, ibid., IX, 174–75.

10. Franklin responded to Deborah's news of Othello's death in a letter of March 18, 1760, ibid., IX, 38; the quotation is from *Observations concerning the Increase of Mankind*.

11. Franklin to John Waring, Dec. 17, 1763, *Papers of Franklin*, X, 396.

12. Lopez and Herbert, *Private Franklin*, 193.

13. *A Conversation between an Englishman, a Scotchman, and an American, on the Subject of Slavery*, in *Papers of Franklin*, XVII, 37–44.

14. Ibid., XIX, 187–88.

15. Franklin to Richard Woodward, April 10, 1773, ibid., XX, 155–56; and Franklin to Rush, July 14, 1773, ibid., XX, 314.

16. On the death of George's wife, see Deborah Franklin to Franklin, June 30, 1772, ibid., XIX, 192.

17. Sarah Bache to Franklin, June 23, 1781, Papers of Benjamin Franklin, Yale University Library. We are indebted to Barbara Oberg of the Franklin Papers for a copy of this letter.

18. Willard Randall, *A Little Revenge: Benjamin Franklin and His Son* (Boston, 1984), 309. Randall provides no documentation for Peter's presence in 1775, and we have been unable to corroborate his claim.

19. *Federal Gazette,* Feb. 17, 1790.

20. Franklin's last will is in Albert Henry Smyth, ed., *The Writings of Benjamin Franklin* (10 vols.; New York, 1905–07), X, 495.

21. *On the Slave Trade,* March 23, 1790, ibid., X, 86–91.

Chapter 1

1. Chester County slave enumerations, 1788–1821, Miscellaneous Slavery Papers, CCHS; "An Act for the Gradual Abolition of Slavery" (1780), James T. Mitchell and Henry Flanders, comps., *The Statutes at Large of Pennsylvania from 1682 to 1801* (Harrisburg, 1896–1915), X, 67–73; Chester Co. slave register, 1780, PAS Papers, Reel 24, HSP.

2. J. Smith Futhey and Gilbert Cope, *History of Chester County, Pennsylvania* (Philadelphia, 1881), 489–491; Chester Co. tax assessment list, 1783, CCA; Morton L. Montgomery, "Early Furnaces and Forges of Berks County, Pennsylvania," *PMHB* 8 (1884): 71–72; Chester Co. Wills, No. 9574. The Chester County wills and inventories for 1715 and after are located in CCA. Most of those before 1715 are included with the Philadelphia probate records.

3. U.S. Bureau of the Census, *A Century of Population Growth from the First Census of the United States to the Twelfth 1790–1900* (Washington, D.C., 1909), 57, 133; U.S. Bureau of the Census, *Fourth Census* (Washington, D.C., 1821); Shane White, "'We Dwell in Safety and Pursue Our Honest Callings': Free Blacks in New York City, 1783–1810," *JAH* 75 (1988): 448.

4. Gary B. Nash, "Slaves and Slaveowners in Colonial Philadelphia," *WMQ,* 3rd ser., 30 (1973): 223–25; Edward Raymond Turner, *Slavery in Pennsylvania* (Baltimore, 1911), 1–2; Jean R. Soderlund et al., eds., *William Penn and the Founding of Pennsylvania, 1680–1684: A Documentary History* (Philadelphia, 1983), 144, 215.

5. James Claypoole to Edward Claypoole, Sept. 23, 1682, published in ibid., 179–81.

6. Nicholas More to William Penn, Dec. 1, 1684, published in Richard S. Dunn et al., eds., *The Papers of William Penn* (5 vols.; Philadelphia, 1981–87), II, 608. More reported that "all the Negroes where sould for redy money, which has Caused Money to be Very scarce." Nash, "Slaves and Slaveowners," 225–26; Susan Mackiewicz, "Philadelphia Flourishing: The Material World of Philadelphians, 1682–1760" (Ph.D. diss., University of Delaware, 1988), 174–97.

7. Richard S. Dunn, *Sugar and Slaves: The Rise of the Planter Class in the English West Indies, 1624–1713* (New York, 1972), 111–16; Peter H. Wood, *Black Majority: Negroes in Colonial South Carolina from 1670 through the Stono Rebellion* (New

York, 1974), 13–34; Russell Menard, "From Servants to Slaves: The Transformation of the Chesapeake Labor System," *Southern Studies* 16 (1977): 355–90; Allan Kulikoff, *Tobacco and Slaves: The Development of Southern Cultures in the Chesapeake, 1680–1800* (Chapel Hill, 1986), 23–44.

8. Dunn et al., eds., *Papers of William Penn,* II, 321; Memorandum book of the Am. debtors of Charles Jones, Jr. & Co. of Bristol Eng., ca. 1685–91, HSP; Phila. Co. Wills, Bk. A, No. 30. Philadelphia probate records of testate decedents are available in photostat for the years 1682–1724 at HSP. The Register of Wills office in Room 185, Philadelphia City Hall, has microfilm copies of the wills and inventories of most testate decedents. The inventories of intestate decedents have not been filmed or copied.

9. Phila. Co. Admins., 1686, No. 60; Hannah Benner Roach, "Philadelphia Business Directory, 1690," *Pennsylvania Genealogical Magazine* 23 (1963–64): 111.

10. Thomas E. Drake, *Quakers and Slavery in America* (New Haven, 1950), 5–10; "Germantown Friends' Protest Against Slavery, 1688," reprinted in J. William Frost, ed., *The Quaker Origins of Antislavery* (Norwood, Pa., 1980), 69 (see Chapter 2 below for further discussion of this protest).

11. Jean R. Soderlund, *Quakers and Slavery: A Divided Spirit* (Princeton, 1985), 34.

12. Dunn et al., eds., *Papers of William Penn,* II, 83, 105, 531, 555, 581, 583, 609; Phila. Co. Wills, Bk. A, No. 34; Bk. A, No. 84; Bk. A, No. 105; Bk. B, No. 3; Phila. Co. Admins., 1700, No. 105.

13. Dunn et al., eds., *Papers of William Penn,* III, 66–67; IV, 113–14; Hannah Penn to James Logan, June 6, 1720, and James Logan to Hannah Penn, May 11, 1721, Penn Papers, Official Correspondence, I, 95, 97, HSP; Samuel M. Janney, *The Life of William Penn* (rprt. ed.; Freeport, N.Y., 1970; orig. pub. 1851), 421; Gary B. Nash, *Forging Freedom: The Formation of Philadelphia's Black Community, 1720–1840* (Cambridge, Mass., 1988), 12.

14. Dunn et al., eds., *Papers of William Penn,* II, 211–27; Gail McKnight Beckman, comp., *The Statutes at Large of Pennsylvania in the Time of William Penn, Volume 1, 1680–1700* (New York, 1976), 34, 225; "An Act for the Better Regulation of Servants in This Province and Territories" (1700), and "An Act for the Trial of Negroes" (1706), Mitchell and Flanders, comps., *Statutes at Large,* II, 54–56, 233–36; A. Leon Higginbotham, Jr., *In the Matter of Color: Race and the American Legal Process, The Colonial Period* (New York, 1978), 269–82.

15. "An Act for the Better Regulating of Negroes in This Province" (1726), Mitchell and Flanders, comps., *Statutes at Large,* IV, 59–64; Higginbotham, *In the Matter of Color,* 50–53, 195–201, 211–12, 253–59, 264–66, 282–88, 303, 305–10.

16. Mitchell and Flanders, comps., *Statutes at Large,* IV, 59–64; "An Act for Regulating of Slaves" (1714), in Bernard Bush, comp., *Laws of the Royal Colony of New Jersey, 1703–1745, New Jersey Archives,* 3rd ser. (Trenton, 1977), II, 136–40; Higginbotham, *In the Matter of Color,* 47–48, 128–31, 175, 282–88, 303, 305–10.

17. Dunn et al., eds., *Papers of William Penn,* II, 96–102, 118–23, 129–30;

Hannah Benner Roach, "The Planting of Philadelphia: A Seventeenth-Century Real Estate Development," *PMHB* 92 (1968): 3–47; James T. Lemon, *The Best Poor Man's Country: A Geographical Study of Early Southeastern Pennsylvania* (Baltimore, 1972), 118–30.

18. Billy G. Smith, "Death and Life in a Colonial Immigrant City: A Demographic Analysis of Philadelphia," *Journal of Economic History* 37 (1977): 863–89; Susan E. Klepp, "Philadelphia in Transition: A Demographic History of the City and Its Occupational Classes, 1720–1830" (Ph.D. diss., University of Pennsylvania, 1980), chap. 4.

19. The absence of adequate tax assessment data before the 1760s and any census for the entire commonwealth before the federal census of 1790 makes measuring the size of the slave population in early Pennsylvania difficult. The probate records—wills and inventories of estates left by colonists when they died—are the only reliable source about who owned slaves and how the institution changed over time. Nevertheless, there are problems associated with these data, most notably a bias toward the more affluent segment of the population which, in the case of slaveholding, may exaggerate the proportion who owned slaves. For general discussion of the risks of using probate data, see Gloria L. Main, "Probate Records as a Source for Early American History," *WMQ*, 3rd ser., 32 (1975): 89–99; and Daniel Scott Smith, "Underregistration and Bias in Probate Records: An Analysis of Data from Eighteenth-Century Hingham, Massachusetts," ibid., 100–10. For discussion of Chester County and Philadelphia probate records, see Soderlund, *Quakers and Slavery*, 202–6.

In Table 1–3, we obtained estimates of the slave population by multiplying the ratio of slaves to inventoried decedents (all decedents, not just slaveholders) by the number of householders. These estimates are necessarily crude and may exaggerate the number of slaves, but since the affluent were overrepresented among householders (even more than among taxpayers), this computation should reduce the inflationary effect of skewed probate data. Additional evidence suggests that these estimates are within reason. The 150 Africans who arrived on the *Isabella* in 1684 could account for most of the estimate for the 1690s, and even if some of these slaves were taken out of the city—as we would expect—slaves brought in from the Caribbean by immigrating owners made up the difference. As for the later estimates, John F. Watson, Philadelphia's first historian, wrote that during the colonial period more than a thousand slaves gathered for festivals in Washington Square (*Annals of Philadelphia* (Philadelphia, 1830), 483). It should also be emphasized that these probate data are for Philadelphia only, where slaveholding was more concentrated than in the Northern Liberties and Southwark. According to the 1767 Philadelphia tax assessment list (Rare Book Room, Van Pelt Library, Univ. of Pennsylvania), 19% of households in the city wards, but only 9% of suburban households, possessed slaves. Mortality statistics, which reported deaths in the city and suburbs and exaggerate the size of the black population in that area because mortality was considerably higher among blacks than among whites, followed the same trend as the probate data (Nash, "Slaves and Slaveholders," 226–27, 230–31; Susan E. Klepp, "Black Mortality in Early Philadelphia, 1722–1859" (Paper Presented at the Annual Meeting of the Social Science History Association, Chicago, Nov. 1988), Appendix A).

20. In comparison with our estimates in Table 1–3, blacks were an estimated 13% of Chesapeake population in 1700, 18% in 1710, and 19% in 1720. John J. McCusker and Russell R. Menard, *The Economy of British America, 1607–1789* (Chapel Hill, 1985), 136.

21. Gary B. Nash, *The Urban Crucible: Social Change, Political Consciousness, and the Origins of the American Revolution* (Cambridge, Mass., 1979), 119–20; Soderlund, *Quakers and Slavery,* 57–60, 64; Darold D. Wax, "Negro Import Duties in Colonial Pennsylvania," *PMHB* 97 (1973): 22–26; Drake, *Quakers and Slavery,* 39; Ralph Sandiford, *The Mystery of Iniquity; In a Brief Examination of the Practice of the Times . . . with Additions* (Philadelphia, 1730), 5. Apparently no duty was imposed from 1731 to 1761.

22. Marianne S. Wokeck, "A Tide of Alien Tongues: The Flow and Ebb of the German Immigration to Pennsylvania, 1683–1776" (Ph.D. diss., Temple University, 1983), 111; Wokeck, "Irish Immigration to the Delaware Valley before the American Revolution," in David B. Quinn, ed., *Ireland and America, 1500 to 1800* (forthcoming); Nash, "Slaves and Slaveowners," 227–32; Darold D. Wax, "The Negro Slave Trade in Colonial Pennsylvania" (Ph.D. diss., University of Washington, 1962), 46, 48; Wax, "Negro Import Duties," 24. The number of white indentured servants in Philadelphia again increased from the late 1760s to the Revolution, but at the same time the total bound labor force (servant and slave) declined in proportion to the city's free labor force. The number of white servants decreased after 1775. Sharon V. Salinger, *"To Serve Well and Faithfully": Labor and Indentured Servitude in Pennsylvania, 1682–1800* (Cambridge, Eng., 1987), 178–80.

23. Soderlund, *Quakers and Slavery,* 58, 64.

24. Phila. Co. Wills, Bk. C, No. 83; Dunn et al., eds., *Papers of William Penn,* II, 608; Roach, "Philadelphia Business Directory," 108.

25. Dunn et al., eds., *Papers of William Penn,* II, 541–42; Phila. Co; Wills, Bk. D, Nos. 1, 251.

26. Phila. Co. Admins., 1710, No. 51; Phila. Co. Wills, Bk. C, No. 137; Darold D. Wax, "Quaker Merchants and the Slave Trade in Colonial Pennsylvania," *PMHB* 86 (1962): 145–56; Jonathan Dickinson Letter Book, 1715–21, LCP collections, on deposit at HSP.

27. Phila. Co. Wills, Bk. E, Nos. 321, 384, 273; Phila. Co. Admins., 1731, No. 77; Soderlund, *Quakers and Slavery,* 59–60.

28. Leonard W. Labaree et al., eds., *The Papers of Benjamin Franklin* (New Haven, 1959–), VI, 425n; VII, 203, 273; IX, 38, 174, 327.

29. Phila. Co. tax assessment list, 1767; Jean R. Soderlund, "Black Women in Colonial Pennsylvania," *PMHB* 107 (1983): 60.

30. Phila. Co. Wills, Bk. C, No. 83; Bk. D, No. 251.

31. Nash, "Slaves and Slaveowners," 249–51.

32. *Pa. Gaz.,* Aug. 2, 1770; July 5, 1770; June 15, 1769. We are grateful to Billy

G. Smith and Richard Wojtowicz for sharing with us their collection of runaway notices from the *Pa. Gaz.* prior to publication of their selected edition, *Blacks Who Stole Themselves: Advertisements for Runaways in the* Pennsylvania Gazette, *1728–1790* (Philadelphia, 1989).

33. Soderlund, "Black Women," 60; *Pa. Gaz.*, Jan. 22, 1767; Jan. 8, 1767; Feb. 25, 1762.

34. Wax, "Quaker Merchants," 143–59; Wax, "Africans on the Delaware: The Pennsylvania Slave Trade, 1759–1765," *Pennsylvania History* 50 (1983): 38–49.

35. Nash, *Forging Freedom*, 8–16.

36. *Pa. Gaz.*, April 10, 1740; May 21, 1747; July 30, 1747; Sept. 1, 1763; June 12, 1776.

37. Russell R. Menard, "The Maryland Slave Population, 1658 to 1730: A Demographic Profile of Blacks in Four Counties," *WMQ*, 3rd ser., 32 (1975): 42–43; Allan Kulikoff, "A 'Prolifick' People: Black Population Growth in the Chesapeake Colonies, 1700–1790," *Southern Studies* 16 (1977): 405–6.

38. For example, Menard found about one girl per woman among slaves on the lower western shore of Maryland by the 1720s; "Maryland Slave Population," 43.

39. Only 58 slave children aged under 10 years were listed on the 1775 constables' returns, which did not include Southwark and the Northern Liberties. Nash, "Slaves and Slaveowners," 239. The mortality statistics do not distinguish between slaves and free blacks.

40. Smith, "Death and Life," 863–89; Klepp, "Black Mortality," Appendix A.

41. Ibid., 10–24.

42. Klepp, "Philadelphia in Transition," 252; Klepp, "'Prudent Resolutions': Fertility and Family Planning in Philadelphia, 1690–1860" (Paper presented to the Northeast Society for Eighteenth-Century Studies Annual Meeting, Philadelphia, Oct. 1986), 5. In "Black Mortality," 22–24, Klepp argued that black fertility was higher than white fertility in Philadelphia, but black infant mortality was higher still.

43. Benezet to Granville Sharp, May 20, 1773, Granville Sharp Letter Book, LCP, quoted in Merle G. Brouwer, "The Negro as a Slave and as a Free Black in Colonial Pennsylvania" (Ph.D. diss., Wayne State University, 1973), 132.

44. Archaeologists have found the bones of infants (or developed fetuses) in eighteenth-century Philadelphia privies; Sharon Ann Burnston, "Babies in the Well: An Underground Insight into Deviant Behavior in Eighteenth-Century Philadelphia," *PMHB* 106 (1982): 151–86.

45. For example, William Masters (d. 1761), Philadelphia's largest slaveholder with 33 blacks, had 17 children listed in his inventory, of whom 11 were bound out, one as far away as Wilmington. Phila. Co. Wills, Bk. M, No. 27.

46. *Pa. Gaz.*, May 21, 1747; July 30, 1747; Oct. 1, 1747; Feb. 2, 1748; Nov. 3, 1763; Oct. 7, 1772; May 1, 1776; July 3, 1776.

47. Roberts Vaux, *Memoirs of the Lives of Benjamin Lay and Ralph Sandiford; Two of the Earliest Public Advocates for the Emancipation of the Enslaved Africans* (Philadelphia, 1815), 27–28.

48. Robert Sutcliff, *Travels in Some Parts of North America, in the Years 1804, 1805, & 1806* (York [Eng.], 1811), 184.

49. *Pa. Gaz.*, May 5, 1748; Whitfield J. Bell, Jr., ed., "Addenda to Watson's *Annals of Philadelphia:* Notes by Jacob Mordecai, 1836," *PMHB* 98 (1974): 139.

50. Soderlund, *Quakers and Slavery*, 153.

51. Labaree et al., eds., *Papers of Franklin*, IV, 229; Darold D. Wax, "Negro Resistance to the Early American Slave Trade," *JNH* 51 (1966): 13–15; Nash, *Forging Freedom*, 11–13; John Smith's Diary, vol. 5, entry for 4M/28/1748, LCP, on deposit at HSP.

52. Billy G. Smith, "The Family Lives of Blacks in Philadelphia, 1750–1800," in Catherine Hutchins, ed., *Shaping a National Culture: The Philadelphia Experience 1750–1800* (New York, forthcoming); Smith, "Fugitives from Slavery in the Mid-Atlantic Region During the Eighteenth Century" (Paper presented to the Philadelphia Center for Early American Studies, Philadelphia, March 1989), 36–43; *Pa. Gaz.*, June 15, 1769; Sept. 21, 1769; Feb. 20, 1772. See also, Merle G. Brouwer, "Marriage and Family Life Among Blacks in Colonial Pennsylvania," *PMHB* 99 (1975): 368–72.

53. *Pa. Gaz.*, Jan. 22, 1767.

54. Records of Christ Church, Philadelphia, Marriages, 1709–1800, Genealogical Society of Pennsylvania transcripts, housed at HSP.

55. Nash, *Forging Freedom*, 19–22; Richard I. Shelling, "William Sturgeon, Catechist to the Negroes of Philadelphia and Assistant Rector of Christ Church, 1747–1766," *Historical Magazine of the Episcopal Church* 8 (1939): 388–401.

56. Nancy Slocum Hornick, "Anthony Benezet and the Africans' School: Toward a Theory of Full Equality," *PMHB* 99 (1975): 399–421.

57. Soderlund, *Quakers and Slavery*, 19, 148, 150, 182–84; Henry J. Cadbury, "Negro Membership in the Society of Friends," *JNH* 21 (1936): 151–213.

58. Nash, *Forging Freedom*, 17–24.

59. Ibid., 21; *Pa. Gaz.*, Nov. 25, 1772; Aug. 23, 1775; Jan. 18, 1770; Aug. 31, 1774.

60. Watson, *Annals of Phila.*, 352, 483.

61. *Pa. Gaz.*, May 5, 1748; Sept. 1, 1763; March 31, 1773; July 2, 1772.

62. Mrs. E. B. Hoskins, "Fanny Saltar's Reminiscences of Colonial Days in Philadelphia," *PMHB* 40 (1916): 187.

63. U.S. Bureau of the Census, *Historical Statistics of the United States, Colonial Times to 1970* (Washington, D.C., 1975), II, 1168; P.M.G. Harris, "The Demographic Development of Colonial Philadelphia in Some Comparative Perspective," *Proceedings of the American Philosophical Society* 133 (1989): 274.

64. Jerome H. Wood, Jr., *Conestoga Crossroads: Lancaster, Pennsylvania, 1730–1790* (Harrisburg, 1979), 162; Paul Erb Doutrich, "The Evolution of an Early American Town: Yorktown, Pennsylvania, 1740–1790" (Ph.D. diss., University of Kentucky, 1985), 75–76.

65. Barry Levy, "From 'Dark Corners' to American Domesticity: The British Social Context of the Welsh and Cheshire Quakers' Familial Revolution in Pennsylvania,

1657–1685," in Richard S. Dunn and Mary Maples Dunn, eds., *The World of William Penn* (Philadelphia, 1986), 218; Lemon, *Best Poor Man's Country*, 150–67, 218–28; Lucy Simler, "Tenancy in Colonial Pennsylvania: The Case of Chester County," *WMQ*, 3rd ser., 43 (1986): 550–53; Chester Co. tax assessment lists, 1765–1800, CCA, microfilm available from PHMC.

66. Thornbury Twp. constables' return, 1726, CCA. In addition, widow Deborah Nayle, who lived as an inmate in another's household, owned a slave woman, probably Bella, whom Nayle freed when she died ca. 1751; Chester Co. Wills, No. 1389.

67. Soderlund, *Quakers and Slavery*, 57, 60, 65–78. These data are not representative of the frequency of ownership of slaves throughout Chester County because the level of slaveholding was higher in these nine eastern townships than in the county as a whole: according to the 1765 tax list, 10.8% of householders in these nine townships owned slaves (close to the 10.6% found in the 1760s probate records) and 6% of all county householders owned slaves. The 1770s probate figure of 19% owning slaves may be inflated because the Revolution interrupted probate proceedings and as a result a smaller percentage of decedents' estates went through probate during this decade than in earlier years, but it may also represent increased importation during the 1760s. In addition, a number of deceased slaveowners in the 1770s freed slaves in their wills, and therefore these blacks did not subsequently appear as slaves on tax lists.

68. Futhey and Cope, *History of Chester County*, 18, 24, 33, 378–79; George Smith, *History of Delaware County, Pennsylvania* (Philadelphia, 1862), 103–4; Dunn et al., eds., *Papers of William Penn*, II, 531–32; Phila. Co. Wills, Bk. A, No. 177; Bk. B, No. 54.

69. Phila. Co. Wills, Bk. C, No. 102; Bk. C, No. 141.

70. Phila. Co. Admins., 1708, No. 29; Phila. Co. Wills, Bk. B, No. 12; Bk. A, No. 114; Chester Co. Wills, Nos. 513, 604, 34, 153, 163, 347, 607.

71. Chester (Pa.) MM mins. (women's), 11M/1713 (Jan. 1714), FHL; Gary B. Nash, *Quakers and Politics: Pennsylvania, 1681–1726* (Princeton, 1968), 251–305; Chester Co. Wills, No. 394; No. 1850.

72. The number of slaves on the 1774 Chester Co. tax list, adjusted to include those not taxable, was 388, a considerable drop from 1765. This list is suspect, however, because at least 44 blacks manumitted during the years 1775 to 1779 do not appear, perhaps because their Quaker owners permitted them to maintain separate households and work for themselves prior to manumission. One such case was that of Sarah Tobias, who went to live with her husband about three years before she was freed. See Chapter 6, below.

73. Lucy Simler generously provided the data on indentured servitude. On the changing labor structure, see Paul G.E. Clemens and Lucy Simler, "Rural Labor and the Farm Household in Chester County, Pennsylvania, 1750–1820," in Stephen Innes, ed., *Work and Labor in Early America* (Chapel Hill, 1988), 106–43.

74. *Pa. Gaz.*, Feb. 18, 1762; Jan. 1, 1767.

75. *Pa. Gaz.*, Oct. 25, 1764; Sept. 22, 1768; June 15, 1769; June 6, 1771.

76. Chester Co. tax assessment list, 1765; Paul F. Paskoff, *Industrial Evolution: Organization, Structure, and Growth of the Pennsylvania Iron Industry, 1750–1860*

(Baltimore, 1983), 14–15; Arthur Cecil Bining, *Pennsylvania Iron Manufacture in the Eighteenth Century,* 2nd ed. (Harrisburg, 1973), 99–102, 171; *Pa. Gaz.,* June 23, 1768.

77. New Pine Forge Time Book, 1760–63, back pages, in Paskoff, *Industrial Evolution,* 14; Phila. Co. Wills, Bk. M, No. 209.

78. *Pa. Gaz.,* April 13, 1769; May 4, 1769; Feb. 8, 1770; Nov. 27, 1760; March 26, 1761; June 14, 1764; Sept. 22, 1768; Jan. 2, 1766; June 23, 1768; July 7, 1768; Aug. 11, 1768; June 19, 1776.

79. Chester Co. slave register; Copy, Lancaster Co. Register of Negroe and Mulatto Slaves and Servants, Lancaster Co. Historical Society, Lancaster, Pa. The original has not been located. The unidentified copyist reconstructed from individual returns two pages of entries that had been torn from the original register. The Bucks Co. Register of Slaves [1780] and Washington Co. Negro Register (1782) are both available on microfilm from PHMC.

80. Chester Co. slave register.

81. Chester Co. slave register.

Chapter 2

1. *PA,* 8th ser. (Harrisburg, 1931), II, 1012–13; Kenneth L. Carroll, "William Southeby, Early Quaker Antislavery Writer," *PMHB* 89 (1965): 416–27; Richard S. Dunn et al., eds., *The Papers of William Penn* (5 vols.; Philadelphia, 1981–87), III, 110; Peter J. Parker, ed., "Rich and Poor in Philadelphia, 1709," *PMHB* 99 (1975): 18.

2. Kenneth Scott, "The Slave Insurrection in New York in 1712," *New-York Historical Society Quarterly* 45 (1961), 43–74; *PA,* 8th ser., II, 1012–13; Darold D. Wax, "The Negro Slave Trade in Colonial Pennsylvania" (Ph.D. diss., University of Washington, 1962), 267–74.

3. Thomas E. Drake, *Quakers and Slavery in America* (New Haven, 1950), 11–20; Jean R. Soderlund, *Quakers and Slavery: A Divided Spirit* (Princeton, 1985), 18–20; Samuel Whitaker Pennypacker, "The Settlement of Germantown Pennsylvania and the Beginning of German Immigration to North America," *The Pennsylvania-German Society Proceedings and Addresses* (Lancaster, Pa., 1899), IX, 196–203; Phila. Co. Wills (see Chapter 1, n. 8, above, for full reference), Bk. D, No. 171; "Germantown Friends' Protest Against Slavery, 1688," reprinted in J. William Frost, ed., *The Quaker Origins of Antislavery* (Norwood, Pa., 1980), 69.

4. Dunn et al., eds., *Papers of William Penn,* III, 357; Pennypacker, "Settlement of Germantown," 203–9; J. William Frost, ed., *The Keithian Controversy in Early Pennsylvania* (Norwood, Pa., 1980), i-xx, 213–18 (quotation on pp. 214–15).

5. Thomas E. Drake, "Cadwalader Morgan: Antislavery Quaker of the Welsh Tract," *Friends Intelligencer* 98 (1941): 575–76; Soderlund, *Quakers and Slavery,* 19; PYM mins., 23/7M/1696, FHL; Phila. Co. Wills, Bk. C, No. 211.

6. Drake, *Quakers and Slavery,* 21; Phila. MM mins., 1697–1717, FHL; Phila. Co. Wills, Bk. D, No. 157; *PA,* 2nd ser., IX, 738.

7. Henry J. Cadbury, "An Early Quaker Anti-slavery Statement," *JNH* 22 (1937): 488–93; *PA*, 2nd ser., IX, 675–76, 683–84.

8. Darold D. Wax, "Quaker Merchants and the Slave Trade in Colonial Pennsylvania," *PMHB* 86 (1962): 143–57.

9. Soderlund, *Quakers and Slavery*, 20–22, 34; John F. Watson, *Annals of Philadelphia, and Pennsylvania, in the Olden Time*, rev. ed. (3 vols.; Philadelphia, 1909), II, 263.

10. Soderlund, *Quakers and Slavery*, 21–26.

11. Drake, *Quakers and Slavery*, 28.

12. Ibid., 24–33, 39–43; Soderlund, *Quakers and Slavery*, 20–26.

13. David Brion Davis, *The Problem of Slavery in Western Culture* (Ithaca, 1966); Davis, *The Problem of Slavery in the Age of Revolution 1770–1823* (Ithaca, 1975); Thomas L. Haskell, "Capitalism and the Origins of the Humanitarian Sensibility, Part 1," *AHR* 90 (1985): 339–61; Part 2, *AHR* 90 (1985): 457–566; Davis, "Reflections on Abolitionism and Ideological Hegemony," *AHR* 92 (1987): 797–812; John Ashworth, "The Relationship between Capitalism and Humanitarianism," *AHR* 92 (1987): 813–28; and Haskell, "Convention and Hegemonic Interest in the Debate over Antislavery: A Reply to Davis and Ashworth," *AHR* 92 (1987): 829–78.

14. Davis, *Problem of Slavery in Western Culture*, 291–332; quotation on p. 324.

15. Davis, *Problem of Slavery in the Age of Revolution*, 233–54.

16. Haskell, "Convention and Hegemonic Interest," 872–78; quotation on p. 875.

17. Davis, "Reflections on Abolitionism," 798.

18. C. Brightwen Rowntree, "Benjamin Lay (1681–1759)," *The Journal of the Friends' Historical Society* 33 (1936): 3–19; Roberts Vaux, *Memoirs of the Lives of Benjamin Lay and Ralph Sandiford; Two of the Earliest Public Advocates for the Emancipation of the Enslaved Africans* (Philadelphia, 1815), 17, 25–28; Drake, *Quakers and Slavery*, 43–47; Davis, *Problem of Slavery in Western Culture*, 321–23.

19. Davis, "Reflections on Abolitionism," 797–812.

20. Jack D. Marietta, *The Reformation of American Quakerism, 1748–1783* (Philadelphia, 1984), 32–96.

21. Phillips P. Moulton, ed., *The Journal and Major Essays of John Woolman* (New York, 1971), 32–33.

22. Ibid., 38.

23. Ibid., 44–45; Soderlund, *Quakers and Slavery*, 34–35.

24. Moulton, ed., *Journal . . . of John Woolman*, 198–209; quotations on pp. 204 and 207.

25. George S. Brookes, *Friend Anthony Benezet* (Philadelphia, 1937), 12–30; PYM mins., 1746–54; Philadelphia tax assessment list, 1774, HSP.

26. Nancy Slocum Hornick, "Anthony Benezet and the Africans' School: Toward a Theory of Full Equality," *PMHB* 99 (1975): 399–421.

27. Quoted in Marietta, *Reformation*, 100.

28. Soderlund, *Quakers and Slavery*, 27; PYM mins., 14–19/9M/1754.

29. Drake, *Quakers and Slavery*, 34–47.

30. Soderlund, *Quakers and Slavery,* 26–28, 34, 43–51; Chapter 1, above.

31. *An Account of the Gospel Labours and Christian Experiences of that Faithful Minister of Christ, John Churchman* (Philadelphia, 1882), 209–10; quoted in Marietta, *Reformation,* 119.

32. Soderlund, *Quakers and Slavery,* 173–77; J. William Frost, "The Origins of the Quaker Crusade against Slavery: A Review of Recent Literature," *Quaker History* 67 (1978): 56–58.

33. PYM mins., 1755–62; Moulton, ed., *Journal . . . of John Woolman,* 94–97, 102, 106, and 117.

34. Marianne S. Wokeck, "A Tide of Alien Tongues: The Flow and Ebb of the German Immigration to Pennsylvania, 1683–1776" (Ph.D. diss., Temple University, 1983), 111; Wokeck, "Irish Immigration to the Delaware Valley before the American Revolution," in David B. Quinn, ed., *Ireland and America, 1500 to 1800* (forthcoming). Wokeck has revised upwards the estimate of Irish arrivals in the Delaware Valley during the late 1750s but suggests that many Irish immigrants disembarked in Delaware before the ships proceeded to Philadelphia.

35. Gary B. Nash, "Slaves and Slaveowners in Colonial Philadelphia," *WMQ,* 3rd ser., 30 (1973): 227–32; Wax, "Negro Slave Trade," 46; Wax, "Negro Import Duties in Colonial Pennsylvania," *PMHB* 97 (1973): 24.

36. Soderlund, *Quakers and Slavery,* 88; Phila. MM mins., 25/1M/1760 and 27/8M/1762.

37. Soderlund, *Quakers and Slavery,* 165.

38. Pemberton to William Reckitt, 2/10M/1758, Reckitt Mss., FHL; Moulton, ed., *Journal . . . of John Woolman,* 92.

39. Most extant manumissions for the period to 1762 are from wills, but a few can be found in the records of the county courts of quarter sessions and in deeds. Manumissions for Philadelphia for the late 17th and 18th century are found in Phila. Co. Wills; PAS Papers, Reels 20–24, originals at HSP; Manumission Book for the Three Philadelphia Monthly Meetings (1772–96), QC; records of the Philadelphia Court of Quarter Sessions, City Hall, Philadelphia; Miscellaneous Deed Books, Philadelphia City Archives; and Letter of Attorney Books, Division of Land Records, Bureau of Archives and History, PHMC.

40. Dunn et al., eds., *Papers of William Penn,* II, 362; Phila. Co. Wills, Bk. A, No. 172; William Wade Hinshaw, ed., *Encyclopedia of American Quaker Genealogy* (5 vols.; Ann Arbor, Mich., 1936–46), II, 234, 445.

41. Phila. Co. Wills, Bk. A, No. 216; Hinshaw, ed., *Encyclopedia,* II, 448, 658; Gary B. Nash, *Quakers and Politics: Pennsylvania, 1681–1726* (Princeton, 1968), 159; Frederick Lewis Weis, *The Colonial Clergy of the Middle Colonies: New York, New Jersey, and Pennsylvania 1628–1776* (Worcester, Mass., 1957), 197–98.

42. Phila. Co. Wills, Bk. B, No. 137; Dunn et al., eds., *Papers of William Penn,* II, 85–86.

43. Phila. Co. Wills, Bk. C, No. 218; Bk. D, No. 13; Parker, "Rich and Poor," 18; Frost, ed., *Keithian Controversy,* 371.

44. Gary B. Nash, *The Urban Crucible: Social Change, Political Consciousness, and the Origins of the American Revolution* (Cambridge, Mass., 1979), 119; Phila. Co. Wills, Bk. D, No. 201.

45. Brittin and his wife were listed as Philadelphia Muggletonians in "An Account of Such as Have Formerly Frequented Friends Meetings and Have Since Followed George Keith or Others," compiled by an unidentified person perhaps in 1700 or 1701, thus identifying them as followers of Lodowick Muggleton (1609–98), a bitter opponent of Quakers. It was reported that in 1708 Roman Catholics gathered at Brittin's house for public Mass. Frost, ed., *Keithian Controversy,* 371–75; Dunn et al., eds., *Papers of William Penn,* I, 87–88; Helen Hutchison Woodroofe, "A Chronological List of Philadelphia Churches and Cemeteries 1642–1790," *Pennsylvania Genealogical Magazine* 30 (1978): 159; Phila. Co. Wills, Bk. D, No. 228; Bk. F, No. 249.

46. Phila. Co. Wills, Bk. D, No. 323.

47. Phila. Co. Wills, Bk. D, No. 312; Bk. D, No. 326; Bk. D, No. 328.

48. Phila. Co. Wills, Bk. E, No. 119; Bk. E, No. 179; Bk. E, No. 366; Bk. E, No. 414.

49. Phila. Co. Wills, Bk. E, No. 412; Bk. G, No. 239.

50. Phila. Co. Wills, Bk. G, No. 41. At about the same time, in 1742, Jeremiah Langhorne of Bucks Co. freed 30 or 40 slaves; Edward Raymond Turner, *Slavery in Pennsylvania* (Baltimore, 1911), 57.

51. Phila. Co. Wills, Bk. G, No. 111; Bk. I, No. 14; Bk. I, No. 5; Bk. K, No. 113.

52. Phila. Co. Wills, Bk. I, No. 285; Bk. K, No. 53; Bk. K, No. 324; Bk. M, No. 82.

53. Phila. Co. Wills, Bk. K, No. 97.

54. Phila. Co. Wills, Bk. H, No. 52; Bk. I, No. 248; Bk. H, No. 191; Bk. K, No. 152; Bk. L, No. 42.

55. Leonard W. Labaree et al., eds., *The Papers of Benjamin Franklin* (New Haven, 1959–), VII, 203.

56. Soderlund, *Quakers and Slavery,* 153.

57. Ibid., 20–25.

58. Phila. Co. Wills, Bk. A, No. 114; Bk. A, No. 177; Soderlund, *Quakers and Slavery,* 153, 155.

59. Tabulated from manumissions granted by residents of Chester County found in Phila. Co. Wills (for the period before 1715); Chester Co. Wills and records of the Chester Co. Court of Quarter Sessions, CCA; Chester Co. Deeds, Recorder of Deeds office, Chester Co. Court House, West Chester; Miscellaneous Slavery Papers and the Buffington and Marshall Papers, No. 452, CCHS. For the period after 1762, Chester County manumissions are also found in the minutes and manumission records of Bradford, Chester, Concord, Darby, Goshen, Kennett, New Garden, Nottingham, Radnor, Sadsbury, and Uwchlan Monthly Meetings, FHL; and Delaware County Wills (beginning 1789), on microfilm at HSP.

60. According to the 1765 Chester County tax assessment list, CCA, the sex ratio of slaves aged 12 to 50 years was 136 males per 100 females. The sex ratio of slaves freed from 1741 to 1762 was 200 for adults and 218 for adults and children.

61. Phila. Co. Wills, 1682–1762; Chester Co. tax assessment list, 1765.

62. Phila. Co. Wills, Bk. B, No. 54; Bk. A, No. 177; Chester Co. Wills, No. 298; No. 632; No. 1389.

63. Chester Co. Wills, No. 394; No. 1850; Chester MM manumissions, 1778.

64. For example, see Jerome S. Handler and John T. Pohlmann, "Slave Manumissions and Freedmen in Seventeenth-Century Barbados," *WMQ*, 3rd ser., 41 (1984): 390-408.

65. *PA*, 8th ser., VI, 5191, 5196, 5197, 5204, 5205–6, 5213–14, 5215, 5217; Wax, "Negro Slave Trade," 274–78.

66. Howard M. Jenkins, "Fragments of a Journal Kept by Samuel Foulke of Bucks County, While a Member of the Colonial Assembly of Pennsylvania, 1762–3–4," *PMHB* 5 (1881): 60; quoted in Wax, "Negro Slave Trade," 265.

67. Gary B. Nash, *Forging Freedom: The Formation of Philadelphia's Black Community, 1720–1840* (Cambridge, Mass., 1988), 12–13; Billy G. Smith, "Fugitives from Slavery in the Mid-Atlantic Region During the Eighteenth Century" (Paper Presented to the Philadelphia Center for Early American Studies, Philadelphia, March 1989), 46–47.

68. Our files of Philadelphia and Chester County slaveowners; *PA*, 8th ser., VI, 5157, 5196; Marietta, *Reformation*, 194–202; Richard Alan Ryerson, *The Revolution Is Now Begun: The Radical Committees of Philadelphia, 1765–1776* (Philadelphia, 1978), 260–62; Alan Tully, *William Penn's Legacy: Politics and Social Structure in Provincial Pennsylvania, 1726–1755* (Baltimore, 1977), 174–80.

69. Davis, *Problem of Slavery in the Age of Revolution*, 214.

Chapter 3

1. Gary B. Nash, "Slaves and Slaveholders in Colonial Philadelphia," *WMQ*, 3rd ser., 30 (1973): 229–31.

2. Thomas Riche Letter Book, 1764–1771, HSP, quoted in Darold D. Wax, "Negro Imports into Pennsylvania, 1720–1766," *Pennsylvania History* 32 (1965): 255.

3. Wax, "The Negro Slave Trade in Colonial Pennsylvania" (Ph.D. diss., University of Washington, 1962), 48; Benezet to Granville Sharp, Feb. 18, 1773, Sharp Letter Book, LCP, cited in Wax, "Negro Imports," 255.

4. "Observations Concerning the Increase in Mankind," in Leonard W. Labaree et al., eds., *The Papers of Benjamin Franklin* (New Haven, 1959–), IV, 231. Franklin's observation received confirmation in 1775 from Boston's Edward Wigglesworth in *Calculations on American Population; with A Table for estimating the annual Increase . . . in the British Colonies* (Boston, 1775), 13.

5. Whitfield J. Bell, ed., "Addenda to Watson's *Annals of Philadelphia:* Notes by Jacob Mordecai, 1836," *PMHB* 98 (1974): 139.

6. *The Journals of Henry Melchior Muhlenberg,* trans. Theodore G. Tappert and John W. Doberstein (3 vols.; Philadelphia, 1942–58), II, 7, 11–12.

7. For data on runaway slave advertisements from the *Pa. Gaz.* we are indebted to Billy G. Smith, Montana State University. To this master list we have added runaway

advertisements in the *Pennsylvania Chronicle, Pennsylvania Journal,* and *Pennsylvania Packet.* Chester County slaveowners, at a distance from Philadelphia, probably had more difficulty in advertising runaway slaves, so it is likely that the number of rural runaway slaves is understated here. Some slaves, of course, were recaptured, but the increase in the number of runaways nonetheless represents a change of consciousness among slaves.

8. Madison to William Bradford, Nov. 26, 1774; Bradford to Madison, Jan. 4, 1775, *The Papers of James Madison,* William T. Hutchinson and William M. E. Rachel, eds. (Chicago, 1962–), I, 129–30, 132.

9. *Pennsylvania Evening Post,* Dec. 14, 1775.

10. Rush to Granville Sharp, Oct. 20, 1773; May 13, 1774; Nov. 1, 1774, in John A. Woods, ed., "Correspondence of Benjamin Rush and Granville Sharp, 1773–1809," *Journal of American Studies* 1 (1967): 3, 5, 13–14.

11. Gary B. Nash, *Forging Freedom: The Formation of Philadelphia's Black Community, 1720–1840* (Cambridge, Mass., 1988), 104–5.

12. Thomas E. Drake, *Quakers and Slavery in America* (New Haven, 1950), 62.

13. *Pennsylvania Chronicle,* Nov. 21–28, 1768, quoted in Darold D. Wax, "Reform and Revolution: The Movement Against Slavery and the Slave Trade in Revolutionary Pennsylvania," *Western Pennsylvania Historical Magazine* 57 (1974): 410–11.

14. Rush, *An Address . . . upon Slavekeeping* (Philadelphia, 1773), 30.

15. Paine, "African Slavery in America," in Philip Foner, ed., *The Complete Writings of Thomas Paine* (2 vols.; New York, 1945), II, 15–19; Paine published a second antislavery essay, "A Serious Thought," in the *Pennsylvania Journal,* Oct. 18, 1775.

16. Quoted in Arthur Zilversmit, *The First Emancipation: The Abolition of Slavery in the North* (Chicago, 1967), 97.

17. For the gathering abolitionist momentum see Duncan J. McLeod, *Slavery, Race, and the American Revolution* (Cambridge, Eng., 1974), chaps. 1–2; and David Brion Davis, *The Problem of Slavery in the Age of Revolution, 1770–1823* (Ithaca, 1975), chaps. 4, 6.

18. Edward R. Turner, "The First Abolition Society in the United States," *PMHB* 36 (1912): 92–109; Edward Needles, *An Historical Memoir of the Pennsylvania Society for Promoting the Abolition of Slavery* (Philadelphia, 1848), 17–18; Manumission Book for the Three Philadelphia Monthly Meetings (1772–96), QC.

19. Rush to Granville Sharp, May 1, 1773, in L. H. Butterfield, ed., *The Letters of Benjamin Rush* (2 vols.; Princeton, 1951), I, 81.

20. Manumission certificate for Cuff and related documents in Society Miscellaneous Collection, Box 11a, HSP.

21. Phila. Co. Admins., 1763, No. 7, City Hall, Philadelphia.

22. In using these data we are not referring to individuals so much as human units in occupational and religious blocs because much shifting of people from one occupational category to another, and even one church to another on occasion, occurred during the decade. Many deaths turned a slaveowning merchant or doctor into a

slaveowning widow; artisans and proprietors sold slaves to mariners and merchants; slave deaths or flight frequently decreased the number of masters represented in a particular religious or occupational grouping without anyone manumitting a slave; and people of one occupational or religious group willed slaves to family members or friends of another occupation or religion. Nonetheless, the data show how the religious, occupational, and wealth structure of slaveholding and manumitting changed over time.

23. Labaree et al., eds., *Papers of Franklin*, IX, 174.

24. For the case of Roberts's slave see Drake, *Quakers and Slavery*, 73.

25. A few of the apparently new slaveowners may have been those with young slaves who reached the taxable age of 12 between 1767 and 1769.

26. Benezet to Granville Sharp, Feb. 18, April 1, 1773, quoted in Wax, "Reform and Revolution," 409.

27. Jean R. Soderlund, *Quakers and Slavery: A Divided Spirit* (Princeton, 1985), chap. 6.

28. Chester MM mins., 6M/1760-2M/1761; Concord MM mins., 1M/1764-1M/1765; these minutes and others cited below are available at FHL.

29. Chester County Quarter Sessions Docket Books A and B, CCA.

30. The constables' returns for the city of Philadelphia have been increased by 20 percent to include Southwark and the Northern Liberties; this is the percentage of slaves in urban Philadelphia held by masters in the two adjacent areas in 1767.

31. Soderlund, *Quakers and Slavery*, 167–71.

32. PYM mins., 26/9M-1/10M/1774.

33. PYM mins., 25-30/9M/1775.

34. Phila. QM mins., 8M/1776.

35. PYM mins., 23-28/9M/1776; Soderlund, *Quakers and Slavery*, 103–9.

36. Thomas Gilpin, "Memorials and Reminiscences in Private Life," 1839, interleaved notes in Hannah Logan Smith, *Collection of Testimonies, etc.* (Philadelphia, 1839), HSP; five of the manumission documents are in Copy of Book of Deeds of Manumission of Slaves (1774–92), Duck Creek Monthly Meeting, Kent, Delaware, Collections of the Genealogical Society of Pennsylvania, HSP.

37. PYM mins., 23–28/9M/1776.

38. Ibid.; Drake, *Quakers and Slavery*, 71–72.

39. Ibid., 74.

40. Philadelphia Yearly Meeting, Meeting for Sufferings minutes, 1 mo/20–21 1780.

41. Adam Smith, *An Inquiry into . . . the Wealth of Nations*, James E. Thorold Rogers, ed. (2 vols.; 2nd ed., Oxford, 1880), I, 391.

42. Charles Varlo [Varley], *Miscellany of Knowledge . . . [with] A Twelve-Month's Tour, of Observations, through America . . .* (2nd ed., London, 1792), 279–80.

43. PYM mins., 9 mo/29–10 mo/4/1783.

44. Petitions of John Hanna and Phebe Hanna, Records of Pennsylvania's Revolutionary Government, microfilm edition, Reel 11, fr962, 1236, PHMC.

45. Bills of sale for slaves, Society Miscellaneous Collection, HSP.

46. Harry Emerson Wildes, *Lonely Midas: The Story of Stephen Girard* (New York, 1943), 26, 99, 323.

47. M. V. Brewington, "The State Ship *General Greene,*" *PMHB* 60 (1936): 233.

48. Petition of Jedidiah Snowden to the Supreme Executive Council, Sept. 27, 1779, Records of Pennsylvania's Revolutionary Governments, 1775–90, microfilm edition, Reel 15, fr1306–7, PHMC.

49. *Muhlenberg Journals,* III, 78.

50. Nash, *Forging Freedom,* 49; in addition to the newspapers listed in note 7 above, runaway advertisements have been compiled from *Pennsylvania Ledger,* 1775–78; *Pennsylvania Evening Post,* 1775–79; and *Royal Pennsylvania Gazette,* 1777–78.

51. *Pennsylvania Packet,* Dec. 12, 1779.

52. Nash, *Forging Freedom,* 56–58; Debra L. Newman, "Black Women in the Era of the American Revolution in Pennsylvania," *JNH* 61 (1976): 276–89.

53. Nash, *Forging Freedom,* 51–55; *Sermon on the Present Situation of the Affairs of America and Great-Britain, Written by a Black, And printed at the Request of several Persons of distinguished Characters* (Philadelphia, 1782), 9, HSP on deposit at LCP.

54. Goshen MM mins., 12 mo./1774; 8 mo./1775; 8 mo./1776.

55. Ibid., 12 mo./1776 to 8 mo./1780.

56. Chester Co. Wills, No. 2881.

57. Chester Co. Wills, Nos. 2980, 3038, 3037.

Chapter 4

1. Peter Force, comp., *American Archives,* 4th ser. (6 vols.; Washington, D.C., 1833–46), II, 172, cited in Arthur Zilversmit, *The First Emancipation: The Abolition of Slavery in the North* (Chicago, 1967), 126.

2. Gordon S. Wood, *The Creation of the American Republic, 1776–1787* (Chapel Hill, 1969), 226.

3. The Constitution of 1776 is reprinted in Theodore Thayer, *Pennsylvania Politics and the Growth of Democracy, 1740–1776* (Harrisburg, 1953), 211–27. The Declaration of Rights is on pp. 212–15.

4. Rush to Anthony Wayne, Sept. 24, 1776; April 2, 1777; May 19, 1777, in Lyman H. Butterfield, ed., *The Letters of Benjamin Rush* (2 vols.; Princeton, 1951), I, 114–15, 136–37, 148, quotation on p. 148.

5. Burton Konkle maintained that some at the convention wanted language explicitly including blacks in the "free and equal" clause, but he cites no evidence. Konkle, *George Bryan and the Constitution of Pennsylvania, 1731–1791* (Philadelphia, 1922), 145.

6. Ibid., chap. 9.

7. Konkle claims that Bryan raised the matter of an antislavery bill in late 1777 when he was vice-president of the Executive Council; *Bryan,* 145.

8. *Journals of the House of Representatives of the Commonwealth of Pennsylvania, . . . 1776–1781* (Philadelphia, 1782), 218.

9. Zilversmit, *First Emancipation,* 126–27; the Council's message to the Assembly is in *PA,* 1st ser., VII (Philadelphia, 1853), 79, and *Pennsylvania Packet,* Nov. 28, 1778.

10. *PA,* 1st ser., VII, 79.

11. *Journals of the House,* 302.

12. The bill was published in the *Penna. Packet,* March 4, 1779.

13. Horace Binney, *Leaders of the Old Philadelphia Bar* (Philadelphia, 1859), 25; six years after Franklin's death in 1790, St. George Tucker, the distinguished Virginia jurist, wrote that "Doctor [Benjamin] Franklin, it is said, drew the bill for the gradual abolition of slavery in Pennsylvania." *A Dissertation on Slavery: with a Proposal for the Gradual Abolition of It, in the State of Virginia* (Philadelphia, 1796), 82. This is highly unlikely since Franklin was in Paris at the time and had been for several years. On Bryan's authorship see Edward Raymond Turner, *The Negro in Pennsylvania: Slavery—Servitude—Freedom, 1639–1861* (Washington, D.C., 1911), 79, and Bryan's obituary in *Pa. Gaz.,* Feb. 2, 1791. Philip Foner calls Paine the author of the preamble and others have followed him in this, misled, it appears, by the fact that Paine was appointed clerk of the assembly on the same day the bill was introduced; Foner, ed., *The Complete Works of Thomas Paine* (2 vols.; New York, 1945), II, 21.

14. *Journals of the House,* Feb. 5, 1779, 303–4.

15. The preamble and law are reprinted in Roger Bruns, ed., *Am I Not a Man and a Brother: The Antislavery Crusade of Revolutionary America, 1688–1788* (New York, 1977), 446–50.

16. Thomas D. Morris, *Free Men All: The Personal Liberty Laws of the North, 1780–1861* (Baltimore, 1974), 5.

17. Owen Ireland, "Germans Against Abolition: A Minority's View of Slavery in Revolutionary Pennsylvania," *Journal of Interdisciplinary History* 3 (1973): 685–706.

18. The Chester County petition is in *Journals of the House,* 365; Bryan, in a letter published in the *Penna. Packet,* Dec. 23, 1779, refuted the argument earlier made by Chester County Presbyterians. Ireland sees the German church people forming the heart of the anti-abolition movement, but his analysis of ten roll calls on the issue indicates that Scots and Scots-Irish opponents of abolition outnumbered German opponents by 18 to 15. "Germans Against Abolition," 689, Table 1.

19. *Penna. Packet,* March 13, 1779.

20. *Journals of the House,* 392, 394, 398.

21. Bruns, ed., *Am I Not a Man and a Brother,* 446.

22. *Penna. Packet,* Jan. 1, 1780.

23. *Pa. Gaz.,* Feb. 2, 1780, for "Phileleutheros," who appears to have been Anthony Benezet; Robert William Fogel and Stanley L. Engerman, "Philanthropy at Bargain Prices: Notes on the Economics of Gradual Emancipation," *Journal of Legal Studies* 3 (1974): 377–401.

24. *Pa. Gaz.,* Feb. 2, 1780.

25. For petitions against adopting the law from Lancaster and Bucks counties see Zilversmit, *First Emancipation*, 128–29.

26. *Journals of the House*, 399.

27. *Penna. Packet*, Dec. 25, 1779.

28. David Brion Davis, *Slavery and Human Progress* (New York, 1984), 81, 107–10, and passim, for the argument that the Revolutionary period brought "a profound change in the basic paradigm of social geography" regarding the evil of slavery (87).

29. *Journals of the House*, 424–25, 435.

30. Robert L. Brunhouse, *The Counter-Revolution in Pennsylvania, 1776–1790* (Harrisburg, 1971), 81.

31. Zilversmit, *First Emancipation*, 131–32; *Journals of the House*, 436; the dissenters were answered in *Penna. Packet*, March 25, 1780.

32. Ireland, "Germans Against Abolition."

33. Marsteller to Bryan, March 13, 1780, George Bryan Papers, HSP. We are grateful to Joseph S. Foster for this reference.

34. Copy, Lancaster County Register of Negro and Mulatto Slaves and Servants, Lancaster County Historical Society, Lancaster, Pa.; the 1779 tax list is published in *PA*, 3rd ser. (Harrisburg, 1898), XVII, 491–685.

35. Edward Needles, *An Historical Memoir of the Pennsylvania Society for Promoting the Abolition of Slavery* . . . (Philadelphia, 1848), 23.

36. For comparisons of the state laws see Fogel and Engerman, "Philanthropy at Bargain Prices," 380–81.

37. "To the Publick," *The New Jersey Journal*, Sept. 20, 1780, in Bruns, ed., *Am I Not a Man and a Brother*, 456–59.

38. J.P. Brissot de Warville, *New Travels in the United States of America* (Dublin, 1792), 277–79.

39. "To the Publick," Bruns, ed., *Am I Not a Man and a Brother*, 446.

40. Brunhouse, *Counter-Revolution in Pennsylvania*, 88–103.

41. *Journals of the House*, 573, 576, 591, 595, for several such cases. Benjamin Rush claimed in 1785 that "many hundreds" of slaves received their freedom in this way; *Consideration Upon the Present Test-law of Pennsylvania*, 2nd ed. (Philadelphia, 1785), 7n.

42. *Penna. Packet*, Dec. 2, 1780, quoted in Zilversmit, *First Emancipation*, 133.

43. *Penna. Journal*, Jan. 31, Feb. 5, 21, 1781, discussed in Zilversmit, *First Emancipation*, 134–35; "Liberalis" answered the proslavery writer in *Penna. Journal*, April 4, 1781.

44. This is discussed in greater detail in Gary B. Nash, *Forging Freedom: The Formation of Philadelphia's Black Community, 1720–1840* (Cambridge, Mass., 1988), chap. 2.

45. *Freedom's Journal*, Sept. 21, 1781.

46. *Journals of the House*, 690, 693, 696; Zilversmit, *First Emancipation*, 136–37.

47. The legislature, however, amended the 1780 law to exempt from its provisions citizens from other states who entered Pennsylvania with their slaves seeking refuge

from the British army. This was passed for the benefit of Virginians on Pennsylvania's southern border.

48. Benezet to George Dillwyn, 1783, QC, in George S. Brookes, *Friend Anthony Benezet* (Philadelphia, 1937), 372–75; *Penna. Packet,* Aug. 3, 1782; Thomas E. Drake, *Quakers and Slavery in America* (New Haven, 1950), 91–93. The 1783 petition is printed in J. William Frost, ed., *The Quaker Origins of Antislavery* (Norwood, Pa., 1980), 262.

49. Rush to Granville Sharp, Nov. 28, 1783, John A. Woods, ed., "The Correspondence of Benjamin Rush and Granville Sharp, 1773–1809," *Journal of American Studies* 1 (1967): 20.

50. Konkle, *Bryan,* 191.

51. Jack D. Marietta, *The Reformation of American Quakerism, 1748–1783* (Philadelphia, 1984), chap. 12.

52. In October 1778, Philadelphia Yearly Meeting urged all quarterly and monthly meetings to promote "the spiritual and temporal welfare of such Negroes and their children who have been restored to freedom," specifically by promoting religious instruction and "pious education" for black children. PYM mins., 9 mo. 16–10 mo. 5, 1778, FHL.

53. Papers of Continental Congress, 1774–89, microfilm edition, reel 57, item 43; Philadelphia Yearly Meeting, Meeting for Sufferings minutes, 11mo./20/1783, FHL.

54. Tench Coxe to David Barclay, March 6, 1787, PAS Papers, I, 59, HSP.

55. Benezet to John Pemberton, Aug. 10, 1783, in Brookes, *Benezet,* 397–98.

56. 1782 Effective Supply Tax, in *PA,* 3rd ser., XVI; Wayne J. Eberly, "The Pennsylvania Abolition Society, 1775–1830" (Ph.D. diss., The Pennsylvania State University, 1973), 25–26; a sketch of Harrison is in L. Maria Child, *Isaac T. Hopper: A True Life* (Boston, 1853), 122–23.

57. David Brion Davis's discussion of the PAS in *The Problem of Slavery in the Age of Revolution, 1770–1823* (Ithaca, 1975), 213–54, is ambiguous on the question of motivation, and Davis has since denied that he was referring to anyone except British political leaders of the period from the 1790s to 1823 when he formulated his argument concerning abolitionism and class interests ("Reflections on Abolitionism and Ideological Hegemony," *AHR* 92 (1987): 797–98); but some historians have concluded that he applied his thesis to all abolitionists of the Revolutionary era. Thomas L. Haskell, criticizing Davis's position, argues that the rise of capitalism and growth of humanitarianism were linked, not because abolitionists tried to bolster their own interests by supporting the wage-labor system but because capitalist activities gave people a "heightened sense of agency" that placed slavery on "the agenda of remediable evils." ("Convention and Hegemonic Interest in the Debate over Anti-slavery: A Reply to Davis and Ashworth," *AHR* 92 (1987): 829–78, quotations on pp. 856, 851). While Haskell's interpretation has considerable merit—and is actually similar to Davis's description in *The Problem of Slavery in Western Culture* (Ithaca, 1966) of how opposition to slavery accompanied the rise of rationalism by the mid-eighteenth century—it fails to explain why some people became abolitionists and others remained

immune to humanitarian sensibility. Specifically, why did some artisans, lawyers, and merchants join abolition societies while others continued to trade in or own slaves? (Davis, "Reflections," 811).

58. PAS Papers, General Meeting Minutes, 1775–87, 9–13, Reel 1.

59. David Donald, "Toward a Reconsideration of the Abolitionists," in Donald, *Lincoln Reconsidered* (New York, 1956), 19–36; Davis, *Problem of Slavery in the Age of Revolution,* chap. 8–9, especially pp. 241–42.

60. Most of those whose ages we have been able to approximate by their date of first marriage began their careers during the period of the Seven Years' War and its aftermath. In their late teens and twenties at that time, they witnessed the influx of slaves during the war and then experienced the shock of postwar depression. Of the 46 men who reestablished the PAS or joined within six weeks of founding, five were 34 years old or younger, seven were between ages 35 and 44, twelve were between 45 and 54, and two were 55 or older.

61. Sharon V. Salinger, "Artisans, Journeymen, and the Transformation of Labor in Late Eighteenth-Century Philadelphia," *WMQ,* 3rd ser., 40 (1983): 62–72; Gary B. Nash, "Slaves and Slaveowners in Colonial Philadelphia," ibid., 30 (1973): 223–56. Salinger directly addresses the reasons for the decline of bound labor, which was only hinted at in the earlier article by Nash. The data on artisan ownership of slaves are in Salinger, p. 67, Table 2, and Nash, p. 249, Table 8.

62. For the complaint of 1707 see Carl Bridenbaugh, *Cities in the Wilderness: The First Century of Urban Life in America, 1625–1742* (New York, 1938), 201. The best-known complaint was contained in Franklin's essay in 1751, "Observations Concerning the Increase in Mankind," *Papers of Franklin,* IV, 225.

63. The early PAS members have been checked against the 1767 and 1772 tax lists and the 1775 and 1780 constables' returns, all of which indicate slaves owned by taxpayers; and against the master list of manumissions in Philadelphia, 1690–1820, compiled by the authors.

64. Registration of Christopher Elliott's slaves, Nov. 1, 1780, PAS Papers, Reel 23.

65. PAS Papers, General Meeting Minutes, 1775–87, 21, Reel 1; Acting Committee Minutes, 1784–88, 12, 17, 23, 49, 53, 63, Reel 4; Indenture Book C, Reel 24.

66. A. J. Dallas, *Reports of Cases Ruled and Adjudged in the Several Courts of the United States, and of Pennsylvania,* (4 vols.; New York, 1905–7), I, 166.

67. Ibid., I, 167–68; PAS Papers, Acting Committee Minutes, 1784–88, 41, Reel 4.

68. Paul Finkelman, *An Imperfect Union: Slavery, Federalism, and Comity* (Chapel Hill, 1981), 50–51, argues that the PAS was seeking the judicial abolition of slavery in *Belt v. Dalby,* but we cannot find support for this in the Abolition Society papers or in the Society's arguments before the state Supreme Court.

69. PAS Papers, Acting Committee Minutes, 1784–88, 63, Reel 4; for a similar case in 1787, involving Jethro and Dinah, age 23 and 25, see ibid., 97–98.

70. PAS Papers, Acting Committee Minutes, 1784–88, 7, Reel 4.

71. Ibid., 76–77; many other cases that apparently did not lead to formal action, "as

related by the different Blacks & not entered" in the Acting Committee minutes, are in Acting Committee, Loose Minutes, 1791–1837, Reel 9.

72. The judge in *Commonwealth v. Lango* (1809) wrote: "It has been customary for negroes in Philadelphia, claimed as slaves by persons living in other states, to bind themselves for . . . periods, not exceeding the age of twenty-eight . . . by way of compromise with their masters; . . . These compromises, especially when the negro has acted under the direction of the abolition society, or any of its members, ought, if possible to be supported." Helen T. Catterall, ed., *Judicial Cases Concerning American Slavery and the Negro* (5 vols.; New York, 1926), IV, 269.

73. Washington to Robert Morris, April 12, 1786, quoted in Finkelman, *Imperfect Union,* 51.

74. Tench Coxe to David Barclay, March 6, 1787, in Bruns, ed., *Am I Not a Man and a Brother,* 510–12.

75. William Wade Hinshaw, ed., *Encyclopedia of American Genealogy* (5 vols.; Ann Arbor, 1936–46), II, 371; a biographical essay on Sarah Harrison is in *Biographical Sketches and Anecdotes of Members of the Religious Society of Friends* (Philadelphia, 1870), 344–65.

76. Child, *Hopper,* 122–23.

77. Eberly, "Penna. Abolition Society," 27–30; after 1786, the Abolition Society's leadership became more dominated by wealthy and prominent men. Jonathan Penrose, with a 1782 assessment of over £3,000, became president in 1786 and was followed in the office by Benjamin Franklin and James Pemberton, a wealthy Quaker and long-time opponent of slavery. Benjamin Rush and Tench Coxe, who both ranked in the top wealth decile in 1785, served as secretaries to the Society beginning in 1787. The committee selected in that year to revise the Society's constitution was composed of Harrison, William Jackson, Penrose, Rush, and Coxe, all of whom were among the wealthiest 10 percent of Philadelphians in the 1785 assessments.

78. *American Museum* 4 (July 1788): 52.

79. PAS Papers, General Meeting Minutes, 1784–87, 30 (April 19, 1787); Minutes, 1787–1800, 10 (May 3, 1787), Reel 1.

80. PAS Papers, Acting Committee Minutes, 1784–88, 173, 175, 182–83, 185–86, Reel 4.

81. Ibid., 148, 152–53, 155.

82. PAS Papers, General Meeting Minutes, 1787–1800, 13, 21–22, 26–27, Reel 1.

83. Zilversmit, *First Emancipation,* 157–58; Wax, "Reform and Revolution," 426–29.

84. Phila. Yearly Meeting, Meeting for Sufferings minutes, 26/12mo/1787; 20/3mo/1788; 17/4mo/1788.

85. Finkelman, *Imperfect Union,* 52–53.

86. James Pennington to William Dillwyn, May 9, 1788, James Pennington File, Dreer Collection, HSP.

87. PAS Papers, CICFB Minute Book, 1790–1803, 1–2, Reel 6; for an account of the PAS reorganization see Wayne Eberly, "Pennsylvania Abolition Society," 47–49.

88. A copy of the first PAS broadside, dated Oct. 26, 1789, is in PAS Papers, Reel 25; for the distribution of handbills among blacks in May 1790, PAS Papers, CICFB Minute Book, 1790–1803, 4, Reel 6; the meeting with blacks, on Oct. 2, 1790, and the appointment of a black committee is noted in ibid., 16–17.

89. PAS Papers, General Meeting Minutes, 1787–1800, 275 (May 3, 1797), Reel 1; for an example of the Committee of Guardians visiting with individual blacks to give them "friendly admonitions against such Improprieties in their Conduct" as disorderly meetings, dancing, and frolicking, see PAS Papers, Committee of Guardians, Minutes, 1787–1800, 46–47 (March 27, 1798), Reel 6.

90. Davis, *Problem of Slavery in the Age of Revolution,* 241–42, may take too instrumentalist a position in arguing that the PAS members, in this and other philanthropic organizations, had two broad goals—"to protect an urban population from disease and disorder, thereby ensuring the smooth functioning of the social and economic system; and to inculcate the lower classes with various moral and economic virtues, so that workers would want to do what the emerging economy required."

91. Brissot de Warville, *New Travels,* 300.

92. Child, *Hopper,* 1–47, passim, on Hopper's life; for "tales of oppression and anecdotes of colored people," 48–212.

93. *Journal of the House, 1792–1793* (Philadelphia, 1793), 39, 42, 45, 55, 60; Zilversmit, *First Emancipation,* 202–3. The Philadelphia newspapers began to carry advertisements of French runaway slaves as early as April 1791; over the next seven years at least 43 slaves fled their masters and mistresses.

94. Francis Thorpe, *The Federal and State Constitutions, Colonial Charter, and Other Organic Laws of the States, Territories, and Colonies . . .* (Washington, D.C.), V, 3099.

95. The committee included George Latimer of Philadelphia and William West of Delaware County; *Journal of the House, 1792–1793,* 195–96, 201, 205, 291.

96. PAS Papers, General Meeting Minutes, 1787–1800, 305 (April 2, 1798), Reel 1.

97. Turner, *Negro in Pennsylvania,* 82–83; Zilversmit, *First Emancipation,* 204–5.

98. *Journal of the House, 1796–1797* (Philadelphia, 1797), 283, 308–9, 354–55; *Journal of the House, 1797–98* (Philadelphia, 1798), 75, 94, 268–69; PAS Papers, General Meeting Minutes, 1787–1800, 305 (April 2, 1798), Reel 1.

99. PAS Papers, General Meeting Minutes, 1787–1800, 336 (Nov. 11, 1799), Reel 1.

100. *Journal of the First Session of the Tenth House of Representatives of the Commonwealth of Pennsylvania* (Lancaster, 1800), 23, 49, 76, 93, 123, 153, 162, 172, 176, 239, 303–6, 309–14, 320, 330, 366–68, 374–76.

101. PAS Papers, General Meeting Minutes, 1787–1800, 356 (March 7, 1800), Reel 1; the memorial to the legislature stating the objections is in PAS Papers, General Meeting Minutes, 1800–18, 13, 16 (Oct. 6, 1800, Jan. 5, 1801), Reel 1.

102. Quoted in Zilversmit, *First Emancipation,* 204.

103. *Respublica v. Betsey,* Dallas, *Reports,* I, 469; Stanley I. Kutler, "Pennsylvania

Courts, the Abolition Act, and Negro Rights," *Pennsylvania History* 30 (1963): 15–17.

104. Kutler, "Penna. Courts," 17.

105. See, for example, *Respublica v. Aberilla Blackmore*, Jasper Yeates, *Reports of Cases Adjudged in the Supreme Court of Pennsylvania* (4 vols.; Philadelphia, 1871), II, 234–36; and *William Thompson v. Richard Stroud and Phillip Price*, 1799, PAS Papers, Acting Committee Minute Book, Vol. 2 (1789–97), 380; Vol. 3 (1798–1810), 7, 15, 18–19, Reel 4.

106. PAS Papers, Committee of Guardians Minute Book, Vol. 2 (1797–1802), 58–59, 62–63, 125, 157, 159, 164–65, 173, 179, 196–97, Reel 6; Acting Committee Minute Book, Vol. 3 (1798–1810), 180, 183, Reel 4.

107. *Silas and Ann Bladen v. Benjamin Mitchell*, PAS Papers, Acting Committee Minute Book, Vol. 3 (1798–1810), 155, 160–61, 163, 187–89, 193, 197, 200, Reels 4 and 5.

108. PAS Papers, Acting Committee Minute Book, Vol. 3 (1798–1810), 241–43, 258, 275, Reel 5; the case is analyzed in Finkelman, *Imperfect Union*, 239–43.

Chapter 5

1. In 1769, for instance, a member of the Assembly reported that owners had not paid duty on slaves brought into York County. The House investigated the matter and discovered that duties were not being collected in York and that the collector in Philadelphia had failed to appoint deputies in Cumberland and Berks counties. *PA*, 8th ser., VII, 6341, 6351.

2. Not including Southwark and the Northern Liberties because the 1780 constables' return does not cover these areas.

3. U.S. Bureau of the Census, *Heads of Families at the First Census of the United States Taken in the Year 1790: Pennsylvania* (Washington, D.C., 1908), 199–245; Philadelphia constables' return, 1779–80, Philadelphia City Archives; U.S., manuscript census, 1800.

4. Chester County slave register, 1780, PAS Papers, Reel 24; Chester Co. tax assessment lists, 1765 and 1774, CCA; U.S. Bureau of the Census, *Heads of Families*, 59–75, 98–104; U.S., manuscript census, 1800.

5. Data on the number of runaway advertisements are from a survey of the *Pa. Gaz.* by Billy Smith and Richard Wojtowicz and our survey of the following newspapers: *Aurora and General Advertiser* (1789–99), *Daily Advertiser* (1796–97), *American Daily Advertiser* (1790–99), *Federal Gazette* (1788–93), *Freeman's Journal* (1781–92), *Independent Gazette* (1782–97), *Gazette of the United States* (1790–99), *National Gazette* (1791–93), *Pennsylvania Chronicle* (1770–74), *Pennsylvania Evening Post* (1775–79), *Pennsylvania Herald* (1775–78), *Pennsylvania Journal* (1770–93), *Pennsylvania Ledger* (1775–78), *Pennsylvania Mercury* (1784–90), *Pennsylvania Packet* (1771–90), *Philadelphia Gazette* (1796–99), *Porcupine's Gazette* (1796–99), *Royal Pennsylvania Gazette* (1777–78), *Universal Gazette* (1797–99). Probably not all masters advertised for runaway slaves, so notices in newspapers undercount the total

number. On the other hand, some slaves were undoubtedly captured and returned to their owners. A few repeat offenders are included in the total number.

6. *Penna. Packet*, Aug. 10, 1784; June 18, 1782.

7. Ibid., Sept. 22, 1786; Jan. 7, 1789.

8. Harry Emerson Wildes, *Lonely Midas: The Story of Stephen Girard* (New York, 1943), 99–102.

9. Gregory B. Keen, "The Descendants of Joran Kyn, the Founder of Upland," *PMHB* 6 (1882): 207–9; *PMHB* 49 (1925): 90; C.P.B. Jefferys, "The Provincial and Revolutionary History of St. Peter's Church, Philadelphia, 1753–1783," *PMHB* 48 (1924): 365.

10. Darold Duane Wax, "The Negro Slave Trade in Colonial Pennsylvania" (Ph.D. diss., University of Washington, 1962), 369; Wax, "Negro Import Duties in Colonial Pennsylvania," *PMHB* 97 (1973): 35–36; *Pennsylvania Colonial Records*, VIII, 576; Philadelphia constables' return, 1775, Philadelphia City Archives; U.S. Bureau of the Census, *Heads of Families*, 237; PAS manumissions.

11. Jefferys, "History of St. Peter's," 359–61; Wax, "Negro Import Duties," 35–36; U.S. Bureau of the Census, *Heads of Families*, 238; U.S., manuscript census, 1800.

12. Harold E. Gillingham, "Some Early Philadelphia Instrument Makers," *PMHB* 51 (1927): 299–301.

13. Milton E. Flower, *John Dickinson: Conservative Revolutionary* (Charlottesville, 1983), 1–9, 20–31, 60–61, 78–80; *PMHB* 5 (1881): 481; William Wade Hinshaw, ed., *Encyclopedia of American Quaker Genealogy* (5 vols.; Ann Arbor, 1936–46), II, 608.

14. Robert R. Logan Family Papers, vol. 34, 93, 110, HSP (information provided by James A. Stewart of the Delaware Bureau of Museum and Historic Sites); R. R. Logan Papers, vol. 6, fldr. 22; vol. 12, 105; vol. 35, 110.

15. R. R. Logan Papers, box 3, fldr. 4, HSP; PAS manumissions.

16. Burton Alva Konkle, *Benjamin Chew 1722–1810* (Philadelphia, 1932), 1–2, 6, 12, 15, 38, 48–52, 64, 67–69.

17. Chew Family Papers, Papers of Benjamin Chew (1722–1810), Box 96: Black History; Receipt Book 1770–1810, HSP.

18. Ibid., Box 96: Black History; Cash Accounts, Cliveden, 1789; Box 3: Correspondence 1778–1809, n.d., HSP.

19. Ibid., Box 96: Black History, HSP.

20. Olive Moore Gambrill, "John Beale Bordley and the Early Years of the Philadelphia Agricultural Society," *PMHB* 66 (1942): 410–39; PAS manumissions; Phila. Wills, 1804, No. 8; J[ohn] B[eale] Bordley, *Essays and Notes on Husbandry and Rural Affairs* (2nd ed. with additions; Philadelphia, 1801), 387, 389–90.

21. Paul G. E. Clemens and Lucy Simler, "Rural Labor and the Farm Household in Chester County, Pennsylvania, 1750–1820," in Stephen Innes, ed., *Work and Labor in Early America* (Chapel Hill, 1988), 106–43.

22. While in 1780 over 80% of Episcopalian and ex-Quaker slaveholders dwelled in the older eastern section of Chester County, 75% of Presbyterians lived in the more recently settled west.

23. Excluded from these data are a number of Philadelphians who manumitted one slave or more in the 1780s but remained owners of at least one slave in 1790.

24. Manumission Book for the Three Philadelphia Monthly Meetings (1772–96), QC; Hinshaw, ed., *Encyclopedia,* II, 331, 382, 451, 565; Hinshaw card file, Philadelphia Southern District Monthly Meeting, FHL.

25. Jean R. Soderlund, *Quakers and Slavery: A Divided Spirit* (Princeton, 1985), 108.

26. Phila. MM manumissions; Hinshaw, ed., *Encyclopedia,* II, 464, 651, 675.

27. Gary B. Nash, *Forging Freedom: The Formation of Philadelphia's Black Community, 1720–1840* (Cambridge, Mass., 1988), 20–24, 126–30; PAS manumissions.

28. In the 1780s, 26% of Episcopalians in Philadelphia who freed adult blacks placed conditions on their freedom but no Presbyterians, Quakers, or ex-Quakers did so.

29. PAS manumissions; Peale to Acting Committee of PAS, July 2, 1787, Lillian B. Miller, ed., *The Selected Papers of Charles Willson Peale and His Family* (New Haven, 1983–), I, 481–82. We have no record of Peale manumitting Phyllis, and Peale is listed as owning two slaves in the 1790 census (U.S. Bureau of the Census, *Heads of Families,* 242). Absalom Jones had similarly carried a subscription paper around the city more than a decade before to obtain the freedom of his wife; William Douglass, *Annals of the First African Church in the United States of America, now styled The African Episcopal Church of St. Thomas* (Philadelphia, 1862), 119–20.

30. Phila. Co. Wills, Register of Wills Office, Philadelphia City Hall. Bk. U, No. 203; Bk. W, No. 82; Phila. Administrations, 1780, No. 9; Phila. MM manumissions.

31. Andrew E. Murray, *Presbyterians and the Negro—A History* (Philadelphia, 1966), 17–18; *Extracts from the Minutes of the General Assembly of the Presbyterian Church, in the United States of America, from A. D. 1789, to A. D. 1802* (Philadelphia, 1803), 3, 77–79.

32. Alison to Ezra Stiles, Oct. 20, 1768, in Franklin B. Dexter, ed., *Extracts from the Itineraries and Other Miscellanies of Ezra Stiles . . . 1755–1794 . . .* (New York, 1916), 434; Phila. Co. Wills, Bk. R, No. 256.

33. Phila. Co. Wills, Bk. T, No. 102; Phila. MM manumissions.

34. Phila. MM manumissions; PAS manumissions.

35. Robert Drew Simpson, ed., *American Methodist Pioneer: The Life and Journals of the Rev. Freeborn Garretson* (Rutland, Vt., 1984), 5, 15; Donald Mathews, *Slavery and Methodism* (Princeton, 1964), chap. 1.

36. Chester Co. slave register, 1780. Two other slaveowners who registered slaves with abbreviated terms were ex-Quakers and none were Presbyterians.

37. Frederick Lewis Weis, *The Colonial Clergy of the Middle Colonies: New York, New Jersey, and Pennsylvania 1628–1776* (Worcester, Mass., 1957), 201; Chester Co. Wills, Nos. 3552, 3433, 2980, 3966, 3692.

38. *Extracts from the Minutes of the General Assembly of the Presbyterian Church,* 5–6; U.S. Bureau of the Census, *Heads of Families,* 67, 70, 101; Chester Co. tax assessment list, 1774; Chester Co. slave register, 1780.

39. See Chapter 6 below on the PAS's role in indenturing freed blacks.

40. Septennial Census Returns 1779–1863, originals in Record Group 7, Records of

the General Assembly, PHMC; microfilm roll No. 1 at CCA, 1800 Chester Co. Septennial Census. The skewed sex ratio in 1800 was also probably a result of more men than women escaping from slavery.

41. From Billy G. Smith and Richard Wojtowicz, *Blacks Who Stole Themselves: Advertisements for Runaways in the* Pennsylvania Gazette, *1728–1790* (Philadelphia, 1989).

Chapter 6

1. Sharon V. Salinger, *"To Serve Well and Faithfully": Labor and Indentured Servants in Pennsylvania, 1682–1800* (New York, 1987), chap. 6.

2. For a fuller analysis of occupations during the early years of freedom for Philadelphia's slaves, see Gary B. Nash, *Forging Freedom: The Formation of Philadelphia's Black Community, 1720–1840* (Cambridge, Mass., 1988), 73–74, 144–54.

3. Ibid., chap. 8.

4. Emma J. Lapsansky, "'Since They Got Those Separate Churches': Afro-Americans and Racism in Jacksonian Philadelphia," *American Quarterly* 32 (1980): 54–78.

5. Nash, *Forging Freedom,* 148.

6. Peter Atall [Robert Waln], *The Hermit in America on a Visit to Philadelphia* (Philadelphia, 1819), 152–53.

7. Nash, *Forging Freedom,* 148–54.

8. Ibid., 248.

9. Ibid., 154–57.

10. For further analysis of impoverishment and self-help, see ibid., 248–53, 267–73. It is possible that black Philadelphians tried to steer clear of white almshouse officials in the early years and that the overseers of the poor did not encourage blacks to apply for aid. Evidence for both phenomena exists for the 1820s and 1830s.

11. The data on free blacks in white households have been compiled from the manuscript censuses and are summarized in Nash, *Forging Freedom,* 161. For a fuller analysis of black family structure in the early nineteenth-century northern cities, see Gary B. Nash, "Forging Freedom: The Emancipation Experience in the Northern Seaport Cities, 1775–1820," in Ira Berlin and Ronald Hoffman, eds., *Slavery and Freedom in the Age of the American Revolution* (Charlottesville, 1983), 31–40.

12. Salinger, *Labor and Indentured Servants,* 178–80, Table A.3.

13. Edward Raymond Turner, *The Negro in Pennsylvania: Slavery—Servitude—Freedom, 1639–1861* (Washington, D.C., 1911), 89.

14. *The Chester and Delaware Federalist* (West Chester, Pa.), Sept. 15, 1813.

15. *Porcupine's Gazette,* Oct. 11, 1798.

16. Robert J. Steinfeld, "The Disappearance of Indentured Servitude and the Invention of Free Labor in the United States," unpublished manuscript, Parts V-VI.

17. Quoted in ibid., 144.

18. The flow of freed slaves into Philadelphia can be followed in the PAS Papers, Indenture Books, Reel 22.

19. *Journal of the Senate, 1832–1833* (2 vols.; Harrisburg, 1832–33), I, 486, quoted in Turner, *Negro in Pennsylvania,* 94n.

20. Nash, *Forging Freedom,* 77.

21. Salinger, *Labor and Indentured Servants,* 80, Table 3.2 for the length of indenture in two eighteenth-century samples.

22. Pennsylvania's slave code of 1726 allowed justices of the peace to bind out children of free blacks to age 24 if male and to age 21 if female and required the indenturing until age 31 of children of mixed marriages who were not slaves. James T. Mitchell and Henry Flanders, comps., *The Statutes at Large of Pennsylvania from 1682 to 1801* (Harrisburg, 1896–1915), IV, 62–63.

23. PAS Papers, Indenture Books, Reel 22; adults were normally indentured for seven years.

24. "Phileleutheros" argued that most people "used to hard labour without doors begin to fail soon after thirty, especially if they have been obliged to live on poor diet." *Pa. Gaz.,* Feb. 2, 1780.

25. The rising mortality rates among Philadelphia African-Americans in the early nineteenth century may have also reduced the years of freedom after release from indentured servitude. According to Susan Klepp's analysis, crude mortality rates (deaths annually per 1000 population) grew from 38 in 1790–99 to 49 in 1800–1809 to 53 in 1810–19. "Black Mortality in Early Philadelphia, 1722–1859," (Paper presented at the Annual Meeting of the Social Science History Association, Chicago, Nov. 5, 1988), Appendix A.

26. The 1769–70 act regulating apprenticing is in Mitchell and Flanders, comps., *Statutes at Large,* VII, 360–63.

27. Quoted in Dennis Clark, "Babes in Bondage: Indentured Irish Children in Philadelphia in the Nineteenth Century," *PMHB* 101 (1977): 477; Turner, citing evidence from 1814 and the early 1830s, concludes that young black males aged 11 to 19, that is with nine to 17 years to serve, brought half the price of a healthy slave; *Negro in Pennsylvania,* 94, 94n.

28. It is impossible to ascertain the completeness of the PAS's recording of indentures, but there is reason to believe they were thorough. Both the manumission and indenture papers, when recorded, became legal evidence of the black person's status, and this could provide the crucial evidence for a later court case. The close connections between PAS leaders and Philadelphia's black clergymen probably ensured that most African-Americans had their manumissions and indentures recorded.

29. Thomas L. Haskell argues that a market orientation increased the "acute sensations of moral responsibility" of early nineteenth-century Anglo-Americans, that capitalism was a source of "humanitarian sensibility"; but our analysis of those who freed their slaves while recapturing their investment by binding them to long-term indentures provides little confirming evidence of this benevolent sensibility. See Haskell, "Convention and Hegemonic Interest in the Debate over Antislavery: A Reply to Davis and Ashworth," *AHR* 92 (1987): passim; the quoted passages are on p. 853.

30. Society Miscellaneous Collection, Box 10, HSP, quoted in Turner, *Negro in Pennsylvania,* 93n.

31. Nash, *Forging Freedom*, 140–42; the manumissions made by the French émigrés are not included in our analysis in Chapter 5 because they were not Philadelphians except as catastrophe had dictated their temporary resettlement in the city.

32. All cases are taken from the PAS Papers, Manumission and Indenture Books, Reels 20–24.

33. In four sampled wards, black adult females living in white households outnumbered black adult males by 555 to 300. For a further discussion see Nash, "Forging Freedom," 31–32.

34. U.S. Bureau of the Census, *Heads of Families at the First Census of the United States Taken in the Year 1790: Pennsylvania* (Washington, D.C., 1908), 59–75, 98–104; U.S., manuscript censuses, 1800, 1810, and 1820.

35. Chester Monthly Meeting manumissions, FHL; Chester Co. Wills, No. 2460; Chester Co. Quarter Sessions Docket Book B, May 31, 1774. CCA.

36. Chester Co. slave register, 1780, PAS Papers, Reel 24; Chester Co. slave enumerations, Miscellaneous Slavery Papers, CCHS; U.S. Bureau of the Census, *Heads of Families*, 69; Chester Co. Wills, No. 4238.

37. Nash, *Forging Freedom*, 139–40; PAS Papers, Committee of Guardians: Indenture papers for Africans, Reels 22–23.

38. Paul G. E. Clemens and Lucy Simler, "Rural Labor and the Farm Household in Chester County, Pennsylvania, 1750–1820" in Stephen Innes, ed., *Work and Labor in Early America* (Chapel Hill, 1988), 128, 137; Martha B. Clark, "Lancaster County's Relation to Slavery," *Lancaster County Historical Society Papers* 15 (1911): 49.

39. U.S., manuscript censuses, 1800 and 1820; Delaware County triennial tax assessments, 1802–4, 1823–25, Neumann College Library, Aston, Pa.; Chester Co. tax assessment list, 1800, and triennial return, 1820, CCA.

40. Calculated from U.S., manuscript census, 1820, and Clemens and Simler, "Rural Labor," 115.

41. Nash, *Forging Freedom*, 135–36.

42. Richard Wojtowicz and Billy G. Smith, "Advertisements for Runaway Slaves, Indentured Servants, and Apprentices in the *Pennsylvania Gazette*, 1795–1796," *Pennsylvania History* 54 (1987): 49, 57, 62, 64–65.

43. Records of the Chester Co. Court of Quarter Sessions, CCA.

44. Chester Co. tax assessment lists, 1783, 1789, 1791; census, 1783; rates, 1790; discounts, 1789; Delaware Co. triennial tax assessments, 1802–4; U.S., manuscript census, 1800.

45. Misc. Slavery Papers, CCHS; Chester Co. Quarter Sessions Docket Book A, Aug. 26, 1766 and May 26, 1767; Delaware Co. Wills, No. 103, microfilm copy at HSP.

46. U.S., manuscript census, 1800; Delaware Co. triennial tax assessments, 1802–4; Chester Co. tax assessment list, 1800.

47. U.S., manuscript census, 1820; Chester Co. triennial return, 1820; Delaware Co. triennial assessments, 1823–25.

48. Our discussion of cottagers and their growing importance in the workforce of rural Pennsylvania is based largely on Clemens and Simler, "Rural Labor," 106–43.

49. Misc. Slavery Papers, CCHS.

50. Chester Co. Wills, Nos. 1389, 2430; Chester Co. tax assessment list, 1765, CCA.

51. Chester Co. Wills, No. 3811.

52. Chester Co. Wills, Nos. 3810, 3812.

53. PAS Papers, manumissions, reels 20–24; Phila. Co. Wills, Philadelphia City Hall, 1804, No. 8; J[ohn] B[eale] Bordley, *Essays and Notes on Husbandry and Rural Affairs* (2nd ed. with additions; Philadelphia, 1801), 387, 389–90.

54. Clemens and Simler, "Rural Labor."

55. Ibid., 115, 121n.

56. Concord MM mins., 9/6mo/1779 and 4/8mo/1779, FHL; Henry J. Cadbury, "Negro Membership in the Society of Friends," *JNH* 21 (1936): 151–213.

57. Misc. Slavery Papers, CCHS.

58. Record of Admissions, Chester Co. Poor House, 1801–26, CCA; Joan M. Jensen, *Loosening the Bonds: Mid-Atlantic Farm Women 1750–1850* (New Haven, 1986), chap. 4; Carl D. Oblinger, "Alms for Oblivion: The Making of a Black Underclass in Southeastern Pennsylvania, 1780–1869," in John E. Bodnar, ed., *The Ethnic Experience in Pennsylvania* (Lewisburg, Pa., 1973), 94–119; esp. 97–98, 104. Oblinger's dissertation, "New Freedoms, Old Miseries: The Emergence and Disruption of Black Communities in Southeastern Pennsylvania, 1780–1860" (Ph.D. diss., Lehigh University, 1988), is an expanded discussion of the lives of black Pennsylvanians in slavery and freedom, but in many instances his analysis of data and interpretation of evidence differ from ours.

59. Records of the Chester Co. Court of Quarter Sessions, CCA.

Chapter 7

1. *Respublica v. Gaoler,* Jasper Yeates, *Reports of Cases Adjudged in the Supreme Court of Pennsylvania* (4 vols.; Philadelphia, 1871), I, 368–69; Stanley I. Kutler, "Pennsylvania Courts, The Abolition Act, and Negro Rights," *Pennsylvania History* 30 (1963): 23; Edward Raymond Turner, *The Negro in Pennsylvania: Slavery—Servitude—Freedom, 1639–1861* (Washington, D.C., 1911), 93–94.

2. Turner, *Negro in Pennsylvania,* 100, citing communication of the PAS in *Minutes of the Seventeenth Session of the American Convention for Promoting the Abolition of Slavery, and Improving the Condition of the African Race* (Philadelphia, 1820), 11.

3. *Miller v. Diviling,* in Thomas Sergeant and William Rawle, Jr., *Reports of Cases Adjudged in the Supreme Court of Pennsylvania* (17 vols.; Philadelphia, 1818–29), XIV, 442–46; *Hazard's Register of Pennsylvania* XI (1833): 158. For other cases involving indentured servants see Paul Finkelman, *An Imperfect Union: Slavery, Federalism, and Comity* (Chapel Hill, 1981), 55–62.

4. *Hester v. Timothy Matlack,* 1811, PAS Papers, Acting Committee Minute Book, Vol. 4 (1810–22), 23–24, Reel 5.

5. *Azor and Polly Golden v. Louis Tousard,* ibid., 10–12.

6. *Commonwealth v. Lambert Smyth,* 1810, PAS Papers, Manumissions, Inden-

tures, and Other Legal Documents Concerning Court Cases in which Slaves were Awarded Freedom, Reel 24, unpaginated.

7. *Minutes of the Proceedings of a Convention of Delegates from the Abolition Societies Established in Different Parts of the United States* . . . (Philadelphia, 1801), 40, cited in Thomas D. Morris, *Free Men All: The Personal Liberty Laws of the North, 1780–1861* (Baltimore, 1974), 26; [Edward Darlington], *Reflections of Slavery* (Philadelphia, 1803), 15–32.

8. Morris, *Free Men All,* 19–21; William M. Wiecek, *The Sources of Antislavery Constitutionalism in America, 1760–1848* (Ithaca, 1977), 97–100. Dwight Dumond calls the Fugitive Slave Act of 1793 "the most flagrantly unconstitutional act of Congress ever enforced by the courts." *Antislavery: The Crusade for Freedom in America* (Ann Arbor, 1961), 58.

9. [Darlington], *Reflections of Slavery,* 22–24.

10. Ibid., 24–27.

11. L. Maria Child, *Isaac T. Hopper: A True Life* (Boston, 1853), 209–19.

12. Morris, *Free Men All,* 27.

13. *Stephenson v. Van Lear,* Sergeant and Rawle, *Cases Adjudged,* I, 247–52; PAS Papers, Acting Committee Minute Book, Vol. 4 (1810–22), 55–56, Reel 5.

14. William R. Leslie, "The Pennsylvania Fugitive Slave Act of 1826," *Journal of Southern History* 18 (1952): 430.

15. *Minutes of the Proceedings of the Fifteenth American Convention for Promoting the Abolition of Slavery* . . . (Philadelphia, 1817), 9–10; Wayne J. Eberly, "The Pennsylvania Abolition Society, 1775–1830" (Ph.D. diss., The Pennsylvania State University, 1973), 5–51, for data on the increase in membership after the War of 1812.

16. *Philadelphia Gazette,* July 25, 1818.

17. Morris, *Free Men All,* 42–46.

18. Ibid.

19. Ibid., 46–53, for the most balanced account, but also see Leslie, "Pennsylvania Fugitive Slave Act," 429–45.

Index

237